AIR FRYER COOKBOOK FOR BEGINNERS

550 Quick and Delicious Air Fryer Recipes for Smart People On a Budget

Emma Gordon

Copyright © 2019 by Emma Gordon

All Right Reserved.

No part of this publication may be reproduced, distributed, or transmitted in any form or by any means, including photocopying, recording, or other electronic or mechanical methods, or by any information storage and retrieval system without the prior written permission of the copyright holder.

Effort has been made to ensure that the information in this book is accurate and complete, however, the author and the publisher do not warrant the accuracy of the information, text and graphics contained within the book due to the rapidly changing nature of science, research, known and unknown facts and internet. The Author and the publisher do not hold any responsibility for errors, omissions or contrary interpretation of the subject matter herein. This book is presented solely for motivational and informational purposes only.

TABLE OF CONTENT

Introduction 1
- Benefits of using air fryer 2
- Getting the Most Out of your Air Fryer 3
- Cleaning and maintenance 4
- Air Fryer - FAQs 5

Breakfast Recipes 6
- Breakfast Potatoes 6
- Sausage and Bacon Bake 6
- Buttermilk Biscuits 6
- Healthy Asparagus Frittata 7
- Breakfast Ham Dish 7
- Spicy Creamy Eggs 7
- Eggs and Tomatoes 8
- Tofu Scramble 8
- Cheesy Sandwich 8
- Turkey and Eggs Casserole 9
- Leek and Potato Frittata 9
- Simple Breakfast 9
- Special Hash Browns 10
- Easy Egg Muffins 10
- Scrambled Eggs 10
- Turkey Burrito 11
- Biscuits Casserole Delight 11
- Cheesy Bread 11
- Polenta Bites 12
- Blackberry French Style Toast 12
- Delicious Doughnuts 12
- Breakfast Casserole 13
- Shrimp Sandwiches 13
- Potato Frittata 13
- Banana Oatmeal Casserole 14
- Morning Egg Bowls 14
- Hash browns 14
- Smoked Sausage Breakfast 15
- Beef Burger 15
- Protein Rich Egg White Omelet 15
- Baked Eggs 16
- Eggs, Sausage and Cheese Mix 16
- Mixed Bell Peppers Frittata 16
- Breakfast Cherries Risotto 17
- Broccoli Quiches 17
- Ham Pie 17
- Cinnamon Toast 18
- Potato Hash 18
- Breakfast Spanish Omelet 18
- Veggie Mix 18
- Ham Rolls 19
- Breakfast Shrimp Frittata 19
- Veggie Burritos Breakfast 19
- Spinach Parcels 20
- Special Corn Flakes Casserole 20
- Breakfast Soufflé 20
- Fried Tomato Quiche 20
- Tuna Sandwiches 21
- Fish Tacos Breakfast 21
- Onion Frittata 21
- Pea Tortilla 22
- Walnuts Pear Oatmeal 22
- Breakfast Raspberry Rolls 22
- Bread Pudding 23
- Bread Rolls 23
- Cream Breakfast Tofu 23
- Potatoes with Bacon 24
- Mushroom Oatmeal Breakfast 24

Smoked Fried Tofu 24

Long Beans Omelet 24

Mushrooms and Tofu 25

Dates Millet Pudding 25

French Beans and Egg Mix 25

Espresso Oatmeal 26

Artichoke Frittata 26

Lunch Recipes 27

Fresh Style Chicken 27

Chicken Salad 27

Cheese and Macaroni 27

Sweet Potato Casserole 28

Beef Meatballs 28

Egg Rolls 28

Different Pasta Salad 29

Cheering Chicken Sandwiches 29

Turkish Style Koftas 29

Turkey Burgers 30

Cheesy Ravioli and Marinara Sauce 30

Chicken Kabobs 30

Stuffed Portobello Mushrooms 30

Japanese Style Chicken 31

Chicken Pie Recipe 31

Chicken Fajitas 31

Lentils Fritters 32

Corn Casserole Recipe 32

Fish and Kettle Chips 32

Steak and Cabbage 33

Chicken Wings 33

Shrimp Croquettes 33

Shrimp Pancake 34

Pork and Potatoes Recipe 34

Lunch Pizzas 34

Asparagus and Salmon 34

Dill and Scallops 35

Beef Cubes 35

Zucchini and Tuna Tortillas 35

Summer Squash Fritters 35

Asian Chicken 36

Parmesan Gnocchi 36

Prosciutto Sandwich 36

Chinese Style Pork 37

Hash Brown Toasts 37

Succulent Turkey Cakes 37

Potato Salad 37

Buttermilk Chicken 38

Cheese Burgers 38

Creamy Chicken Stew Recipe 38

Tasty Hot Dogs 39

Chicken Corn Casserole 39

Veggie Toasts 39

Succulent Turkey Breast 39

Bell Pepper and Sausage 40

Fried Thai Salad 40

Seafood Stew 40

Bacon Garlic Pizzas 41

Chicken, Quinoa, Corn, Beans and Casserole 41

Meatballs, Tomato Sauce 41

Chicken and kale Recipe 42

Meatballs Sandwich Delight 42

Zucchini Casseroles 42

Bacon Sandwiches 43

Chicken and Coconut Casserole 43

Italian Style Eggplant Sandwich 43

Beef Stew 44

Stuffed Meatballs 44

Bacon Pudding 44

Chicken Zucchini 45

Poultry Recipes 46

Italian Chicken Recipe 46
Chicken Cacciatore Recipe 46
Fried Japanese Duck Breasts 46
Chicken and Asparagus Recipe 47
Chinese Chicken Wings Recipe 47
Herbed Chicken Recipe 47
Chicken Thighs and Apple 47
Coconut Creamy Chicken 48
Creamy Chicken, Peas and Rice 48
Chicken Salad Recipe 48
Chicken Breasts and Tomatoes Sauce 49
Chicken and Green Onions Sauce Recipe 49
Chicken Tenders and Flavored Sauce Recipe 49
Chicken Wings and Mint Sauce Recipe 50
Chicken Parmesan Recipe 50
Chicken and Coconut Sauce Recipe 51
Chicken Thighs Recipe 51
Chicken and Creamy Mushrooms Recipe 51
Turkey Quarters and Veggies Recipe 52
Chinese Duck Legs Recipe 52
Chicken & Parsley Sauce 52
Mexican Chicken Recipe 53
Chinese Stuffed Chicken Recipe 53
Duck Breasts Recipe 53
Chicken and Lentils Casserole Recipe 54
Honey Duck Breasts Recipe 54
Pepperoni Chicken Recipe 54
Fall Fried Chicken 55
Duck and Plum Sauce Recipe 55
Cheese Crusted Chicken Recipe 55
Lemony Chicken 56
Turkey, Mushrooms and Peas Casserole 56
Duck Breast with Fig Sauce Recipe 56

Chicken Thighs and Baby Potatoes 57
Chicken and Apricot Sauce Recipe 57
Creamy Chicken Casserole Recipe 57
Chicken and Garlic Sauce Recipe 58
Duck and Veggies Recipe 58
Chicken and Cauliflower Rice Mix Recipe 58
Greek Chicken Recipe 59
Marinated Duck Breasts Recipe 59
Chicken Breasts with Passion Fruit Sauce 59
Duck Breasts and Mango Mix Recipe 60
Chicken and Chestnuts Mix Recipe 60
Duck and Cherries Recipe 60
Chicken Breasts and BBQ Chili Sauce Recipe 61
Tea Glazed Chicken Recipe 61
Cider Glazed Chicken Recipe 61
Duck Breasts with Red Wine and Orange Sauce Recipe 62
Veggie Stuffed Chicken Breasts Recipe 62
Duck and Tea Sauce Recipe 62
Chicken and Peaches Recipe 63
Chicken and Creamy Veggie Mix Recipe 63
Duck Breasts Recipe 63
Chicken and Spinach Salad Recipe 64
Duck Breasts with Endives Recipe 64
Chicken and Capers Recipe 64
Chicken and Black Olives Sauce Recipe 65

Fish and Seafood Recipes 66

Asian Style Salmon 66
Trout Fillet & Orange Sauce 66
Cod Fillets with Grapes and Fennel Salad 66
Shrimp and Cauliflower Recipe 67
Vinaigrette and Cod 67
Tangy Saba Fish 67
Cod with Pearl Onions Recipe 68

Salmon Thyme and Parsley 68
East Trout and Butter Sauce 68
Flavored Fried Salmon 69
Pollock Recipe 69
Oriental Fish Recipe 69
Peas and Cod Fillets 70
Shrimp and Crab Recipe 70
Asian Style Halibut 70
Salmon with Mash and Capers 71
Tabasco Shrimp Recipe 71
Salmon and Avocado Salsa 71
Air Fried Cod 72
Roasted Cod & Prosciutto 72
Cod Steaks with Plum Sauce 72
Tuna and Chimichurri Sauce 73
Creamy-Shrimp and Veggies 73
Coconut Tilapia Recipe 74
Mustard Salmon Recipe 74
Squid and Guacamole 74
Salmon and Lemon Relish Recipe 75
Chinese Style Cod 75
Catfish Fillets Recipe 75
Halibut and Sun Dried Tomatoes 76
Salmon & Chives Vinaigrette 76
Italian Barramundi Fillets 76
Marinated Salmon Recipe 77
Buttery Shrimp Skewers 77
Fish and Couscous Recipe 77
Delightful French Cod 78
Hawaiian Salmon Recipe 78
Salmon and Avocado Sauce Recipe 78
Tasty Catfish 79
Salmon and Orange Marmalade Recipe 79
Salmon & Blackberry Glaze 79

Stuffed Salmon Delight 80
Honey Sea Bass Recipe 80
Snapper Fillets and Veggies Recipe 80
Black Cod & Plum Sauce 81
Creamy Salmon Recipe 81
Spanish Salmon Recipe 81
Flavored Jamaican Salmon Recipe 82
Fried Branzino 82
Crusted Salmon Recipe 82
Lemon Sole & Swiss Chard 83
Stuffed Calamari Recipe 83
Swordfish and Mango Salsa 83
Red Snapper Recipe 84
Tilapia & Chives Sauce 84
Chili Salmon Recipe 84
Salmon and Avocado Salad Recipe 85
Salmon and Greek Yogurt Sauce Recipe 85

Meat Recipes 86

Marinated Pork Chops and Onions Recipe 86
Beef and Cabbage Mix Recipe 86
Lamb and Lemon Sauce Recipe 86
Lamb Shanks and Carrots Recipe 87
Chinese Steak and Broccoli Recipe 87
Beef Roast and Wine Sauce Recipe 87
Braised Pork Recipe 88
Beef Fillets with Garlic Mayo Recipe 88
Fennel Flavored Pork Roast Recipe 88
Coffee Flavored Steaks Recipe 89
Provencal Pork Recipe 89
Creamy Pork Recipe 89
Lamb Roast and Potatoes Recipe 90
Lemony Lamb Leg Recipe 90
Oriental Fried Lamb Recipe 90
Greek Beef Meatballs Salad Recipe 91

Beef Brisket and Onion Sauce Recipe 91
Pork with Couscous Recipe 92
Lamb Ribs Recipe 92
Rib Eye Steak Recipe 92
Garlic and Bell Pepper Beef Recipe 93
Beef Strips with Snow Peas and Mushrooms Recipe 93
Beef and Green Onions Marinade Recipe 93
Crispy Lamb Recipe 94
Ham and Cauliflower Mix Recipe 94
Pork Chops and Green Beans Recipe 94
Asian Pork Recipe 95
Beef Medallions Mix Recipe 95
Fried Pork Shoulder Recipe 95
Mexican Beef Mix Recipe 96
Garlic Lamb Chops Recipe 96
Sausage and Kale Recipe 96
Lamb and Spinach Mix Recipe 96
Short Ribs and Beer Sauce Recipe 97
Beef Stuffed Squash Recipe 97
Burgundy Beef Mix Recipe 97
Beef Curry Recipe 98
Pork Chops and Roasted Peppers Recipe 98
Lamb and Creamy Brussels Sprouts Recipe 98
Mustard Marinated Beef Recipe 99
Tasty Ham and Greens Recipe 99
Sirloin Steaks and Pico De Gallo Recipe 99
Pork Chops and Mushrooms Mix Recipe 100
Beef Kabobs Recipe 100
Creamy Lamb Recipe 100
Beef Casserole Recipe 101
Ham and Veggie Air Fried Mix Recipe 101
Lamb Shanks Recipe 101
Lamb and Green Pesto Recipe 102
Stuffed Pork Steaks Recipe 102

Mediterranean Steaks and Scallops Recipe 102
Filet Mignon and Mushrooms Sauce Recipe ... 103
Fried Sausage and Mushrooms Recipe 103
Short Ribs and Sauce Recipe 103
Pork Chops and Sage Sauce Recipe 104
Lamb Racks and Fennel Mix Recipe 104
Balsamic Beef Recipe 104
Beef Patties and Mushroom Sauce Recipe 105

Side Dish Recipes 106
Sweet Potato Fries 106
Roasted Parsnips Dish 106
Roasted Pumpkin Side Dish 106
Creamy Endives 106
Eggplant Fries Dish 107
Herbed Tomatoes Dish 107
Mushrooms and Cream 107
Cauliflower Cakes 108
Cauliflower Rice Dish 108
Coconut Potatoes 108
Veggie Fries Dish 109
Vermouth White Mushrooms 109
Delightful Cauliflower and Broccoli 109
Parmesan Button Mushrooms 110
Green Beans Dish 110
Hassel-Back Potatoes 110
Greek Veggie Dish 110
Potato Wedges 111
Creamy Fried Potato Dish 111
Brussels Sprouts Dish 111
Potato Chips 112
Garlic Potatoes 112
Lemony Artichokes Side Dish 112
Cajun Onion Wedges Dish 112
Artichokes and Tarragon Sauce Dish 113

Button Mushroom Dish 113
Fried Creamy Cabbage 113
Rice and Mushroom Risotto 113
Air Fried Tomatoes 114
Roasted Eggplant Dish 114
Tortilla Chips 114
Roasted Carrots 114
Pumpkin Rice Dish 115
Yummy Biscuits 115
Mushroom Cakes 115
Carrots and Rhubarb Dish 116
Potato Casserole Dish 116
Tasty Barley Risotto 116
Zucchini Fries Dish 117
Avocado Fries Dish 117
Maple Glazed Beets 117
Beet Wedges Dish 117
Eggplant Dish 118
Zucchini Croquettes 118
Air Fried Red Cabbage 118
Yellow Squash and Zucchinis Dish 119
Tasty Potatoes Patties 119
Colored Veggie Rice Recipe 119
Brussels Sprouts and Pomegranate Seeds Dish 120
Corn with Cheese and Lime 120
Fried Broccoli 120
Onion Rings Dish 120
Roasted Peppers Dish 121
Creamy Brussels Sprouts Side Dish 121
Flavored Cauliflower Dish 121
Creamy Potatoes Dish 122
Brussels Sprouts and Potatoes 122
Roasted Peppers Dish 122
Wild Rice Pilaf 123

Rice and Sausage Dish 123
Cauliflower Bars 123

Vegetable Recipes 124

Beet, Tomato and Goat Cheese Mix Recipe 124
Flavored Fennel Recipe 124
Broccoli Salad Recipe 124
Brussels Sprouts and Butter Sauce Recipe 125
Collard Greens and Turkey Wings Recipe 125
Swiss Chard and Sausage Recipe 125
Collard Greens and Bacon Recipe 126
Green Beans Recipe 126
Cheesy Brussels Sprouts Recipe 126
Okra and Corn Salad Recipe 126
Artichokes and Sauce Recipe 127
Eggplant Hash Recipe 127
Brussels Sprouts and Tomatoes Mix Recipe 127
Potatoes and Tomatoes Mix Recipe 128
Spinach Pie Recipe 128
Cherry Tomatoes Skewers Recipe 128
Stuffed Baby Peppers Recipe 129
Beet Salad and Parsley Dressing Recipe 129
Herbed Eggplant and Zucchini Mix Recipe 129
Peppers Stuffed with Beef Recipe 130
Beets and Blue Cheese Salad Recipe 130
Radish Hash Recipe 130
Flavored Fried Tomatoes Recipe 131
Mexican Peppers Recipe 131
Balsamic Artichokes Recipe 131
Beets and Arugula Salad Time Recipe 132
Sesame Mustard Greens Recipe 132
Garlic Tomatoes Recipe 132
Broccoli and Tomatoes Fried Stew Recipe 132
Cheesy Artichokes Recipe 133
Stuffed Eggplants Recipe 133

Fried Asparagus Recipe 133
Collard Greens Mix Recipe 134
Spanish Greens Recipe 134
Stuffed Tomatoes Recipe 134
Zucchini Mix Recipe 135
Broccoli Hash Recipe 135
Crispy Potatoes and Parsley Recipe 135
Sweet Baby Carrots Dish Recipe 135
Zucchini Noodles Recipe 136
Creamy Green Beans Recipe 136
Greek Potato Mix Recipe 136
Portobello Mushrooms Recipe 137
Green Beans and Parmesan Recipe 137
Asian Turnips Salad Recipe 137
Green Beans and Potatoes Recipe 138
Swiss Chard Salad Recipe 138
Green Beans and Tomatoes Recipe 138
Rutabaga and Cherry Tomatoes Mix Recipe 138
Stuffed Poblano Peppers Recipe 139
Balsamic Potatoes Recipe 139
Sweet Potatoes Mix Recipe 139
Asian Potatoes Recipe 140
Tomato and Basil Tart Recipe 140
Tomatoes and Bell Pepper Sauce Recipe 140
Spicy Cabbage Recipe 141
Potatoes and Tomato Sauce Recipe 141
Italian Eggplant Stew Recipe 141

Snack and Appetizer Recipes 142

Spicy Fish Nuggets 142
Cauliflower Snack 142
Tasty Banana Snack 142
Chestnut and Shrimp Rolls 143
Chicken Breast Sticks 143
Honey Chicken Wings 143

Pesto Crackers 144
Salmon Meatballs Snack 144
Sweet Popcorn Snack 144
Cabbage Spring Rolls 145
Salmon Patties 145
Tasty Crab Sticks 145
Zucchini Chips 146
Coco Chicken Bites 146
Beef Rolls 146
Jerky Beef Snack 146
Delightful Chickpeas Snack 147
Tasty Apple Chips 147
Zucchini Cakes 147
Fried Dill Pickles 147
Succulent Chicken Dip 148
Olives Balls 148
Cheering Chicken Breast Rolls 148
Sweet Potato Spread 149
Cheese Sticks 149
Banana Chips 149
Mexican Style Apple Snack 150
Greek Style Lamb Meatballs 150
Bacon Jalapeno Balls 150
Chicken Wings 150
Broccoli Patties 151
Seafood Appetizer 151
White Mushrooms Appetizer 151
Shrimp Muffins 152
Stuffed Peppers 152
Herbed Tomatoes 152
Spicy Stuffed Peppers 153
Fish Sticks 153
Traditional Sweet Bacon Snack 153
Special Empanadas 154

Appetizing Cajun Shrimp 154
Bread Sticks Snack 154
Roasted Pepper Rolls 154
Crispy Shrimp Snack 155
Radish Chips 155
Healthy Spinach Balls 155
Shrimp and Calamari Snack 156
Holyday Beef Patties 156
Sausage Balls Snack 156
Party Beef Rolls 157
Cheesy Chicken Wings 157
Tuna Cakes 157
Cheesy Zucchini Snack 158
Pure Pumpkin Muffins 158
Kale and Celery Crackers 158
Cheesy Chicken Rolls 158
Egg White Chips Snack 159
Party Pork Rolls 159
Wrapped Shrimp 159

Dessert Recipes 160

Mini Lava Cakes Recipe 160
Tomato Cake Recipe 160
Lentils and Dates Brownies Recipe 160
Plum Cake Recipe 161
Strawberry Cobbler Recipe 161
Carrot Cake Recipe 161
Banana Bread Recipe 162
Banana Cake Recipe 162
Blueberry Scones Recipe 162
Strawberry Donuts Recipe 163
Chocolate Cookies Recipe 163
Bread Dough and Amaretto Dessert Recipe 163
Plum and Currant Tart Recipe 164
Strawberry Pie Recipe 164

Pears and Espresso Cream Recipe 165
Pumpkin Cookies Recipe 165
Coffee Cheesecakes Recipe 165
Cheesecake Recipe 166
Cinnamon Rolls and Cream Cheese Dip Recipe 166
Granola Recipe 166
Chocolate Cake Recipe 167
Lemon Bars Recipe 167
Orange Cake Recipe 167
Peach Pie Recipe 168
Cocoa Cake Recipe 168
Apple Bread Recipe 168
Bread Pudding Recipe 169
Fried Bananas Recipe 169
Macaroons Recipe 169
Walnuts Brownies 169
Rhubarb Pie Recipe 170
Crispy Apples Recipe 170
Pumpkin Pie Recipe 170
Black Tea Cake Recipe 171
Cocoa Cookies Recipe 171
Mandarin Pudding Recipe 172
Figs and Coconut Butter Mix Recipe 172
Strawberry Shortcakes Recipe 172
Lemon Tart Recipe 173
Chocolate and Pomegranate Bars Recipe 173
Sweet Squares Recipe 173
Wrapped Pears Recipe 174
Tangerine Cake Recipe 174
Lentils Cookies Recipe 174
Plum Bars Recipe 175
Sweet Potato Cheese Cake Recipe 175
Berries Mix Recipe 175
Ginger Cheesecake Recipe 176

Cocoa and Almond Bars Recipe 176
Fried Apples Recipe 176
Cashew Bars Recipe 176
Brown Butter Cookies Recipe 177
Blueberry Pudding Recipe 177
Sponge Cake Recipe 177
Ricotta and Lemon Cake Recipe 178

Orange Cookies Recipe 178
Poppyseed Cake Recipe 178
Passion Fruit Pudding Recipe 179
Maple Cupcakes Recipe 179

Introduction

An air fryer uses superheated airflow above and around your food to convert tiny amounts of moisture into mist. The extra-hot cooking chamber lets dry heat penetrate the food from the outside in, yielding the familiar crispy texture food gets with a bath in the deep fryer.

Traditionally, deep frying food is very messy. You end up with a lot of dirty pans, grimy utensils, and a greasy coating on everything around the fryer. Air fryers, on the other hand, are relatively clean. The cooking basket is completely enclosed, which eliminates splattering and all the fat, grease, and oil in your food drips down into the oil pan below.

This cookbook presents a carefully hank-picked 550 easy and delicious recipes that you can cook in your air fryer. Just Pick the best recipes you like and start cooking with your air fryer now. You will be amazed at how simple it is to use. The machine plays with you, but you need to make sure to handle it with care. It gives you healthy food with all the nutrients your body requires. Thus, you can feed your family with healthy meals without stressing yourself too much or spending long hours inside the kitchen.

The recipes are simple and easy to understand. By using this cookbook Anyone can make the delicious recipes with the air fryer. You just need to know the right measurements, and you will have a great recipe ready for you. You do not have to deal with fire or flames on the stoves, air fryer has made life easier for the people now.

Benefits of using air fryer

Healthier Cooking:

Air frying is a healthy cooking method. It gives the food the same crispy texture as deep frying but without heavy oils or fats. By using a spray of cooking oil, you can cook any amount of food in this air fryer, such as, you can cook frozen fries, onion rings, wings and more, and still get really crispy results without the extra oil.

Great Time Saver:

With only 24 hours to complete everyday routine tasks, the time has become a genuinely luxury in our fast paced lifestyle. Air Fryers are designed to save your precious cooking time by serving you crunchy snacks and fried cuisines in a matter of minutes. If you are always on a tight schedule, Air Fryer is no less than a time savior

Ease of Use:

Air fryers are really easy to use just select the temperature and the cooking time, add food and shake a few times while cooking. No need to fuss or stir like using the stove top.

The baskets make shaking your food simple and fast as well, and the unit doesn't lose a lot of heat when you open it. So feel free to peek while cooking if you want! Unlike an oven, you won't be slowing things down if you do.

Ease of Clean Up:

One part of cooking that most of us don't enjoy is the clean-up. With an air fryer, you just have a basket and pan to clean, and many are even dishwasher safe. With non-stick coated parts, food usually isn't stuck to the pan and instead slides right off onto your plate. It takes just a few minutes to wash up after using.

Superfast Heating:

Unlike traditional frying method, Air Fryers takes only a few minutes to heat and prepare foods. They are always ready to make meals whenever you crave for fried foods. Most Air Fryer models get ready in only 3 minutes to heat up properly and they can also go as high as 400 degrees F to make you crispy meals

Versatility:

You can cook fresh and frozen foods and even reheat leftovers in them. It can be done with meats, fish, casseroles, sandwiches and a lot of different veggies. Some fryers come with extra features, like a rotisserie rack, grill pan or elevated cooking rack. Dividable baskets mean you can cook several things at the same time as well. It is impressive that a single unit can cook so many things in so many ways.

Depending on the size of your fryer, there are a lot of different accessories you can buy. Cake and pizza pans, kabob skewers and steamer inserts are just a few of the accessories

Getting the Most Out of your Air Fryer

To maximize the benefits of using an air fryer, here are some tips that you should not overlook:

Getting Started

- Place your air fryer on a level and heatproof kitchen top, if you have granite surfaces this is perfect
- Avoid putting it close to the wall as this will dissipate the heat causing slower cooking times. Leave a space of at least five inches between the wall and the air fryer
- Oven-safe baking sheets and cake pans may be used in the air fryer on the condition that they can fit inside easily and the door can close

Before Cooking

- If you can, always preheat your air fryer for 3 minutes before cooking. Once the timer goes off it will be ready to rock and roll
- Use a hand pumped spray bottle for applying the oil. Adopting this method will cause you to use less oil and is an easier option when compared to brushing or drizzling. **Avoid canned aerosol brands as they tend to have a lot of nasty chemicals**
- Always Bread if necessary. This breading step should not be missed. Be sure to press the breading firmly onto the meat or vegetable so the crumbs do not fall off easily

Whilst Cooking

- Adding water to the air fryer drawer while cooking high-fat foods to will prevent excessive smoke and heat. Use this technique when cooking burgers, bacon, sausage and similar foods
- Secure light foods such as bread slices with toothpicks so they don't get blown around
- Avoid putting too many food items into the air fryer basket. Overcrowding will result in uneven cooking and will also prevent the food from getting that glorious crispy texture that we all love.
- Shaking the fryer and flipping the food halfway through the cooking process is advised to make sure that everything inside cooks evenly
- Opening the air fryer a few times to check how the food is doing won't affect the cooking time, so don't worry.

Once done:

- Remove the basket from the drawer before taking out the food to prevent the oil remaining on the food that you just fried.
- The juices in the air fryer drawer can be used to make delicious marinades and sauces. If you find it too greasy you can always reduce it in a saucepan to get rid of the excess liquid.
- Cleaning both the basket and drawer after every use is imperative

Cleaning and maintenance

Like all other kitchen gadgets, you should properly clean and maintain your air fryer though. If you don't clean your air fryer, it won't perform as optimally. Plus, it can accumulate smells and flavors, and those old flavors can transfer into other foods. Dirty air fryers can also build up grease, and that grease can cause your air fryer to smoke and reduce the quality of your food. Here are the steps to clean your air fryer

1. Always unplug the device before you start cleaning. Do not touch the device immediately after it is finished cooking. Allow it to cool at room temperature and handle it with care.
2. The first important step to clean the device is to take out all of the removable parts. Remove the air fryer basket, the crisper plate, and the multilayer rack if they were used.
3. All of these removable items are dishwasher safe so you can safely wash them in the dishwasher. To be more cautious, they can be hand-washed using dish soap and water. Avoid rubbing or scraping the interior of the basket with abrasive scrubs or brushes. Wash them gently and use a soft cloth or sponge to clean the grease off the basket. Treat the crisper plate in the same manner.
4. Once all these removable items are washed, make sure to let them completely dry before putting them back into their places.
5. As they dry, you can clean the area around the air fryer and wipe off the base unit if you see it's dirty. Sometimes the food inside the basket can leave a stain on the underside of the base unit, directly above the food. This needs to be cleaned, but not by washing it in the sink. Instead, wipe it off using a clean cloth. If the stain is stubborn, use a damp cloth.
6. Never immerse the base unit in water and don't let water touch any of its parts as it can damage the electrical heating system. You can only use a damp cloth over the exterior of this device and on the underside of the unit as described in the previous step.
7. To clean the dirt off the plug of the device, wipe it with a cloth.
8. Once the device is completely clean and dry, put all the parts back where they belong and store the device where you like between uses.

Air Fryer - FAQs

1. How long does it take to preheat, and how will I know when it's done?
We recommend 3 minutes of preheating. You can use the built-in timer to set a 3-minute countdown.

2. Should I add my ingredients before or after preheating?
It is recommended to let the unit preheat for 3 minutes before adding ingredients.

3. Why the food is burned?
For best results, check progress throughout cooking, and remove food when desired level of brownness has been achieved. Remove food immediately after the cook time is complete to avoid overcooking.

4. Why is my food blowing around when air frying?
Occasionally, the fan from the air fryer will blow lightweight foods around. To alleviate this, secure foods (like the top slice of bread on a sandwich) with toothpicks.

5. How many items can be cooked at a go in an air fryer?
You can easily cook two different items at a go in an air fryer but make sure to use the divider. This will help in proper cooking and less time will be consumed.

6. Can we cook different varieties of food in an air fryer?
Yes, you can easily cook different varieties of food in an air fryer. One of the best things about cooking food in an air fryer is that it is healthy and free from oil. Items such as meat, potatoes, poultry and French fries can be easily cooked. Apart from these items you can also bake brownies and grill different vegetables.

7. Do we need to preheat the air fryer?
No, there is no need to preheat the air fryer. However, pre-heating the air fryer for about 3 minutes can help in significant reduction of the cooking time.

8. Does air fryer help in making food crispy and tasty?
Yes, the food that you cook in an air fryer is as tasty and crispy as it is with frying. One of the main reasons why air fryer cooks tasty and crispy food is because it helps in keeping the outer layer of the food crisp and the inside gets soft.

9. Can we add more ingredients while the food is getting cooked in an air fryer?
Yes, you can add more ingredients while the food is getting cooked in an air fryer but make sure to add the ingredients immediately otherwise the heat loss may lead to more time consumption for cooking the food.

10. How much time an air fryer takes to cook frozen foods?
One of the best things to do while cooking frozen food in an air fryer is to use the knob as per the food that you are cooking. It normally takes some more time to cook frozen foods as compared to other food items.

11. What is the input power range of an air fryer?
For the European market the input power range is 220 v and for USA market it is 110 v.

12. Is it possible to use baking paper or aluminium foil in an air fryer?
Yes, you can use a baking paper or aluminium foil but you need to make sure that appropriate space is given so that the steam can pass easily.

13. Is there any specific type of oil required for air fryer?
No, there is no special oil which is required for cooking in an air fryer. You can use any type of oil such as olive oil, peanut oil. ***Avoid canned aerosol sprays as they tend to have a lot of nasty chemicals***

Breakfast Recipes

Breakfast Potatoes

(Prep + Cook Time: 45 Minutes | **Servings:** 4)

Ingredients:
- 3 potatoes; cubed
- 1 yellow onion; chopped.
- 2 tbsp. olive oil
- 1 red bell pepper; chopped
- 1 tsp. garlic powder
- 1 tsp. sweet paprika
- 1 tsp. onion powder
- Salt and black pepper to the taste

Instructions:
1. Grease your air fryer's basket with olive oil; add potatoes, toss and season with salt and pepper.
2. Add onion, bell pepper, garlic powder, paprika and onion powder, toss well, cover and cook at 370 °F, for 30 minutes. Divide potatoes mix on plates and serve for breakfast.

Nutrition Facts: Calories: 214; Fat: 6g; Fiber: 8g; Carbs: 15g; Protein: 4g

Sausage and Bacon Bake

(Prep + Cook Time: 30 Minutes | **Servings:** 4)

Ingredients:
- 1 lb. breakfast sausage; casings removed and chopped.
- 4 bacon slices; cooked and crumbled
- 2 cups milk
- 2 eggs
- 2 ½ cups cheddar cheese; shredded
- 1/2 tsp. onion powder
- 3 tbsp. parsley; chopped.
- Salt and black pepper to the taste
- Cooking spray

Instructions:
1. In a bowl; mix eggs with milk, cheese, onion powder, salt, pepper and parsley and whisk well.
2. Spray cooking spray into your air fryer basket and Pre-heat your air fryer 320 °F
3. Add bacon and sausage. Add eggs mix spread and cook for 20 minutes. Divide among plates and serve.

Nutrition Facts: Calories: 214; Fat: 5g; Fiber: 8g; Carbs: 12g; Protein: 12g

Buttermilk Biscuits

(Prep + Cook Time: 18 Minutes | **Servings:** 4)

Ingredients:
- 4 tbsp. butter; cold and cubed+ 1 tbsp. melted butter
- 3/4 cup buttermilk
- 1 ¼ cup white flour
- 1/2 cup self-rising flour
- 1/4 tsp. baking soda
- 1/2 tsp. baking powder
- 1 tsp. sugar
- Maple syrup for serving

Instructions:
1. In a bowl; mix white flour with self-rising flour, baking soda, baking powder and sugar and stir.
2. Add cold butter and stir using your hands.
3. Add buttermilk, stir until you obtain a dough and transfer to a floured working surface.
4. Roll your dough and cut 10 pieces using a round cutter.
5. Arrange biscuits in your air fryer's cake pan; brush them with melted butter and cook at 400 °F, for 8 minutes. Serve them for breakfast with some maple syrup on top.

Nutrition Facts: Calories: 192; Fat: 6g; Fiber: 9g; Carbs: 12g; Protein: 3g

Healthy Asparagus Frittata

(Prep + Cook Time: 15 Minutes | Servings: 2)

Ingredients:
- 10 asparagus tips; steamed
- 4 eggs; whisked
- 2 tbsp. parmesan; grated
- 4 tbsp. milk
- Salt and black pepper to the taste
- Cooking spray

Instructions:
1. In a bowl; mix eggs with parmesan, milk, salt and pepper and whisk well.
2. Pre-heat your air fryer at 400 °F and Spray cooking spray into your air fryer basket.
3. Add asparagus, add eggs mix; toss a bit and cook for 5 minutes. Divide frittata on plates and serve for breakfast.

Nutrition Facts: Calories: 312; Fat: 5g; Fiber: 8g; Carbs: 14g; Protein: 2g

Breakfast Ham Dish

(Prep + Cook Time: 25 Minutes | Servings: 6)

Ingredients:
- 10 oz. ham; cubed
- 6 cups French bread; cubed
- 4 oz. green chilies; chopped.
- 2 cups milk
- 5 eggs
- 1 tbsp. mustard
- 4 oz. cheddar cheese; shredded
- Salt and black pepper to the taste
- Cooking spray

Instructions:
1. Pre-heat your air fryer at 350 °F and Spray cooking spray into your air fryer basket.
2. In a bowl; mix eggs with milk, cheese, mustard, salt and pepper and stir.
3. Add bread cubes in your air fryer and mix with chilies and ham.
4. Add eggs mix; spread and cook for 15 minutes. Divide among plates and serve.

Nutrition Facts: Calories: 200; Fat: 5g; Fiber: 6g; Carbs: 12g; Protein: 14g

Spicy Creamy Eggs

(Prep + Cook Time: 22 Minutes | Servings: 4)

Ingredients:
- 4 eggs
- 2 ham slices
- 2 tsp. butter; soft
- 3 tbsp. parmesan; grated
- 2 tsp. chives; chopped
- 2 tbsp. heavy cream
- Salt and black pepper to the taste
- A pinch of smoked paprika

Instructions:
1. Grease your air fryer's pan with the butter; line it with the ham and add it to your air fryer's basket.
2. In a bowl; mix 1 egg with heavy cream, salt and pepper, whisk well and add over ham.
3. Crack the rest of the eggs in the pan, sprinkle parmesan and cook the mix for 12 minutes at 320 degrees F. Sprinkle paprika and chives all over; divide among plates and serve for breakfast.

Nutrition Facts: Calories: 263; Fat: 5g; Fiber: 8g; Carbs: 12g; Protein: 5g

Eggs and Tomatoes

(Prep + Cook Time: 15 Minutes | **Servings:** 4)

Ingredients:
- 4 eggs
- 8 cherry tomatoes; halved
- 2 oz. milk
- 2 tbsp. parmesan; grated
- Salt and black pepper to the taste
- Cooking spray

Instructions:
1. Spray cooking spray into your air fryer basket and Pre-heat your air fryer at 200 degrees F.
2. In a bowl; mix eggs with cheese, milk, salt and pepper and whisk.
3. Add this mix to your air fryer and cook for 6 minutes. Add tomatoes; cook your scrambled eggs for 3 minutes, divide among plates and serve.

Nutrition Facts: Calories: 200; Fat: 4g; Fiber: 7g; Carbs: 12g; Protein: 3g

Tofu Scramble

(Prep + Cook Time: 35 Minutes | **Servings:** 4)

Ingredients:
- 2½ cup red potatoes; cubed
- 1 tofu block; cubed
- 1/2 cup yellow onion; chopped.
- 2 tbsp. soy sauce
- 1 tsp. turmeric; ground
- 1/2 tsp. garlic powder
- 2 tbsp. extra virgin olive oil
- 4 cups broccoli florets
- 1/2 tsp. onion powder
- Salt and black pepper to the taste

Instructions:
1. Mix tofu with 1 tbsp. olive oil, salt, pepper, soy sauce, garlic powder, onion powder, turmeric and onion in a bowl; stir and leave aside.
2. In a separate bowl; combine potatoes with the rest of the olive oil, a pinch of salt and pepper and toss to coat.
3. Put the potatoes in your air fryer Basket and bake at 350 °F for 15 minutes; shaking once for every 5 minutes.
4. Add tofu and its marinade to the air fryer Basket and bake for another 15 minutes.
5. Add broccoli to the fryer and cook everything for 5 minutes more. One done, Serve right away.

Nutrition Facts: Calories: 140; Fat: 4g; Fiber: 3g; Carbs: 10g; Protein: 14g

Cheesy Sandwich

(Prep + Cook Time: 18 Minutes | **Servings:** 1)

Ingredients:
- 2 bread slices
- 2 cheddar cheese slices
- 2 tsp. butter
- A pinch of sweet paprika

Instructions:
1. Spread butter on bread slices, add cheddar cheese on one, sprinkle paprika, top with the other bread slices, cut into 2 halves; arrange them in your air fryer basket and cook at 370 °F, for 8 minutes.
2. Flipping them once, arrange on a plate and serve.

Nutrition Facts: Calories: 130; Fat: 3g; Fiber: 5g; Carbs: 9g; Protein: 3g

Turkey and Eggs Casserole

(**Prep + Cook Time:** 35 Minutes | **Servings:** 6)

Ingredients:
- 12 eggs
- 1 lb. turkey; ground
- 1 sweet potato; cubed
- 1 cup baby spinach
- 1 tbsp. olive oil
- 1/2 tsp. chili powder
- 2 tomatoes; chopped for serving
- Salt and black pepper to the taste

Instructions:
1. In a bowl; mix eggs with salt, pepper, chili powder, potato, spinach, turkey and sweet potato and whisk well.
2. Pre-heat your air fryer at 350 degrees F; add oil and heat it up.
3. Add eggs mix, spread into your air fryer; cover and cook for 25 minutes. Divide among plates and serve for breakfast.

Nutrition Facts: Calories: 300; Fat: 5g; Fiber: 8g; Carbs: 13g; Protein: 6g

Leek and Potato Frittata

(**Prep + Cook Time:** 28 Minutes | **Servings:** 4)

Ingredients:
- 2 gold potatoes; boiled, peeled and chopped.
- 2 leeks; sliced
- 1/4 cup whole milk
- 10 eggs; whisked
- 5 oz. fromage blanc; crumbled
- 2 tbsp. butter
- Salt and black pepper to the taste

Instructions:
1. Heat up a pan that fits your air fryer with the butter over medium heat, add leeks; stir and cook for 4 minutes.
2. Add potatoes, salt, pepper, eggs, cheese and milk, whisk well; cook for 1 minute more,
3. Place the mixture in your air fryer basket and cook at 350 °F, for 13 minutes. Slice frittata, divide among plates and serve.

Nutrition Facts: Calories: 271; Fat: 6g; Fiber: 8g; Carbs: 12g; Protein: 6g

Simple Breakfast

(**Prep + Cook Time:** 23 Minutes | **Servings:** 4)

Ingredients:
- 8 tomatoes; halved
- 4 eggs
- 7 oz. baby spinach
- 8 chestnuts mushrooms; halved
- 1 garlic clove; minced
- 4 chipolatas
- 4 bacon slices; chopped.
- Salt and black pepper to the taste
- Cooking spray

Instructions:
1. Grease a cooking pan with the oil and add tomatoes, garlic and mushrooms.
2. Add bacon and chipolatas, also add spinach and crack eggs at the end.
3. Season with salt and pepper; place pan in the cooking basket of your air fryer and cook for 13 minutes at 350 degrees F. Divide among plates and serve for breakfast.

Nutrition Facts: Calories: 312; Fat: 6g; Fiber: 8g; Carbs: 15g; Protein: 5g

Special Hash Browns
(Prep + Cook Time: 30 Minutes | **Servings:** 6)

Ingredients:
- 2 lbs. hash browns
- 1 cup whole milk
- 1 cup cheddar cheese; shredded
- 6 green onions; chopped
- 8 bacon slices; chopped
- 6 eggs
- 9 oz. cream cheese
- 1 yellow onion; chopped
- Salt and black pepper to the taste
- Cooking spray

Instructions:
1. Pre-heat your air fryer at 350 °F and grease it with cooking spray.
2. In a bowl; mix eggs with milk, cream cheese, cheddar cheese, bacon, onion, salt and pepper and whisk well.
3. Add hash browns to your air fryer; add eggs mix over them and cook for 20 minutes. Divide among plates and serve.

Nutrition Facts: Calories: 261; Fat: 6g; Fiber: 9g; Carbs: 8g; Protein: 12g

Easy Egg Muffins
(Prep + Cook Time: 25 Minutes | **Servings:** 4)

Ingredients:
- 3.5 oz. white flour
- 1 tbsp. baking powder
- 2 oz. parmesan; grated
- 3 tbsp. milk
- 1 egg
- 2 tbsp. olive oil
- A splash of Worcestershire sauce

Instructions:
1. In a bowl; mix egg with flour, oil, baking powder, milk, Worcestershire and parmesan; whisk well and divide into 4 silicon muffin cups.
2. Arrange cups in your air fryer's cooking basket; cover and cook at 392, °F, for 15 minutes. Serve warm for breakfast.

Nutrition Facts: Calories: 251; Fat: 6g; Fiber: 8g; Carbs: 9g; Protein: 3g

Scrambled Eggs
(Prep + Cook Time: 20 Minutes | **Servings:** 2)

Ingredients:
- 2 eggs
- 2 tbsp. butter
- 1 red bell pepper; chopped.
- Salt and black pepper to the taste
- A pinch of sweet paprika

Instructions:
1. In a bowl; mix eggs with salt, pepper, paprika and red bell pepper and whisk well.
2. Pre-heat your air fryer at 140 degrees F; add butter and melt it.
3. Add eggs mix; stir and cook for 10 minutes. Divide scrambled eggs on plates and serve.

Nutrition Facts: Calories: 200; Fat: 4g; Fiber: 7g; Carbs: 10g; Protein: 3g

Turkey Burrito

(Prep + Cook Time: 20 Minutes | **Servings:** 2)

Ingredients:
- 4 slices turkey breast already cooked
- 1/2 red bell pepper; sliced
- 2 eggs
- 1/8 cup mozzarella cheese; grated
- 1 small avocado; peeled; pitted and sliced
- 2 tbsp. salsa
- Salt and black pepper to the taste
- Tortillas for serving

Instructions:
1. In a bowl; whisk eggs with salt and pepper to the taste, pour them in a pan and place it in the air fryer's basket.
2. Cook at 400 °F, for 5 minutes; take pan out of the fryer and transfer eggs to a plate.
3. Arrange tortillas on a working surface, divide eggs on them; also divide turkey meat, bell pepper, cheese, salsa and avocado.
4. Roll your burritos and place them in your air fryer after you've lined it with some tin foil. Heat up the burritos at 300 °F, for 3 minutes; divide them on plates and serve.

Nutrition Facts: Calories: 349; Fat: 23g; Fiber: 11g; Carbs: 20g; Protein: 21g

Biscuits Casserole Delight

(Prep + Cook Time: 25 Minutes | **Servings:** 8)

Ingredients:
- 12 oz. biscuits; quartered
- 3 tbsp. flour
- 1/2 lb. sausage; chopped.
- 2 ½ cups milk
- A pinch of salt and black pepper
- Cooking spray

Instructions:
1. Spray cooking spray into your air fryer basket and Pre-heat your air fryer at 350 degrees F.
2. Add biscuits on the bottom and mix with sausage.
3. Add flour, milk, salt and pepper; toss a bit and cook for 15 minutes. Divide among plates and serve for breakfast.

Nutrition Facts: Calories: 321; Fat: 4g; Fiber: 7g; Carbs: 12g; Protein: 5g

Cheesy Bread

(Prep + Cook Time: 18 Minutes | **Servings:** 3)

Ingredients:
- 6 bread slices
- 5 tbsp. butter; melted
- 3 garlic cloves; minced
- 6 tsp. sun dried tomato pesto
- 1 cup mozzarella cheese; grated

Instructions:
1. Arrange bread slices on a working surface.
2. Spread butter all over; divide tomato paste, garlic and top with grated cheese.
3. Add bread slices to your pre-heated air fryer and cook them at 350 °F, for 8 minutes. Divide among plates and serve.

Nutrition Facts: Calories: 187; Fat: 5g; Fiber: 6g; Carbs: 8g; Protein: 3g

Polenta Bites
(Prep + Cook Time: 30 Minutes | **Servings:** 4)

Ingredients:
For the polenta:
- 1 cup cornmeal
- 1 tbsp. butter
- 3 cups water
- Salt and black pepper to the taste

For the polenta bites:
- 2 tbsp. powdered sugar
- Cooking spray

Instructions:
1. In a pan; mix water with cornmeal, butter, salt and pepper, stir, bring to a boil over medium heat; cook for 10 minutes, take off heat; whisk one more time and keep in the fridge until it's cold.
2. Scoop 1 tbsp. of polenta, shape a ball and place on a working surface.
3. Repeat with the rest of the polenta; arrange all the balls in the cooking basket of your air fryer, spray them with cooking spray; cover and cook at 380 °F, for 8 minutes. Arrange polenta bites on plates; sprinkle sugar all over and serve for breakfast.

Nutrition Facts: Calories: 231; Fat: 7g; Fiber: 8g; Carbs: 12g; Protein: 4g

Blackberry French Style Toast
(Prep + Cook Time: 30 Minutes | **Servings:** 6)

Ingredients:
- 1 cup blackberry jam; warm
- 2 cups half and half
- 1/2 cup brown sugar
- 1 tsp. vanilla extract
- 12 oz. bread loaf; cubed
- 8 oz. cream cheese; cubed
- 4 eggs
- 1 tsp. cinnamon powder
- Cooking spray

Instructions:
1. Spray cooking spray into your air fryer basket and Pre-heat your air fryer at 300 degrees F.
2. Add blueberry jam on the bottom, layer half of the bread cubes, then add cream cheese and top with the rest of the bread.
3. In a bowl; mix eggs with half and half, cinnamon, sugar and vanilla; whisk well and add over bread mix.
4. Air fry for 20 minutes; divide among plates and serve for breakfast.

Nutrition Facts: Calories: 215; Fat: 6g; Fiber: 9g; Carbs: 16g; Protein: 6g

Delicious Doughnuts
(Prep + Cook Time: 28 Minutes | **Servings:** 6)

Ingredients:
- 2 ¼ cups white flour
- 1/2 cup sugar
- 1/3 cup caster sugar
- 4 tbsp. butter; soft
- 1 ½ tsp. baking powder
- 1 tsp. cinnamon powder
- 2 egg yolks
- 1/2 cup sour cream

Instructions:
1. In a bowl; mix 2 tablespoon butter with simple sugar, egg yolks and whisk well.
2. Add half of the sour cream and stir.
3. In another bowls; mix flour with baking powder, stir and also add to eggs mix.
4. Stir well until you obtain a dough, transfer it to a floured working surface; roll it out and cut big circles with smaller ones in the middle.
5. Brush doughnuts with the rest of the butter; Pre-heat your air fryer at 360 degrees F; place doughnuts inside and cook them for 8 minutes.
6. In a bowl; mix cinnamon with caster sugar and stir. Arrange doughnuts on plates and dip them in cinnamon and sugar before serving.

Nutrition Facts: Calories: 182; Fat: 3g; Fiber: 7g; Carbs: 8g; Protein: 3g

Breakfast Casserole
(Prep + Cook Time: 40 Minutes | **Servings:** 4)

Ingredients:
- 1/2 cup flour
- 3 tbsp. brown sugar
- 4 tbsp. butter
- 2 tbsp. white sugar
- 1/2 tsp. cinnamon powder

For the casserole:
- 2 eggs
- 2 tbsp. white sugar
- 2 ½ cups white flour
- 1 tsp. baking soda
- 1 tsp. baking powder
- 2 eggs
- 1/2 cup milk
- 2 cups buttermilk
- 4 tbsp. butter
- 1 ⅔ cup blueberries
- Zest from 1 lemon; grated

Instructions:
1. In a bowl; mix eggs with 2 tbsp. white sugar, 2 ½ cups white flour, baking powder, baking soda, 2 eggs, milk, buttermilk, 4 tbsp. butter, lemon zest and blueberries; stir and pour in a pan that fits your air fryer.
2. In another bowls; mix 3 tbsp. brown sugar with 2 tbsp. white sugar, 4 tbsp. butter, 1/2 cup flour and cinnamon, stir until you obtain a crumble and spread over blueberries mix.
3. Place in preheated air fryer and bake at 300 °F, for 30 minutes. Divide among plates and serve for breakfast.

Nutrition Facts: Calories: 214; Fat: 5g; Fiber: 8g; Carbs: 12g; Protein: 5g

Shrimp Sandwiches
(Prep + Cook Time: 15 Minutes | **Servings:** 4)

Ingredients:
- 6 oz. canned tiny shrimp; drained
- 1 ¼ cups cheddar; shredded
- 2 tbsp. green onions; chopped.
- 4 whole wheat bread slices
- 3 tbsp. mayonnaise
- 2 tbsp. butter; soft

Instructions:
1. In a bowl; mix shrimp with cheese, green onion and mayo and stir well.
2. Spread this on half of the bread slices; top with the other bread slices, cut into halves diagonally and spread butter on top.
3. Place sandwiches in your air fryer and cook at 350 °F, for 5 minutes. Divide shrimp sandwiches on plates and serve them for breakfast.

Nutrition Facts: Calories: 162; Fat: 3g; Fiber: 7g; Carbs: 12g; Protein: 4g

Potato Frittata
(Prep + Cook Time: 30 Minutes | **Servings:** 6)

Ingredients:
- 16 potato wedges
- 6 oz. jarred roasted red bell peppers; chopped.
- 12 eggs; whisked
- 2 tbsp. chives; chopped.
- 6 tbsp. ricotta cheese
- 1/2 cup parmesan; grated
- 3 garlic cloves; minced
- 2 tbsp. parsley; chopped.
- Salt and black pepper to the taste
- Cooking spray

Instructions:
1. In a bowl; mix eggs with red peppers, garlic, parsley, salt, pepper and ricotta and whisk well.
2. Pre-heat your air fryer at 300 °F and Spray cooking spray into your air fryer basket.
3. Add half of the potato wedges on the bottom and sprinkle half of the parmesan all over.
4. Add half of the egg mix; add the rest of the potatoes and the rest of the parmesan.

5. Add the rest of the eggs mix; sprinkle chives and cook for 20 minutes. Divide among plates and serve for breakfast.

Nutrition Facts: Calories: 312; Fat: 6g; Fiber: 9g; Carbs: 16g; Protein: 5g

Banana Oatmeal Casserole
(Prep + Cook Time: 30 Minutes | Servings: 8)

Ingredients:
- 1 banana; peeled and mashed
- 2 cups rolled oats
- 1 tsp. baking powder
- 1/2 cup chocolate chips
- 2/3 cup blueberries
- 1/3 cup brown sugar
- 1 tsp. cinnamon powder
- 2 cups milk
- 1 eggs
- 2 tbsp. butter
- 1 tsp. vanilla extract
- Cooking spray

Instructions:
1. In a bowl; mix sugar with baking powder, cinnamon, chocolate chips, blueberries and banana and stir.
2. In a separate bowl; mix eggs with vanilla extract and butter and stir.
3. Pre-heat your air fryer at 320 degrees F; Spray cooking spray into your air fryer basket and add oats on the bottom.
4. Add cinnamon mix and eggs mix; toss and cook for 20 minutes. Stir one more time, divide into bowls and serve for breakfast.

Nutrition Facts: Calories: 300; Fat: 4g; Fiber: 7g; Carbs: 12g; Protein: 10g

Morning Egg Bowls
(Prep + Cook Time: 30 Minutes | Servings: 4)

Ingredients:
- 4 eggs
- 4 dinner rolls; tops cut off and insides scooped out
- 4 tbsp. mixed chives and parsley
- 4 tbsp. parmesan; grated
- 4 tbsp. heavy cream
- Salt and black pepper to the taste

Instructions:
1. Arrange dinner rolls on a baking pan and crack an egg in each.
2. Divide heavy cream, mixed herbs in each roll and season with salt and pepper.
3. Sprinkle parmesan on top of your rolls; place them in your air fryer and cook at 350 °F, for 20 minutes. Divide your bread bowls on plates and serve for breakfast.

Nutrition Facts: Calories: 238; Fat: 4g; Fiber: 7g; Carbs: 14g; Protein: 7g

Hash browns
(Prep + Cook Time: 25 Minutes | Servings: 6)

Ingredients:
- 16 oz. hash browns
- 1/4 cup olive oil
- 1/2 tsp. paprika
- 1/2 tsp. garlic powder
- 1 egg; whisked
- 2 tbsp. chives; chopped
- 1 cup cheddar; shredded
- Salt and black pepper to the taste

Instructions:
1. Add oil to your air fryer basket and Pre-heat your air fryer at 350 °F.
2. Add hash browns. add paprika, garlic powder, salt, pepper and egg; toss and cook for 15 minutes. Add cheddar and chives, toss; divide among plates and serve.

Nutrition Facts: Calories: 213; Fat: 7g; Fiber: 8g; Carbs: 12g; Protein: 4g

Smoked Sausage Breakfast
(Prep + Cook Time: 40 Minutes | **Servings:** 4)

Ingredients:
- 1 ½ lbs. smoked sausage; chopped and browned
- 1 ½ cups grits
- 1 ½ tsp. thyme; chopped.
- 1/4 tsp. garlic powder
- 4 ½ cups water
- 16 oz. cheddar cheese; shredded
- 1 cup milk
- 4 eggs; whisked
- A pinch of salt and black pepper
- Cooking spray

Instructions:
1. Pour the water in a pot; bring it to boil over medium heat, add grits, stir and cover, cook for 5 minutes and take off heat.
2. Add milk, thyme, salt, pepper, garlic powder and eggs and cheese, stir until cheese melts and whisk really well.
3. Pre-heat your air fryer at 300 degrees F; Spray cooking spray into your air fryer basket and add browned sausage and grits mix; spread and cook for 25 minutes.
4. Divide among plates and serve for breakfast.

Nutrition Facts: Calories: 321; Fat: 6g; Fiber: 7g; Carbs: 17g; Protein: 4g

Beef Burger
(Prep + Cook Time: 55 Minutes | **Servings:** 4)

Ingredients:
- 1 lb. beef; ground
- 1 yellow onion; chopped
- 1 tbsp. cheddar cheese; grated
- 1 tsp. parsley; chopped
- 1 tsp. tomato puree
- 1 tsp. garlic; minced
- 1 tsp. mustard
- 1 tsp. basil; dried
- Salt and black pepper to the taste
- 4 bread buns; for serving

Instructions:
1. In a bowl; mix beef with onion, tomato puree, garlic, mustard, basil, parsley, cheese, salt and pepper; stir well and shape 4 burgers out of this mix.
2. Pre-heat your air fryer at 400 degrees F; add burgers and cook them for 25 minutes.
3. Reduce temperature to 350 °F and bake burgers for 20 minutes more. Arrange them on bread buns and serve.

Nutrition Facts: Calories: 234; Fat: 5g; Fiber: 8g; Carbs: 12g; Protein: 4g

Protein Rich Egg White Omelet
(Prep + Cook Time: 25 Minutes | **Servings:** 4)

Ingredients:
- 1 cup egg whites
- 1/4 cup mushrooms; chopped
- 2 tbsp. chives; chopped
- 1/4 cup tomato; chopped
- 2 tbsp. skim milk
- Salt and black pepper to the taste

Instructions:
1. In a bowl; mix egg whites with tomato, milk, mushrooms, chives, salt and pepper; whisk well and pour into your air fryer's pan.
2. Cook at 320 °F, for 15 minutes; cool omelet down, slice, divide among plates and serve.

Nutrition Facts: Calories: 100; Fat: 3g; Fiber: 6g; Carbs: 7g; Carbs: 4

Baked Eggs

(Prep + Cook Time: 30 Minutes | **Servings:** 4)

Ingredients:
- 4 eggs
- 1 lb. baby spinach; torn
- 4 tbsp. milk
- 1 tbsp. olive oil
- 7 oz. ham; chopped.
- Cooking spray
- Salt and black pepper to the taste

Instructions:
1. Heat up a pan with the oil over medium heat; add baby spinach, stir cook for a couple of minutes and take off heat.
2. Grease 4 ramekins with cooking spray and divide baby spinach and ham in each.
3. Crack an egg in each ramekin, also divide milk, season with salt and pepper; place ramekins in preheated air fryer at 350 °F and bake for 20 minutes. Serve baked eggs for breakfast.

Nutrition Facts: Calories: 321; Fat: 6g; Fiber: 8g; Carbs: 15g; Protein: 12g

Eggs, Sausage and Cheese Mix

(Prep + Cook Time: 30 Minutes | **Servings:** 4)

Ingredients:
- 10 oz. sausages; cooked and crumbled
- 8 eggs; whisked
- 1 cup milk
- 1 cup cheddar cheese; shredded
- 1 cup mozzarella cheese; shredded
- Salt and black pepper to the taste
- Cooking spray

Instructions:
1. In a bowl; mix sausages with cheese, mozzarella, eggs, milk, salt and pepper and whisk well.
2. Pre-heat your air fryer at 380 degrees F; spray cooking oil, add eggs and sausage mix and cook for 20 minutes. Divide among plates and serve.

Nutrition Facts: Calories: 320; Fat: 6g; Fiber: 8g; Carbs: 12g; Protein: 5g

Mixed Bell Peppers Frittata

(Prep + Cook Time: 30 Minutes | **Servings:** 4)

Ingredients:
- 1/2 lbs. chicken sausage; casings removed and chopped.
- 1 sweet onion; chopped
- 1 red bell pepper; chopped
- 2 tbsp. olive oil
- 1 orange bell pepper; chopped
- 1 green bell pepper; chopped
- 8 eggs; whisked
- 1/2 cup mozzarella cheese; shredded
- 2 tsp. oregano; chopped
- Salt and black pepper to the taste

Instructions:
1. Add 1 tablespoon of olive oil to your air fryer; add sausage, heat up at 320 °F and brown for 1 minute.
2. Add the rest of the olive oil, onion, red bell pepper, orange and green one; stir and cook for 2 minutes more.
3. Add oregano, salt, pepper and eggs; stir and cook for 15 minutes. Add mozzarella, leave frittata aside for a few minutes; divide among plates and serve.

Nutrition Facts: Calories: 212; Fat: 4g; Fiber: 6g; Carbs: 8g; Protein: 12g

Breakfast Cherries Risotto

(Prep + Cook Time: 22 Minutes | **Servings:** 4)

Ingredients:
- 1/2 cup cherries; dried
- 1/3 cup brown sugar
- 1 ½ cup Arborio rice
- 1 ½ tsp. cinnamon powder
- 1 cup apple juice
- 3 cups milk
- 2 tbsp. butter
- 2 apples; cored and sliced
- A pinch of salt

Instructions:
1. Heat up a pan that fist your air fryer with the butter over medium heat, add rice; stir and cook for 4-5 minutes.
2. Add sugar, apples, apple juice, milk, cinnamon and cherries and stir, Place the mixture in your air fryer basket and cook at 350 °F, for 8 minutes. Divide into bowls and serve for breakfast.

Nutrition Facts: Calories: 162; Fat: 12g; Fiber: 6g; Carbs: 23g; Protein: 8g

Broccoli Quiches

(Prep + Cook Time: 30 Minutes | **Servings:** 2)

Ingredients:
- 1 broccoli head; florets separated and steamed
- 1 tomato; chopped.
- 1 tsp. thyme; chopped
- 3 carrots; chopped and steamed
- 2 oz. cheddar cheese; grated
- 2 oz. milk
- 1 tsp. parsley; chopped
- 2 eggs
- Salt and black pepper to the taste

Instructions:
1. In a bowl; mix eggs, milk, parsley, thyme, salt and pepper and whisk well.
2. Put the broccoli, carrots and tomato in your air fryer.
3. Add eggs mix on top, spread cheddar cheese; lock the basket and cook at 350 °F, for 20 minutes. Divide among plates and serve for breakfast.

Nutrition Facts: Calories: 214; Fat: 4g; Fiber: 7g; Carbs: 12g; Protein: 3g

Ham Pie

(Prep + Cook Time: 35 Minutes | **Servings:** 6)

Ingredients:
- 2 cups ham; cooked and chopped.
- 16 oz. crescent rolls dough
- 1 tbsp. parmesan; grated
- 2 eggs; whisked
- 2 cups cheddar cheese; grated
- Salt and black pepper to the taste
- Cooking spray

Instructions:
1. Spray cooking spray into your air fryer basket and press half of the crescent rolls dough on the bottom.
2. In a bowl; mix eggs with cheddar cheese, parmesan, salt and pepper; whisk well and add over dough.
3. Spread ham, cut the rest of the crescent rolls dough in strips, arrange them over ham and cook at 300 °F, for 25 minutes. Slice pie and serve for breakfast.

Nutrition Facts: Calories: 400; Fat: 27g; Fiber: 7g; Carbs: 22g; Protein: 16g

Cinnamon Toast

(Prep + Cook Time: 15 Minutes | **Servings:** 6)

Ingredients:
- 12 bread slices
- 1 ½ tsp. cinnamon powder
- 1 stick butter; soft
- 1 ½ tsp. vanilla extract
- 1/2 cup sugar

Instructions:
1. In a bowl; mix soft butter with sugar, vanilla and cinnamon and whisk well.
2. Spread this on bread slices; place them in your air fryer and cook at 400 °F, for 5 minutes; divide among plates and serve.

Nutrition Facts: Calories: 221; Fat: 4g; Fiber: 7g; Carbs: 12g; Protein: 8g

Potato Hash

(Prep + Cook Time: 35 Minutes | **Servings:** 4)

Ingredients:
- 1 ½ potatoes; cubed
- 1 yellow onion; chopped.
- 2 tsp. olive oil
- 2 eggs
- 1/2 tsp. thyme; dried
- 1 green bell pepper; chopped
- Salt and black pepper to the taste

Instructions:
1. Pre-heat your air fryer at 350 degrees F; add oil, add onion, bell pepper, salt and pepper; stir and cook for 5 minutes.
2. Add potatoes, thyme and eggs, stir, cover and cook at 360 °F, for 20 minutes. Divide among plates and serve.

Nutrition Facts: Calories: 241; Fat: 4g; Fiber: 7g; Carbs: 12g; Protein: 7g

Breakfast Spanish Omelet

(Prep + Cook Time: 20 Minutes | **Servings:** 4)

Ingredients:
- 3 eggs
- 1/2 chorizo; chopped
- 1 tbsp. parsley; chopped.
- 1 tbsp. feta cheese; crumbled
- 1 potato; peeled and cubed
- 1/2 cup corn
- 1 tbsp. olive oil
- Salt and black pepper to the taste

Instructions:
1. Pre-heat your air fryer at 350 °F and add oil.
2. Add chorizo and potatoes; stir and brown them for a few seconds.
3. In a bowl; mix eggs with corn, parsley, cheese, salt and pepper and whisk.
4. Pour this over chorizo and potatoes; spread and cook for 5 minutes. Divide omelet on plates and serve for breakfast.

Nutrition Facts: Calories: 300; Fat: 6g; Fiber: 9g; Carbs: 12g; Protein: 6g

Veggie Mix

(Prep + Cook Time: 35 Minutes | **Servings:** 6)

Ingredients:
- 1 gold potato; chopped.
- 1 yellow onion; sliced
- 1 red bell pepper; chopped.
- 2 tbsp. olive oil
- 8 eggs
- 2 tbsp. mustard
- 3 cups milk
- 8 oz. brie; trimmed and cubed
- 12 oz. sourdough bread; cubed
- 4 oz. parmesan; grated
- Salt and black pepper to the taste

Instructions:
1. Pre-heat your air fryer at 350 degrees F; add oil, onion, potato and bell pepper and cook for 5 minutes.
2. In a bowl; mix eggs with milk, salt, pepper and mustard and whisk well.
3. Add bread and brie to your air fryer; add half of the eggs mix and add half of the parmesan as well.
4. Add the rest of the bread and parmesan; toss just a little bit and cook for 20 minutes.
5. Divide among plates and serve.

Nutrition Facts: Calories: 231; Fat: 5g; Fiber: 10g; Carbs: 20g; Protein: 12g

Ham Rolls
(Prep + Cook Time: 20 Minutes | Servings: 4)

Ingredients:
- 8 ham slices; chopped
- 1 sheet puff pastry
- 4 handful gruyere cheese; grated
- 4 tsp. mustard

Instructions:
1. Roll out puff pastry on a working surface, divide cheese, ham and mustard, roll tight and cut into medium rounds.
2. Place all rolls in your air fryer and cook for 10 minutes at 370 degrees F. Divide rolls on plates and serve.

Nutrition Facts: Calories: 182; Fat: 4g; Fiber: 7g; Carbs: 9g; Protein: 8g

Breakfast Shrimp Frittata
(Prep + Cook Time: 25 Minutes | Servings: 4)

Ingredients:
- 1/2 cup shrimp; cooked, peeled, deveined and chopped.
- 4 eggs
- 1/2 cup baby spinach; chopped.
- 1/2 tsp. basil; dried
- Cooking spray
- Salt and black pepper to the taste
- 1/2 cup rice; cooked
- 1/2 cup Monterey jack cheese; grated

Instructions:
1. In a bowl; mix eggs with salt, pepper and basil and whisk well.
2. Spray cooking spray into your air fryer basket and add rice, shrimp and spinach.
3. Add eggs mix, sprinkle cheese all over and cook in your air fryer at 350 °F, for 10 minutes. Divide among plates and serve.

Nutrition Facts: Calories: 162; Fat: 6g; Fiber: 5g; Carbs: 8g; Protein: 4g

Veggie Burritos Breakfast
(Prep + Cook Time: 20 Minutes | Servings: 4)

Ingredients:
- 1/2 cup sweet potatoes; steamed and cubed
- 1/2 small broccoli head; florets separated and steamed
- 2 tbsp. cashew butter
- 2 tbsp. tamari
- 2 tbsp. water
- 2 tbsp. liquid smoke
- 4 rice papers
- 7 asparagus stalks
- 8 roasted red peppers; chopped
- A handful kale; chopped

Instructions:
1. In a bowl; mix cashew butter with water, tamari and liquid smoke and whisk well.
2. Wet rice papers and arrange them on a working surface.
3. Divide sweet potatoes, broccoli, asparagus, red peppers and kale; wrap burritos and dip each in cashew mix.
4. Arrange burritos in your air fryer basket and cook them at 350 °F, for 10 minutes. Divide veggie burritos on plates and serve.

Nutrition Facts: Calories: 172; Fat: 4g; Fiber: 7g; Carbs: 8g; Protein: 3g

Spinach Parcels

(Prep + Cook Time: 14 Minutes | **Servings:** 2)

Ingredients:
- 1 lb. baby spinach leaves; roughly chopped
- 4 sheets filo pastry
- 1/2 lb. ricotta cheese
- 2 tbsp. pine nuts
- 1 eggs; whisked
- Zest from 1 lemon; grated
- Greek yogurt for serving
- Salt and black pepper to the taste

Instructions:
1. In a bowl; mix spinach with cheese, egg, lemon zest, salt, pepper and pine nuts and stir.
2. Arrange filo sheets on a working surface, divide spinach mix; fold diagonally to shape your parcels.
3. Place them in your preheated air fryer at 400 degrees F. Bake parcels for 4 minutes; divide them on plates and serve them with Greek yogurt on the side.

Nutrition Facts: Calories: 182; Fat: 4g; Fiber: 8g; Carbs: 9g; Protein: 5g

Special Corn Flakes Casserole

(Prep + Cook Time: 18 Minutes | **Servings:** 5)

Ingredients:
- 1 ½ cups corn flakes; crumbled
- 1/3 cup milk
- 4 tbsp. cream cheese; whipped
- 1/4 tsp. nutmeg; ground
- 1/4 cup blueberries
- 3 tsp. sugar
- 2 eggs; whisked
- 5 bread slices

Instructions:
1. In a bowl; mix eggs with sugar, nutmeg and milk and whisk well.
2. In another bowl; mix cream cheese with blueberries and whisk well.
3. Put the corn flakes in a third bowl.
4. Spread blueberry mix on each bread slice; then dip in eggs mix and dredge in corn flakes at the end.
5. Place bread in your air fryer's basket; heat up at 400 °F and bake for 8 minutes. Divide among plates and serve.

Nutrition Facts: Calories: 300; Fat: 5g; Fiber: 7g; Carbs: 16g; Protein: 4g

Breakfast Soufflé

(Prep + Cook Time: 18 Minutes | **Servings:** 4)

Ingredients:
- 4 eggs; whisked
- 4 tbsp. heavy cream
- 2 tbsp. parsley; chopped.
- 2 tbsp. chives; chopped.
- A pinch of red chili pepper; crushed
- Salt and black pepper to the taste

Instructions:
1. In a bowl; mix eggs with salt, pepper, heavy cream, red chili pepper, parsley and chives; stir well and divide into 4 soufflé dishes.
2. Arrange dishes in your air fryer and cook soufflés at 350 °F, for 8 minutes. Serve them hot.

Nutrition Facts: Calories: 300; Fat: 7g; Fiber: 9g; Carbs: 15g; Protein: 6g

Fried Tomato Quiche

(Prep + Cook Time: 40 Minutes | **Servings:** 1)

Ingredients:
- 1/4 cup tomatoes; chopped.
- 2 tbsp. yellow onion; chopped.
- 1/2 cup gouda cheese; shredded
- 2 eggs
- 1/4 cup milk
- Salt and black pepper to the taste
- Cooking spray

Instructions:
1. Spray the ramekin with cooking spray.
2. Crack eggs, add onion, milk, cheese, tomatoes, salt and pepper and stir. Place the ramekin in your air fryer's basket and cook at 340 °F, for 30 minutes.

Nutrition Facts: Calories: 241; Fat: 6g; Fiber: 8g; Carbs: 14g; Protein: 6g

Tuna Sandwiches
(Prep + Cook Time: 15 Minutes | **Servings:** 4)

Ingredients:
- 16 oz. canned tuna; drained
- 2 green onions; chopped.
- 3 English muffins; halved
- 1/4 cup mayonnaise
- 2 tbsp. mustard
- 1 tbsp. lemon juice
- 3 tbsp. butter
- 6 provolone cheese

Instructions:
1. In a bowl; mix tuna with mayo, lemon juice, mustard and green onions and stir.
2. Grease muffin halves with the butter, place them in preheated air fryer and bake them at 350 °F, for 4 minutes.
3. Spread tuna mix on muffin halves; top each with provolone cheese, return sandwiches to air fryer and cook them for 4 minutes; divide among plates and serve hot.

Nutrition Facts: Calories: 182; Fat: 4g; Fiber: 7g; Carbs: 8g; Protein: 6g

Fish Tacos Breakfast
(Prep + Cook Time: 23 Minutes | **Servings:** 4)

Ingredients:
- 4 white fish fillets; skinless and boneless
- 4 big tortillas
- 1 red bell pepper; chopped
- 1/2 cup salsa
- 1 yellow onion; chopped
- 1 cup corn
- A handful mixed romaine lettuce; spinach and radicchio
- 4 tbsp. parmesan; grated

Instructions:
1. Place the fish fillets in your air fryer and cook at 350 °F, for 6 minutes.
2. Meanwhile; heat up a pan over medium high heat, add bell pepper, onion and corn; stir and cook for 1-2 minutes.
3. Arrange tortillas on a working surface, divide fish fillets, spread salsa over them; divide mixed veggies and mixed greens and spread parmesan on each at the end.
4. Roll your tacos; place them in preheated air fryer and cook at 350 °F, for 6 minutes more. Divide fish tacos on plates and serve.

Nutrition Facts: Calories: 200; Fat: 3g; Fiber: 7g; Carbs: 9g; Protein: 5g

Onion Frittata
(Prep + Cook Time: 30 Minutes | **Servings:** 6)

Ingredients:
- 2 yellow onions; chopped
- 1 lb. small potatoes; chopped
- 10 eggs; whisked
- 1 tbsp. olive oil
- 1 oz. cheddar cheese; grated
- 1/2 cup sour cream
- Salt and black pepper to the taste

Instructions:
1. In a large bowl; mix eggs with potatoes, onions, salt, pepper, cheese and sour cream and whisk well.
2. Grease your air fryer's pan with the oil, add eggs mix; place in air fryer and cook for 20 minutes at 320 degrees F. Slice frittata, divide among plates and serve.

Nutrition Facts: Calories: 231; Fat: 5g; Fiber: 7g; Carbs: 8g; Protein: 4g

Pea Tortilla

(Prep + Cook Time: 17 Minutes | **Servings:** 8)

Ingredients:
- 1/2 lb. baby peas
- 1 ½ cup yogurt
- 8 eggs
- 1/2 cup mint; chopped.
- 4 tbsp. butter
- Salt and black pepper to the taste

Instructions:
1. Heat up a pan that fits your air fryer with the butter over medium heat, add peas; stir and cook for a couple of minutes.
2. Meanwhile; in a bowl, mix half of the yogurt with salt, pepper, eggs and mint and whisk well.
3. Pour this over the peas, toss, close the air fryer basket and cook at 350 °F, for 7 minutes. Spread the rest of the yogurt over your tortilla; slice and serve.

Nutrition Facts: Calories: 192; Fat: 5g; Fiber: 4g; Carbs: 8g; Protein: 7g

Walnuts Pear Oatmeal

(Prep + Cook Time: 17 Minutes | **Servings:** 4)

Ingredients:
- 1 cup rolled oats
- 1/2 cup walnuts; chopped.
- 1 tbsp. butter; soft
- 1/4 cups brown sugar
- 1 cup water
- 1/2 cup raisins
- 1/2 tsp. cinnamon powder
- 2 cups pear; peeled and chopped.

Instructions:
1. In a heat proof dish that fits your air fryer; mix milk with sugar, butter, oats, cinnamon, raisins, pears and walnuts; stir well.
2. Now Place the pan in your fryer and cook at 360 °F, for 12 minutes. Divide into bowls and serve.

Nutrition Facts: Calories: 230; Fat: 6g; Fiber: 11g; Carbs: 20g; Protein: 5g

Breakfast Raspberry Rolls

(Prep + Cook Time: 50 Minutes | **Servings:** 6)

Ingredients:
- 3 ¼ cups flour
- 1 cup milk
- 1/4 cup sugar

For the filling:
- 8 oz. cream cheese; soft
- 12 oz. raspberries
- 1 tsp. vanilla extract
- 1 egg
- 4 tbsp. butter
- 2 tsp. yeast

- 5 tbsp. sugar
- 1 tbsp. cornstarch
- Zest from 1 lemon; grated

Instructions:
1. In a bowl; mix flour with sugar and yeast and stir.
2. Add milk and egg, stir until you obtain a dough, leave it aside to rise for 30 minutes; transfer dough to a working surface and roll well.
3. In a bowl; mix cream cheese with sugar, vanilla and lemon zest; stir well and spread over dough.
4. In another bowl; mix raspberries with cornstarch, stir and spread over cream cheese mix.
5. Roll the dough, cut into medium pieces, place them in your air fryer; spray them with cooking spray and cook them at 350 °F, for 30 minutes. Serve your rolls for breakfast.

Nutrition Facts: Calories: 261; Fat: 5g; Fiber: 8g; Carbs: 9g; Protein: 6g

Bread Pudding
(Prep + Cook Time: 32 Minutes | Servings: 4)

Ingredients:
- 1/2 lb. white bread; cubed
- 3/4 cup milk
- 3/4 cup water
- 2 tsp. cinnamon powder
- 1 ⅓ cup flour
- 3/5 cup brown sugar
- 2 tsp. cornstarch
- 1/2 cup apple; peeled; cored and roughly chopped.
- 5 tbsp. honey
- 1 tsp. vanilla extract
- 3 oz. soft butter

Instructions:
1. In a bowl; mix bread with apple, milk with water, honey, cinnamon, vanilla and cornstarch and whisk well.
2. In a separate bowl; mix flour with sugar and butter and stir until you obtain a crumbled mixture.
3. Press half of the crumble mix on the bottom of your air fryer; add bread and apple mix, add the rest of the crumble and cook everything at 350 °F, for 22 minutes. Divide bread pudding on plates and serve.

Nutrition Facts: Calories: 261; Fat: 7g; Fiber: 7g; Carbs: 8g; Protein: 5g

Bread Rolls
(Prep + Cook Time: 22 Minutes | Servings: 4)

Ingredients:
- 5 potatoes; boiled; peeled and mashed
- 1/2 tsp. turmeric powder
- 2 curry leaf springs
- 1/2 tsp. mustard seeds
- 8 bread slices; white parts only
- 1 coriander bunch; chopped.
- 2 green chilies; chopped
- 2 small yellow onions; chopped.
- 2 tbsp. olive oil
- Salt and black pepper to the taste

Instructions:
1. Heat up a pan with 1 teaspoon oil; add mustard seeds, onions, curry leaves and turmeric, stir and cook for a few seconds.
2. Add mashed potatoes, salt, pepper, coriander and chilies, stir well; take off heat and cool it down.
3. Divide potatoes mix into 8 parts and shape ovals using your wet hands.
4. Wet bread slices with water; press in order to drain excess water and keep one slice in your palm.
5. Add a potato oval over bread slice and wrap it around it.
6. Repeat with the rest of the potato mix and bread.
7. Pre-heat your air fryer at 400 degrees F; add the rest of the oil, add bread rolls; cook them for 12 minutes. Divide bread rolls on plates and serve.

Nutrition Facts: Calories: 261; Fat: 6g; Fiber: 9g; Carbs: 12g; Protein: 7g

Cream Breakfast Tofu
(Prep + Cook Time: 35 Minutes | Servings: 4)

Ingredients:
- 1 block firm tofu; pressed and cubed
- 1 tsp. rice vinegar
- 2 tbsp. soy sauce
- 1 tbsp. potato starch
- 2 tsp. sesame oil
- 1 cup Greek yogurt

Instructions:
1. In a bowl; mix tofu cubes with vinegar, soy sauce and oil, toss, and leave aside for 15 minutes.
2. Dip tofu cubes in potato starch, toss, transfer to your air fryer; heat up at 370 °F and cook for 20 minutes shake the basket every few minutes to ensure even cooking. Divide into bowls and serve for breakfast with some Greek yogurt on the side.

Nutrition Facts: Calories: 110; Fat: 4g; Fiber: 5g; Carbs: 8g; Protein: 4g

Potatoes with Bacon

(Prep + Cook Time: 30 Minutes | **Servings:** 4)

Ingredients:
- 4 potatoes; peeled and cut into medium cubes
- 4 bacon slices; chopped
- 6 garlic cloves; minced
- 2 eggs; whisked
- 2 rosemary springs; chopped
- 1 tbsp. olive oil
- Salt and black pepper to the taste

Instructions:
1. In your air fryer's pan, mix oil with potatoes, garlic, bacon, rosemary, salt, pepper and eggs and whisk.
2. Cook potatoes at 400 °F, for 20 minutes; divide everything on plates and serve.

Nutrition Facts: Calories: 211; Fat: 3g; Fiber: 5g; Carbs: 8g; Protein: 5g

Mushroom Oatmeal Breakfast

(Prep + Cook Time: 30 Minutes | **Servings:** 4)

Ingredients:
- 8 oz. mushroom; sliced
- 1 small yellow onion; chopped.
- 1 cup steel cut oats
- 2 garlic cloves; minced
- 2 tbsp. extra virgin olive oil
- 1/2 cup gouda cheese; grated
- 2 tbsp. butter
- 1/2 cup water
- 14 oz. canned chicken stock
- 3 thyme springs; chopped.
- Salt and black pepper to the taste

Instructions:
1. Heat up a pan that fits your air fryer with the butter over medium heat, add onions and garlic; stir and cook for 4 minutes.
2. Add oats, water, salt, pepper, stock and thyme; stir, close the air fryer basket and cook at 360 °F, for 16 minutes.
3. Meanwhile; heat up a pan with the olive oil over medium heat, add mushrooms, cook them for 3 minutes; add to oatmeal and cheese; stir, divide into bowls and serve.

Nutrition Facts: Calories: 284; Fat: 8g; Fiber: 8g; Carbs: 20g; Protein: 17g

Smoked Fried Tofu

(Prep + Cook Time: 22 Minutes | **Servings:** 2)

Ingredients:
- 1 tofu block; pressed and cubed
- 1 tbsp. smoked paprika
- 1/4 cup cornstarch
- Salt and black pepper to the taste
- Cooking spray

Instructions:
1. Grease your air fryer's basket with cooking spray and heat the fryer at 370 degrees F.
2. In a bowl; mix tofu with salt, pepper, smoked paprika and cornstarch and toss well.
3. Add tofu to you air fryer's basket and cook for 12 minutes, shaking the fryer basket for every 4 minutes. Divide into bowls and serve for breakfast.

Nutrition Facts: Calories: 172; Fat: 4g; Fiber: 7g; Carbs: 12g; Protein: 4g

Long Beans Omelet

(Prep + Cook Time: 20 Minutes | **Servings:** 3)

Ingredients:
- 4 long beans; trimmed and sliced
- 1/2 tsp. soy sauce
- 1 tbsp. olive oil
- 3 eggs; whisked
- 4 garlic cloves; minced
- A pinch of salt and black pepper

Instructions:
1. In a bowl; mix eggs with a pinch of salt, black pepper and soy sauce and whisk well.
2. Pre-heat your air fryer at 320 degrees F; add oil and garlic, stir and brown for 1 minute.
3. Add long beans and eggs mix; spread and cook for 10 minutes. Divide omelet on plates and serve for breakfast.

Nutrition Facts: Calories: 200; Fat: 3g; Fiber: 7g; Carbs: 9g; Protein: 3g

Mushrooms and Tofu
(Prep + Cook Time: 20 Minutes | **Servings:** 2)

Ingredients:
- 1 tofu block; pressed and cut into medium pieces
- 1 tbsp. mushrooms; minced
- 1 cup panko bread crumbs
- 1/2 tbsp. flour
- 1 egg
- Salt and black pepper to the taste

Instructions:
1. In a bowl; mix egg with mushrooms, flour, salt and pepper and whisk well.
2. Dip tofu pieces in egg mix; then dredge them in panko bread crumbs.
3. Place them in your air fryer and cook at 350 °F, for 10 minutes. Serve them right away.

Nutrition Facts: Calories: 142; Fat: 4g; Fiber: 6g; Carbs: 8g; Protein: 3g

Dates Millet Pudding
(Prep + Cook Time: 25 Minutes | **Servings:** 4)

Ingredients:
- 14 oz. milk
- 4 dates; pitted
- 7 oz. water
- 2/3 cup millet
- Honey for serving

Instructions:
1. Put the millet in a pan that fits your air fryer; add dates, milk and water; stir.
2. Close the air fryer basket and cook at 360 °F, for 15 minutes. Divide among plates; drizzle honey on top and serve for breakfast.

Nutrition Facts: Calories: 231; Fat: 6g; Fiber: 6g; Carbs: 18g; Protein: 6g

French Beans and Egg Mix
(Prep + Cook Time: 20 Minutes | **Servings:** 3)

Ingredients:
- 3 oz. French beans; trimmed and sliced diagonally
- 2 eggs; whisked
- 1/2 tsp. soy sauce
- 1 tbsp. olive oil
- 4 garlic cloves; minced
- Salt and white pepper to the taste

Instructions:
1. In a bowl; mix eggs with soy sauce, salt and pepper and whisk well.
2. Pre-heat your air fryer at 320 degrees F; add oil and heat it up as well.
3. Add garlic and brown for 1 minute.
4. Add French beans and egg mix; toss and cook for 10 minutes. Divide among plates and serve for breakfast.

Nutrition Facts: Calories: 182; Fat: 3g; Fiber: 6g; Carbs: 8g; Protein: 3g

Espresso Oatmeal
(Prep + Cook Time: 27 Minutes | **Servings:** 4)

Ingredients:
- 1 cup steel cut oats
- 1 cup milk
- 1 tsp. espresso powder
- 2 tsp. vanilla extract
- 2 ½ cups water
- 2 tbsp. sugar

Instructions:
1. In a pan that fits your air fryer, mix oats with water, sugar, milk and espresso powder; stir, close the air fryer basket and cook at 360 °F, for 17 minutes.
2. Add vanilla extract, stir; leave everything aside for 5 minutes; divide into bowls and serve for breakfast.

Nutrition Facts: Calories: 261; Fat: 7g; Fiber: 6g; Carbs: 39g; Protein: 6g

Artichoke Frittata
(Prep + Cook Time: 25 Minutes | **Servings:** 6)

Ingredients:
- 3 canned artichokes hearts; drained and chopped
- 1/2 tsp. oregano; dried
- 2 tbsp. olive oil
- Salt and black pepper to the taste
- 6 eggs; whisked

Instructions:
1. In a bowl; mix artichokes with oregano, salt, pepper and eggs and whisk well.
2. Add the oil to your air fryer's pan; add eggs mix and cook at 320 °F, for 15 minutes. Divide frittata on plates and serve for breakfast.

Nutrition Facts: Calories: 136; Fat: 6g; Fiber: 6g; Carbs: 9g; Protein: 4g

Lunch Recipes

Fresh Style Chicken

(Prep + Cook Time: 32 Minutes | **Servings:** 4)

Ingredients:
- 2 chicken breasts; skinless, boneless and cubed
- 1/2 tsp. thyme; dried
- 10 oz. alfredo sauce
- 8 button mushrooms; sliced
- 1 red bell pepper; chopped
- 1 tbsp. olive oil
- 6 bread slices
- 2 tbsp. butter; soft

Instructions:
1. In your air fryer Basket, mix chicken, mushrooms, bell pepper and olive oil; toss to coat well and cook at 350 °F, for 15 minutes.
2. Transfer chicken mix to a bowl; add thyme and alfredo sauce, toss, return to air fryer and cook at 350 °F, for 4 minutes more.
3. Spread butter on bread slices; add it to the fryer, butter side up and cook for 4 minutes more.
4. Arrange toasted bread slices on a platter; top each with chicken mix and serve.

Nutrition Facts: Calories: 172; Fat: 4g; Fiber: 9g; Carbs: 12g; Protein: 4g

Chicken Salad

(Prep + Cook Time: 30 Minutes | **Servings:** 4)

Ingredients:
- 1 lb. chicken tenders; boneless
- 12 cherry tomatoes; sliced
- 2 ears of corn; hulled
- 1/4 cup ranch dressing
- 3 tbsp. BBQ sauce
- 1 tsp. sweet paprika
- 1 tbsp. brown sugar
- 3 tbsp. cilantro; chopped.
- 1/2 tsp. garlic powder
- 1/2 iceberg lettuce head; cut into medium strips
- 1/2 romaine lettuce head; cut into medium strips
- 1 cup canned black beans; drained
- 1 cup cheddar cheese; shredded
- 4 green onions; chopped.
- Olive oil as needed
- Salt and black pepper to the taste

Instructions:
1. Put the corn in your air fryer basket; drizzle some oil, toss, cook at 400 °F, for 10 minutes; transfer to a plate and set aside.
2. Put the chicken pieces in your air fryer's basket, add salt, pepper, brown sugar, paprika and garlic powder; toss, drizzle some more oil, cook at 400 °F, for 10 minutes; flipping them halfway, transfer tenders to a cutting board and chop them.
3. Cur kernels off the cob, transfer corn to a bowl; add chicken, iceberg lettuce, romaine lettuce, black beans, cheese, cilantro, tomatoes, onions, BBQ sauce and ranch dressing; toss well and serve for lunch.

Nutrition Facts: Calories: 372; Fat: 6g; Fiber: 9g; Carbs: 17g; Protein: 6g

Cheese and Macaroni

(Prep + Cook Time: 40 Minutes | **Servings:** 3)

Ingredients:
- 1 ½ cups favorite macaroni
- 1/2 cup heavy cream
- 1/2 cup mozzarella cheese; shredded
- 1/4 cup parmesan; shredded
- 1 cup chicken stock
- 3/4 cup cheddar cheese; shredded
- Salt and black pepper to the taste
- Cooking spray

Instructions:
1. Spray a pan with cooking spray; add macaroni, heavy cream, stock, cheddar cheese, mozzarella and parmesan but also salt and pepper; toss well.
2. Place the pan in your air fryer's basket and cook for 30 minutes. Divide among plates and serve.

Nutrition Facts: Calories: 341; Fat: 7g; Fiber: 8g; Carbs: 18g; Protein: 4g

Sweet Potato Casserole
(Prep + Cook Time: 60 Minutes | **Servings:** 6)

Ingredients:
- 3 big sweet potatoes; pricked with a fork
- 1 cup chicken stock
- 1/4 tsp. nutmeg; ground
- 1/3 cup coconut cream
- Salt and black pepper to the taste
- A pinch of cayenne pepper

Instructions:
1. Place the sweet potatoes in your air fryer basket; cook them at 350 °F, for 40 minutes; cool them down, peel, roughly chop and transfer to a pan that fits your air fryer.
2. Add stock, salt, pepper, cayenne and coconut cream; toss, Close the air fryer and cook at 360 °F, for 10 minutes. Divide casserole into bowls and serve.

Nutrition Facts: Calories: 245; Fat: 4g; Fiber: 5g; Carbs: 10g; Protein: 6g

Beef Meatballs
(Prep + Cook Time: 25 Minutes | **Servings:** 4)

Ingredients:
- 1/2 lb. beef; ground
- 1/2 tsp. garlic powder
- 1/2 tsp. onion powder
- 1/2 lb. Italian sausage; chopped.
- 1/2 cup cheddar cheese; grated
- Mashed potatoes for serving
- Salt and black pepper to the taste

Instructions:
1. In a bowl; mix beef with sausage, garlic powder, onion powder, salt, pepper and cheese; stir well and shape 16 meatballs out of this mix.
2. Place meatballs in your air fryer and cook them at 370 °F, for 15 minutes.
3. Serve your meatballs with some mashed potatoes on the side.

Nutrition Facts: Calories: 333; Fat: 23g; Fiber: 1g; Carbs: 8g; Protein: 20g

Egg Rolls
(Prep + Cook Time: 25 Minutes | **Servings:** 4)

Ingredients:
- 1/2 cup mushrooms; chopped
- 1/2 cup carrots; grated
- 1/2 cup zucchini; grated
- 8 egg roll wrappers
- 1 eggs; whisked
- 2 green onions; chopped.
- 2 tbsp. soy sauce
- 1 tbsp. cornstarch

Instructions:
1. In a bowl; mix carrots, mushrooms, zucchini, green onions and soy sauce and stir well.
2. Arrange egg roll wrappers on a working surface; divide veggie mix on each and roll well.
3. In a bowl; mix cornstarch with egg, whisk well and brush eggs rolls with this mix.
4. Seal edges, place all rolls in your preheated air fryer and cook them at 370 °F, for 15 minutes. Arrange them on a platter and serve.

Nutrition Facts: Calories: 172; Fat: 6g; Fiber: 6g; Carbs: 8g; Protein: 7g

Different Pasta Salad

(Prep + Cook Time: 22 Minutes | Servings: 6)

Ingredients:
- 1 lb. penne rigate; already cooked
- 1 zucchini; sliced in half and roughly chopped.
- 1 orange bell pepper; roughly chopped.
- 1 green bell pepper; roughly chopped.
- 1 cup cherry tomatoes; halved
- 1/2 cup kalamata olive; pitted and halved
- 1/4 cup olive oil
- 1 red onion; roughly chopped.
- 4 oz. brown mushrooms; halved
- 1 tsp. Italian seasoning
- 3 tbsp. balsamic vinegar
- 2 tbsp. basil; chopped.
- Salt and black pepper to the taste

Instructions:
1. In a bowl; mix zucchini with mushrooms, orange bell pepper, green bell pepper, red onion, salt, pepper, Italian seasoning and oil; toss well, transfer to preheated air fryer at 380 °F and cook them for 12 minutes.
2. In a large salad bowl; mix pasta with cooked veggies, cherry tomatoes, olives, vinegar and basil; toss and serve for lunch.

Nutrition Facts: Calories: 200; Fat: 5g; Fiber: 8g; Carbs: 10g; Protein: 6g

Cheering Chicken Sandwiches

(Prep + Cook Time: 20 Minutes | Servings: 4)

Ingredients:
- 2 chicken breasts; skinless, boneless and cubed
- 1/2 cup Italian seasoning
- 1/2 tsp. thyme; dried
- 1 red onion; chopped.
- 1 red bell pepper; sliced
- 2 cups butter lettuce; torn
- 4 pita pockets
- 1 cup cherry tomatoes; halved
- 1 tbsp. olive oil

Instructions:
1. In your air fryer basket, mix chicken, onion, bell pepper, Italian seasoning and oil; toss and cook at 380 °F, for 10 minutes. Transfer chicken mix to a bowl; add thyme, butter lettuce and cherry tomatoes, toss well; stuff pita pockets with this mix and serve.

Nutrition Facts: Calories: 126; Fat: 4g; Fiber: 8g; Carbs: 14g; Protein: 4g

Turkish Style Koftas

(Prep + Cook Time: 25 Minutes | Servings: 2)

Ingredients:
- 1 leek; chopped
- 2 tbsp. feta cheese; crumbled
- 1 tbsp. parsley; chopped
- 1 tsp. garlic; minced
- 1/2 lb. lean beef; minced
- 1 tbsp. cumin; ground
- 1 tbsp. mint; chopped
- Salt and black pepper to the taste

Instructions:
1. In a bowl; mix beef with leek, cheese, cumin, mint, parsley, garlic, salt and pepper; stir well, shape your koftas and place them on sticks.
2. Add koftas to your preheated air fryer at 360 °F and cook them for 15 minutes. Serve them with a side salad for lunch.

Nutrition Facts: Calories: 281; Fat: 7g; Fiber: 8g; Carbs: 17g; Protein: 6g

Turkey Burgers

(Prep + Cook Time: 18 Minutes | **Servings:** 4)

Ingredients:
- 1 lb. turkey meat; ground
- 1 shallot; minced
- A drizzle of olive oil
- 1 small jalapeno pepper; minced
- 2 tsp. lime juice
- Zest from 1 lime; grated
- 1 tsp. cumin; ground
- 1 tsp. sweet paprika
- Salt and black pepper to the taste
- Guacamole for serving

Instructions:
1. In a bowl; mix turkey meat, salt, pepper, cumin, paprika, shallot, jalapeno, lime juice and zest; stir well,
2. Shape burgers from this mix, drizzle the oil over them; transfer to the preheated air fryer and cook them at 370 °F, for 8 minutes on each side. Divide among plates and serve with guacamole on top.

Nutrition Facts: Calories: 200; Fat: 12g; Fiber: 0g; Carbs: 0g; Protein: 12g

Cheesy Ravioli and Marinara Sauce

(Prep + Cook Time: 18 Minutes | **Servings:** 6)

Ingredients:
- 20 oz. cheese ravioli
- 10 oz. marinara sauce
- 1/4 cup parmesan; grated
- 1 tbsp. olive oil
- 1 cup buttermilk
- 2 cups bread crumbs

Instructions:
1. Put the buttermilk in a bowl and breadcrumbs in another bowl.
2. Dip ravioli in buttermilk, then in breadcrumbs and place them in your air fryer on a baking pan.
3. Drizzle olive oil over them; cook at 400 °F, for 5 minutes; divide them on plates, sprinkle parmesan on top and serve.

Nutrition Facts: Calories: 270; Fat: 12g; Fiber: 6g; Carbs: 12g; Protein: 15g

Chicken Kabobs

(Prep + Cook Time: 30 Minutes | **Servings:** 2)

Ingredients:
- 2 chicken breasts; skinless, boneless and roughly cubed
- 3 orange bell peppers; cut into squares
- 1/4 cup honey
- 1/3 cup soy sauce
- Cooking spray
- 6 mushrooms; halved
- Salt and black pepper to the taste

Instructions:
1. In a bowl; mix chicken, salt, pepper, honey, say sauce and spray cooking spray and toss well.
2. Thread chicken, bell peppers and mushrooms on skewers; place them in your air fryer and cook at 338 °F, for 20 minutes. Divide among plates and serve.

Nutrition Facts: Calories: 261; Fat: 7g; Fiber: 9g; Carbs: 12g; Protein: 6g

Stuffed Portobello Mushrooms

(Prep + Cook Time: 30 Minutes | **Servings:** 4)

Ingredients:
- 4 big Portobello mushroom caps
- 1/3 cup bread crumbs
- 1/4 tsp. rosemary; chopped.
- 1 tbsp. olive oil
- 1/4 cup ricotta cheese
- 5 tbsp. parmesan; grated
- 1 cup spinach; torn

Instructions:
1. Rub mushrooms caps with the oil; place them in your air fryer's basket and cook them at 350 °F, for 2 minutes.

2. Meanwhile; in a bowl, mix half of the parmesan with ricotta, spinach, rosemary and bread crumbs and stir well.
3. Stuff mushrooms with this mix; sprinkle the rest of the parmesan on top; place them in your air fryer's basket again and cook at 350 °F, for 10 minutes. Divide them on plates and serve.

Nutrition Facts: Calories: 152; Fat: 4g; Fiber: 7g; Carbs: 9g; Protein: 5g

Japanese Style Chicken

(**Prep + Cook Time:** 18 Minutes | **Servings:** 2)

Ingredients:
- 2 chicken thighs; skinless and boneless
- 1/8 cup sake
- 1/2 tsp. sesame oil
- 1/8 cup water
- 2 ginger slices; chopped
- 3 garlic cloves; minced
- 1/4 cup soy sauce
- 1/4 cup mirin
- 2 tbsp. sugar
- 1 tbsp. cornstarch mixed with 2 tbsp. water
- Sesame seeds for serving

Instructions:
1. In a bowl; mix chicken thighs with ginger, garlic, soy sauce, mirin, sake, sesame oil, water, sugar and cornstarch; toss well, transfer to the preheated air fryer and cook at 360 °F, for 8 minutes.
2. Divide among plates; sprinkle sesame seeds on top and serve.

Nutrition Facts: Calories: 300; Fat: 7g; Fiber: 9g; Carbs: 17g; Protein: 10g

Chicken Pie Recipe

(**Prep + Cook Time:** 29 Minutes | **Servings:** 4)

Ingredients:
- 2 chicken thighs; boneless, skinless and cubed
- 1 carrot; chopped
- 1 tsp. Worcestershire sauce
- 1 tbsp. flour
- 1 tbsp. milk
- 2 puff pastry sheets
- 1 tbsp. butter; melted
- 1 yellow onion; chopped
- 2 potatoes; chopped
- 2 mushrooms; chopped
- 1 tsp. soy sauce
- Salt and black pepper to the taste
- 1 tsp. Italian seasoning
- 1/2 tsp. garlic powder

Instructions:
1. Heat up a pan over medium high heat, add potatoes, carrots and onion; stir and cook for 2 minutes.
2. Add chicken and mushrooms, salt, soy sauce, pepper, Italian seasoning, garlic powder, Worcestershire sauce, flour and milk; stir really well and take off heat.
3. Place 1 puff pastry sheet on the bottom of your air fryer's pan and trim edge excess.
4. Add chicken mix, top with the other puff pastry sheet; trim excess as well and brush pie with butter.
5. Place in your air fryer and cook at 360 °F, for 6 minutes. Leave pie to cool down; slice and serve..

Nutrition Facts: Calories: 300; Fat: 5g; Fiber: 7g; Carbs: 14g; Protein: 7g

Chicken Fajitas

(**Prep + Cook Time:** 20 Minutes | **Servings:** 4)

Ingredients:
- 1 lb. chicken breasts; cut into strips
- 1 tsp. garlic powder
- 1/4 tsp. cumin; ground
- 1/2 tsp. chili powder
- 1 green bell pepper; sliced
- 1 yellow onion; chopped.
- 1 tbsp. lime juice
- 1/4 tsp. coriander; ground
- 1 red bell pepper; sliced
- Salt and black pepper to the taste
- Cooking spray
- 4 tortillas; warmed up
- Salsa for serving
- 1 cup lettuce leaves; torn for serving
- Sour cream for serving

Instructions:
1. In a bowl; mix chicken, garlic powder, cumin, chili, salt, pepper, coriander, lime juice, red bell pepper, green bell pepper and onion; toss, leave aside for 10 minutes, transfer to your air fryer and drizzle some cooking spray all over.
2. Toss and cook at 400 °F, for 10 minutes. Arrange tortillas on a working surface, divide chicken mix, also add salsa, sour cream and lettuce; wrap and serve.

Nutrition Facts: Calories: 317; Fat: 6g; Fiber: 8g; Carbs: 14g; Protein: 4g

Lentils Fritters
(Prep + Cook Time: 20 Minutes | **Servings:** 2)

Ingredients:
- 1 cup yellow lentils; soaked in water for 1 hour and drained
- 1 hot chili pepper; chopped.
- 1-inch ginger piece; grated
- 1/2 tsp. turmeric powder
- 1 tsp. garam masala
- 1 tsp. baking powder
- 2 tsp. olive oil
- 1/3 cup water
- 1/2 cup cilantro; chopped
- 1 ½ cup spinach; chopped
- 4 garlic cloves; minced
- 3/4 cup red onion; chopped
- Salt and black pepper to the taste
- Mint chutney for serving

Instructions:
1. In your blender; mix lentils with chili pepper, ginger, turmeric, garam masala, baking powder, salt, pepper, olive oil, water, cilantro, spinach, onion and garlic, blend well and shape medium balls out of this mix.
2. Place them all in your preheated air fryer at 400 °F and cook for 10 minutes and serve.

Nutrition Facts: Calories: 142; Fat: 2g; Fiber: 8g; Carbs: 12g; Protein: 4g

Corn Casserole Recipe
(Prep + Cook Time: 25 Minutes | **Servings:** 4)

Ingredients:
- 2 cups corn
- 1/2 cup light cream
- 1/2 cup Swiss cheese; grated
- 2 tbsp. butter
- 3 tbsp. flour
- 1 egg
- 1/4 cup milk
- Salt and black pepper to the taste
- Cooking spray

Instructions:
1. In a bowl; mix corn with flour, egg, milk, light cream, cheese, salt, pepper and butter and stir well.
2. Grease your air fryer's pan with cooking spray, pour cream mix; spread and cook at 320 °F, for 15 minutes. Serve warm.

Nutrition Facts: Calories: 281; Fat: 7g; Fiber: 8g; Carbs: 9g; Protein: 6g

Fish and Kettle Chips
(Prep + Cook Time: 22 Minutes | **Servings:** 2)

Ingredients:
- 2 medium cod fillets; skinless and boneless
- 1/4 cup buttermilk
- 3 cups kettle chips; cooked
- Salt and black pepper to the taste

Instructions:
1. In a bowl mix fish with salt, pepper and buttermilk; toss and leave aside for 5 minutes.
2. Put the chips in your food processor, crush them and spread them on a plate.
3. Add fish and press well on all sides.
4. Transfer fish to your air fryer's basket and cook at 400 °F, for 12 minutes. Serve hot for lunch.

Nutrition Facts: Calories: 271; Fat: 7g; Fiber: 9g; Carbs: 14g; Protein: 4g

Steak and Cabbage
(**Prep + Cook Time:** 20 Minutes | **Servings:** 4)

Ingredients:
- 1/2 lb. sirloin steak; cut into strips
- 2 green onions; chopped.
- 2 garlic cloves; minced
- 2 tsp. cornstarch
- 1 tbsp. peanut oil
- 2 cups green cabbage; chopped
- 1 yellow bell pepper; chopped
- Salt and black pepper to the taste

Instructions:
1. In a bowl; mix cabbage, salt, pepper and peanut oil; toss, transfer to air fryer's basket, cook at 370 °F, for 4 minutes and transfer to a bowl.
2. Add steak strips to your air fryer; also add green onions, bell pepper, garlic, salt and pepper, toss and cook for 5 minutes. Add over cabbage; toss, divide among plates and serve.

Nutrition Facts: Calories: 282; Fat: 6g; Fiber: 8g; Carbs: 14g; Protein: 6g

Chicken Wings
(**Prep + Cook Time:** 55 Minutes | **Servings:** 4)

Ingredients:
- 3 lbs. chicken wings
- 3/4 cup potato starch
- 1 tsp. lemon juice
- 1/2 cup butter
- 1 tbsp. old bay seasoning
- Lemon wedges for serving

Instructions:
1. In a bowl; mix starch with old bay seasoning and chicken wings and toss well.
2. Place chicken wings in your air fryer's basket and cook them at 360 °F, for 35 minutes shake the basket every 5 minutes.
3. Increase temperature to 400 degrees F; cook chicken wings for 10 minutes more and divide them on plates.
4. Heat up a pan over medium heat; add butter and melt it.
5. Add lemon juice; stir well, take off heat and drizzle over chicken wings. Serve the chicken wings with lemon wedges on the side.

Nutrition Facts: Calories: 271; Fat: 6g; Fiber: 8g; Carbs: 18g; Protein: 18g

Shrimp Croquettes
(**Prep + Cook Time:** 18 Minutes | **Servings:** 4)

Ingredients:
- 2/3 lb. shrimp; cooked; peeled; deveined and chopped.
- 1 ½ cups bread crumbs
- 1 egg; whisked
- 2 tbsp. olive oil
- 2 tbsp. lemon juice
- 3 green onions; chopped.
- 1/2 tsp. basil; dried
- Salt and black pepper to the taste

Instructions:
1. In a bowl; mix half of the bread crumbs with egg and lemon juice and stir well. Add green onions, basil, salt, pepper and shrimp and stir really well.
2. In a separate bowl; mix the rest of the bread crumbs with the oil and toss well.
3. Shape round balls out of shrimp mix, dredge them in bread crumbs; place them in preheated air fryer and cook for 8 minutes at 400 degrees F. Serve them with a dip.

Nutrition Facts: Calories: 142; Fat: 4g; Fiber: 6g; Carbs: 9g; Protein: 4g

Shrimp Pancake

(Prep + Cook Time: 20 Minutes | **Servings:** 2)

Ingredients:
- 1 cup small shrimp; peeled and deveined
- 1 tbsp. butter
- 3 eggs; whisked
- 1/2 cup flour
- 1/2 cup milk
- 1 cup salsa

Instructions:
1. Preheat your air fryer at 400 degrees F; add fryer's pan, add 1 tbsp. butter and melt it.
2. In a bowl; mix eggs with flour and milk, whisk well and pour into air fryer's pan, spread, cook at 350 degrees for 12 minutes and transfer to a plate.
3. In a bowl; mix shrimp with salsa; stir and serve your pancake with this on the side.

Nutrition Facts: Calories: 200; Fat: 6g; Fiber: 8g; Carbs: 12g; Protein: 4g

Pork and Potatoes Recipe

(Prep + Cook Time: 35 Minutes | **Servings:** 2)

Ingredients:
- 2 lbs. pork loin
- 2 red potatoes; cut into medium wedges
- 1/2 tsp. garlic powder
- 1/2 tsp. red pepper flakes
- 1 tsp. parsley; dried
- A drizzle of balsamic vinegar
- Salt and black pepper to the taste

Instructions:
1. In your air fryer's pan; mix pork with potatoes, salt, pepper, garlic powder, pepper flakes, parsley and vinegar; toss and cook at 390 °F, for 25 minutes.
2. Slice pork, divide it and potatoes on plates and serve.

Nutrition Facts: Calories: 400; Fat: 15g; Fiber: 7g; Carbs: 27g; Protein: 20g

Lunch Pizzas

(Prep + Cook Time: 17 Minutes | **Servings:** 4)

Ingredients:
- 1 cup grape tomatoes; sliced
- 3/4 cup pizza sauce
- 2 green onions; chopped
- 2 cup mozzarella; grated
- 4 pitas
- 1 tbsp. olive oil
- 4 oz. jarred mushrooms; sliced
- 1/2 tsp. basil; dried

Instructions:
1. Spread pizza sauce on each pita bread; sprinkle green onions and basil, divide mushrooms and top with cheese.
2. Arrange pita pizzas in your air fryer and cook them at 400 °F, for 7 minutes. Top each pizza with tomato slices; divide among plates and serve.

Nutrition Facts: Calories: 200; Fat: 4g; Fiber: 6g; Carbs: 7g; Protein: 3g

Asparagus and Salmon

(Prep + Cook Time: 33 Minutes | **Servings:** 4)

Ingredients:
- 1 lb. asparagus; trimmed
- 1 tbsp. olive oil
- A pinch of sweet paprika
- A pinch of garlic powder
- A pinch of cayenne pepper
- 1 red bell pepper; cut into halves
- 4 oz. smoked salmon
- Salt and black pepper to the taste

Instructions:
1. Put asparagus spears and bell pepper on a lined baking pan that fits your air fryer.
2. Add salt, pepper, garlic powder, paprika, olive oil, cayenne pepper, toss to coat.

3. Now place the pan in your air fryer; cook at 390 °F, for 8 minutes, flip and cook for 8 minutes more. Add salmon, cook for 5 minutes more; divide everything on plates and serve.

Nutrition Facts: Calories: 90; Fat: 1g; Fiber: 1g; Carbs: 1.2g; Protein: 4g

Dill and Scallops
(Prep + Cook Time: 15 Minutes | Servings: 4)

Ingredients:
- 1 lb. sea scallops; debearded
- 1 tsp. dill; chopped.
- 2 tsp. olive oil
- 1 tbsp. lemon juice
- Salt and black pepper to the taste

Instructions:
1. In your air fryer basket, mix scallops with dill, oil, salt, pepper and lemon juice; cover and cook at 360 °F, for 5 minutes. Discard unopened ones, divide scallops and dill sauce on plates and serve.

Nutrition Facts: Calories: 152; Fat: 4g; Fiber: 7g; Carbs: 19g; Protein: 4g

Beef Cubes
(Prep + Cook Time: 22 Minutes | Servings: 4)

Ingredients:
- 1 lb. sirloin; cubed
- 16 oz. jarred pasta sauce
- 1 ½ cups bread crumbs
- 1/2 tsp. marjoram; dried
- 2 tbsp. olive oil
- White rice; already cooked for serving

Instructions:
1. In a bowl; mix beef cubes with pasta sauce and toss well.
2. In another bowl; mix bread crumbs with marjoram and oil and stir well.
3. Dip beef cubes in this mix, place them in your air fryer and cook at 360 °F, for 12 minutes. Divide among plates and serve with white rice.

Nutrition Facts: Calories: 271; Fat: 6g; Fiber: 9g; Carbs: 18g; Protein: 12g

Zucchini and Tuna Tortillas
(Prep + Cook Time: 20 Minutes | Servings: 4)

Ingredients:
- 1 cup zucchini; shredded
- 1/3 cup mayonnaise
- 2 tbsp. mustard
- 4 corn tortillas
- 4 tbsp. butter; soft
- 6 oz. canned tuna; drained
- 1 cup cheddar cheese; grated

Instructions:
1. Spread butter on tortillas; place them in your air fryer's basket and cook them at 400 °F, for 3 minutes.
2. Meanwhile; in a bowl, mix tuna with zucchini, mayo and mustard and stir.
3. Divide this mix on each tortilla, top with cheese, roll tortillas; place them in the air fryer's basket and cook them at 400 °F, for 4 minutes and serve.

Nutrition Facts: Calories: 162; Fat: 4g; Fiber: 8g; Carbs: 9g; Protein: 4g

Summer Squash Fritters
(Prep + Cook Time: 17 Minutes | Servings: 4)

Ingredients:
- 1 yellow summer squash; grated
- 3 oz. cream cheese
- 1 egg; whisked
- 1/2 tsp. oregano; dried
- 1/3 cup carrot; grated
- 2/3 cup bread crumbs
- A pinch of salt and black pepper
- 2 tbsp. olive oil

Instructions:
1. In a bowl; mix cream cheese with salt, pepper, oregano, egg, breadcrumbs, carrot and squash and stir well.
2. Shape medium patties out of this mix and brush them with the oil.
3. Place squash patties in your air fryer and cook them at 400 °F, for 7 minutes and serve.

Nutrition Facts: Calories: 200; Fat: 4g; Fiber: 7g; Carbs: 8g; Protein: 6g

Asian Chicken
(Prep + Cook Time: 40 Minutes | **Servings:** 4)

Ingredients:
- 2 chicken breasts; skinless, boneless and sliced
- 1 tsp. olive oil
- 1 yellow onion; sliced
- 1 tbsp. Worcestershire sauce
- 14 oz. pizza dough
- 1 ½ cups cheddar cheese; grated
- 1/2 cup jarred cheese sauce
- Salt and black pepper to the taste

Instructions:
1. Preheat your air fryer at 400 degrees F; add ½ teaspoon olive oil, 1 onion and fry them for 8 minutes, stirring once.
2. Add chicken pieces, Worcestershire sauce, salt and pepper; toss, air fry for 8 minutes more, stirring once and transfer everything to a bowl.
3. Roll pizza dough on a working surface and shape a rectangle.
4. Spread half of the cheese all over, add chicken and onion mix and top with cheese sauce.
5. Roll your dough and shape into a U.
6. Place your roll in your air fryer's basket, brush with the rest of the oil and cook at 370 degrees for 12 minutes, flipping the roll halfway. Slice your roll when it's warm and serve.

Nutrition Facts: Calories: 300; Fat: 8g; Fiber: 17g; Carbs: 20g; Protein: 6g

Parmesan Gnocchi
(Prep + Cook Time: 27 Minutes | **Servings:** 4)

Ingredients:
- 1/4 cup parmesan; grated
- 1 yellow onion; chopped
- 16 oz. gnocchi
- 1 tbsp. olive oil
- 3 garlic cloves; minced
- 8 oz. spinach pesto

Instructions:
1. Grease your air fryer's pan with olive oil, add gnocchi, onion and garlic, toss; put the pan in your air fryer and cook at 400 °F, for 10 minutes.
2. Add pesto, toss and cook for 7 minutes more at 350 degrees F. Divide among plates and serve.

Nutrition Facts: Calories: 200; Fat: 4g; Fiber: 4g; Carbs: 12g; Protein: 4g

Prosciutto Sandwich
(Prep + Cook Time: 15 Minutes | **Servings:** 1)

Ingredients:
- 2 bread slices
- 2 prosciutto slices
- 2 basil leaves
- 1 tsp. olive oil
- 2 mozzarella slices
- 2 tomato slices
- A pinch of salt and black pepper

Instructions:
1. Arrange mozzarella and prosciutto on a bread slice.
2. Season with salt and pepper; place in your air fryer and cook at 400 °F, for 5 minutes.
3. Drizzle oil over prosciutto, add tomato and basil; cover with the other bread slice, cut sandwich in half and serve.

Nutrition Facts: Calories: 172; Fat: 3g; Fiber: 7g; Carbs: 9g; Protein: 5g

Chinese Style Pork

(Prep + Cook Time: 22 Minutes | **Servings:** 4)

Ingredients:
- 2 lbs. pork; cut into medium cubes
- 2 eggs
- 1 cup cornstarch
- 1 tsp. sesame oil
- A pinch of Chinese five spice
- 3 tbsp. canola oil
- Sweet tomato sauce for serving
- Salt and black pepper to the taste

Instructions:
1. In a bowl; mix five spice with salt, pepper and cornstarch and stir.
2. In another bowl; mix eggs with sesame oil and whisk well.
3. Dredge pork cubes in cornstarch mix; then dip in eggs mix and place them in your air fryer which you've greased with the canola oil.
4. Cook at 340 °F, for 12 minutes; shake the basket in the middle of the cooking to ensure even cooking. Serve pork for lunch with the sweet tomato sauce on the side.

Nutrition Facts: Calories: 320; Fat: 8g; Fiber: 12g; Carbs: 20g; Protein: 5g

Hash Brown Toasts

(Prep + Cook Time: 17 Minutes | **Servings:** 4)

Ingredients:
- 4 hash brown patties; frozen
- 1 tbsp. olive oil
- 1 tbsp. balsamic vinegar
- 1 tbsp. basil; chopped.
- 1/4 cup cherry tomatoes; chopped.
- 3 tbsp. mozzarella; shredded
- 2 tbsp. parmesan; grated

Instructions:
1. Put the hash brown patties in your air fryer; drizzle the oil over them and cook them at 400 °F, for 7 minutes.
2. In a bowl; mix tomatoes with mozzarella, parmesan, vinegar and basil and stir well. Divide hash brown patties on plates; top each with tomatoes mix and serve for lunch.

Nutrition Facts: Calories: 199; Fat: 3g; Fiber: 8g; Carbs: 12g; Protein: 4g

Succulent Turkey Cakes

(Prep + Cook Time: 20 Minutes | **Servings:** 4)

Ingredients:
- 6 mushrooms; chopped
- 1 tsp. garlic powder
- 1 tsp. onion powder
- 1 ¼ lbs. turkey meat; ground
- Cooking spray
- Tomato sauce for serving
- Salt and black pepper to the taste

Instructions:
1. In your blender, mix mushrooms with salt and pepper, pulse well and transfer to a bowl.
2. Add turkey, onion powder, garlic powder, salt and pepper; stir and shape cakes out of this mix.
3. Spray them with cooking spray; transfer them to your air fryer and cook at 320 °F, for 10 minutes. Serve them with tomato sauce on the side and a tasty side salad.

Nutrition Facts: Calories: 202; Fat: 6g; Fiber: 3g; Carbs: 17g; Protein: 10g

Potato Salad

(Prep + Cook Time: 35 Minutes | **Servings:** 4)

Ingredients:
- 2 lb. red potatoes; halved
- 2 tbsp. olive oil
- 1/3 cup lemon juice
- 3 tbsp. mustard
- Salt and black pepper to the taste
- 2 green onions; chopped
- 1 red bell pepper; chopped

Instructions:
1. In your air fryer's basket; mix potatoes with half of the olive oil, salt and pepper and cook at 350 °F, for 25 minute, shake the basket every few minutes to ensure even cooking.
2. In a bowl; mix onions with bell pepper and roasted potatoes and toss.
3. In a small bowl; mix lemon juice with the rest of the oil and mustard and whisk well. Add this to potato salad; toss well and serve.

Nutrition Facts: Calories: 211; Fat: 6g; Fiber: 8g; Carbs: 12g; Protein: 4g

Buttermilk Chicken
(Prep + Cook Time: 28 Minutes | **Servings:** 4)

Ingredients:
- 1 ½ lbs. chicken thighs
- 2 cups buttermilk
- 1 tbsp. baking powder
- 1 tbsp. sweet paprika
- A pinch of cayenne pepper
- 2 cups white flour
- 1 tbsp. garlic powder
- Salt and black pepper to the taste

Instructions:
1. In a bowl; mix chicken thighs with buttermilk, salt, pepper and cayenne; toss and leave aside for 6 hours.
2. In a separate bowl; mix flour with paprika, baking powder and garlic powder and stir.
3. Drain chicken thighs, dredge them in flour mix; arrange them in your air fryer and cook at 360 °F, for 8 minutes.
4. Flip chicken pieces, cook them for 10 minutes more; arrange on a platter and serve.

Nutrition Facts: Calories: 200; Fat: 3g; Fiber: 9g; Carbs: 14g; Protein: 4g

Cheese Burgers
(Prep + Cook Time: 30 Minutes | **Servings:** 2)

Ingredients:
- 12 oz. lean beef; ground
- 4 tsp. ketchup
- 3 tbsp. yellow onion; chopped.
- 2 tsp. mustard
- 4 cheddar cheese slices
- 2 burger buns; halved
- Salt and black pepper to the taste

Instructions:
1. In a bowl; mix beef with onion, ketchup, mustard, salt and pepper; stir well and shape 4 patties out of this mix.
2. Divide cheese on 2 patties and top with the other 2 patties.
3. Place them in preheated air fryer at 370 °F and fry them for 20 minutes. Divide cheeseburger on 2 bun halves; top with the other 2 and serve.

Nutrition Facts: Calories: 261; Fat: 6g; Fiber: 10g; Carbs: 20g; Protein: 6g

Creamy Chicken Stew Recipe
(Prep + Cook Time: 35 Minutes | **Servings:** 4)

Ingredients:
- 1 ½ cups canned cream of celery soup
- 6 chicken tenders
- 1 tbsp. milk
- 1 egg yolk
- 1/2 cup heavy cream
- 2 potatoes; chopped
- 1 bay leaf
- 1 thyme spring; chopped
- Salt and black pepper to the taste

Instructions:
1. In a bowl; mix chicken with cream of celery, potatoes, heavy cream, bay leaf, thyme, salt and pepper; toss, pour into your air fryer's pan and cook at 320 °F, for 25 minutes.
2. Leave your stew to cool down a bit; discard bay leaf, divide among plates and serve right away.

Nutrition Facts: Calories: 300; Fat: 11g; Fiber: 2g; Carbs: 23g; Protein: 14g

Tasty Hot Dogs
(Prep + Cook Time: 17 Minutes | Servings: 2)
Ingredients:
- 2 hot dog buns
- 1 tbsp. Dijon mustard
- 2 hot dogs
- 2 tbsp. cheddar cheese; grated

Instructions:
1. Put the hot dogs in preheated air fryer and cook them at 390 °F, for 5 minutes.
2. Divide hot dogs into hot dog buns, spread mustard and cheese; return everything to your air fryer and cook for 2 minutes more at 390 degrees F and serve.

Nutrition Facts: Calories: 211; Fat: 3g; Fiber: 8g; Carbs: 12g; Protein: 4g

Chicken Corn Casserole
(Prep + Cook Time: 40 Minutes | Servings: 6)
Ingredients:
- 2 lbs. chicken breasts; skinless, boneless and cubed
- 1 cup clean chicken stock
- 6 oz. canned coconut milk
- 1 ½ cups green lentils
- 1/3 cup cilantro; chopped
- 3 cups corn
- 3 handfuls spinach
- 3 green onions; chopped
- 2 tsp. garlic powder
- Salt and black pepper to the taste

Instructions:
1. In a pan that fits your air fryer; mix chicken stock with coconut milk, salt, pepper, garlic powder, chicken and lentils.
2. Add corn, green onions, cilantro and spinach; stir well, close the air fryer basket and cook at 350 °F, for 30 minutes.

Nutrition Facts: Calories: 345; Fat: 12g; Fiber: 10g; Carbs: 20g; Protein: 25g

Veggie Toasts
(Prep + Cook Time: 25 Minutes | Servings: 4)
Ingredients:
- 1 red bell pepper; cut into thin strips
- 1 cup cremini mushrooms; sliced
- 4 bread slices
- 2 tbsp. butter; soft
- 1 yellow squash; chopped.
- 2 green onions; sliced
- 1 tbsp. olive oil
- 1/2 cup goat cheese; crumbled

Instructions:
1. In a bowl; mix red bell pepper with mushrooms, squash, green onions and oil, toss; transfer to your air fryer, cook them at 350 °F, for 10 minutes (shake the basket in the middle of cooking) and transfer them to a bowl.
2. Spread butter on bread slices; place them in air fryer and cook them at 350 °F, for 5 minutes. Divide veggie mix on each bread slice, top with crumbled cheese and serve.

Nutrition Facts: Calories: 152; Fat: 3g; Fiber: 4g; Carbs: 7g; Protein: 2g

Succulent Turkey Breast
(Prep + Cook Time: 57 Minutes | Servings: 4)
Ingredients:
- 1 big turkey breast
- 2 tsp. olive oil
- 1/2 tsp. smoked paprika
- 1 tsp. thyme; dried
- 1/2 tsp. sage; dried
- 2 tbsp. mustard
- 1/4 cup maple syrup
- 1 tbsp. butter; soft
- Salt and black pepper to the taste

Instructions:
1. Brush turkey breast with the olive oil; season with salt, pepper, thyme, paprika and sage, rub, place in your air fryer's basket and fry at 350 °F, for 25 minutes.
2. Flip turkey; cook for 10 minutes more; flip one more time and cook for another 10 minutes.
3. Meanwhile; heat up a pan with the butter over medium heat, add mustard and maple syrup; stir well, cook for a couple of minutes and take off heat. Slice turkey breast, divide among plates and serve with the maple glaze drizzled on top.

Nutrition Facts: Calories: 280; Fat: 2g; Fiber: 7g; Carbs: 16g; Protein: 14g

Bell Pepper and Sausage

(Prep + Cook Time: 20 Minutes | **Servings:** 4)

Ingredients:
- 1 lb. sausages; sliced
- 1 red bell pepper; cut into strips
- 1/2 cup yellow onion; chopped.
- 1/2 cup chicken stock
- 1/3 cup ketchup
- 3 tbsp. brown sugar
- 2 tbsp. mustard
- 2 tbsp. apple cider vinegar

Instructions:
1. In a bowl; mix sugar with ketchup, mustard, stock and vinegar and whisk well.
2. In your air fryer's pan; mix sausage slices with bell pepper, onion and sweet and sour mix; toss and cook at 350 °F, for 10 minutes. Divide into bowls and serve.

Nutrition Facts: Calories: 162; Fat: 6g; Fiber: 9g; Carbs: 12g; Protein: 6g

Fried Thai Salad

(Prep + Cook Time: 15 Minutes | **Servings:** 4)

Ingredients:
- 12 big shrimp; cooked, peeled and deveined
- 1 cup carrots; grated
- 1 cup red cabbage; shredded
- A handful cilantro; chopped.
- 1 small cucumber; chopped.
- Juice from 1 lime
- 2 tsp. red curry paste
- A pinch of salt and black pepper

Instructions:
1. In a pan, mix cabbage with carrots, cucumber and shrimp; toss, close the air fryer basket and cook at 360 °F, for 5 minutes.
2. Add salt, pepper, cilantro, lime juice and red curry paste; toss again, divide among plates and serve.

Nutrition Facts: Calories: 172; Fat: 5g; Fiber: 7g; Carbs: 8g; Protein: 5g

Seafood Stew

(Prep + Cook Time: 30 Minutes | **Servings:** 4)

Ingredients:
- 3 oz. sea bass fillet; skinless, boneless and chopped.
- 5 oz. white rice
- 2 oz. peas
- 1 red bell pepper; chopped.
- 14 oz. white wine
- 3 oz. water
- 2 oz. squid pieces
- 7 oz. mussels
- 6 scallops
- 3.5 oz. clams
- 4 shrimp
- 4 crayfish
- 1 tbsp. olive oil
- Salt and black pepper to the taste

Instructions:
1. In your air fryer's pan; mix sea bass with shrimp, mussels, scallops, crayfish, clams and squid.
2. Add the oil, salt and pepper and toss to coat.
3. In a bowl; mix peas salt, pepper, bell pepper and rice and stir.

4. Add this over seafood, also add wine and water, place pan in your air fryer and cook at 400 °F, for 20 minutes; stirring halfway. Divide into bowls and serve.

Nutrition Facts: Calories: 300; Fat: 12g; Fiber: 2g; Carbs: 23g; Protein: 25g

Bacon Garlic Pizzas
(Prep + Cook Time: 20 Minutes | Servings: 4)

Ingredients:
- 8 bacon slices; cooked and chopped.
- 4 dinner rolls; frozen
- 1 ¼ cups cheddar cheese; grated
- 4 garlic cloves minced
- 1/2 tsp. oregano dried
- 1/2 tsp. garlic powder
- 1 cup tomato sauce
- Cooking spray

Instructions:
1. Place dinner rolls on a working surface and press them to obtain 4 ovals.
2. Spray each oval with cooking spray; transfer them to your air fryer and cook them at 370 °F, for 2 minutes.
3. Spread tomato sauce on each oval, divide garlic, sprinkle oregano and garlic powder and top with bacon and cheese.
4. Return pizzas to your heated air fryer and cook them at 370 °F, for 8 minutes more and serve them warm.

Nutrition Facts: Calories: 217; Fat: 5g; Fiber: 8g; Carbs: 12g; Protein: 4g

Chicken, Quinoa, Corn, Beans and Casserole
(Prep + Cook Time: 40 Minutes | Servings: 8)

Ingredients:
- 3 cups chicken breast; cooked and shredded
- 1 cup quinoa; already cooked
- 2 tsp. chili powder
- 2 tsp. cumin; ground
- 3 cups mozzarella cheese; shredded
- 14 oz. canned black beans
- 12 oz. corn
- 1/2 cup cilantro; chopped.
- 6 kale leaves; chopped.
- 1/2 cup green onions; chopped.
- 1 cup clean tomato sauce
- 1 cup clean salsa
- 1 tbsp. garlic powder
- Cooking spray
- 2 jalapeno peppers; chopped.

Instructions:
1. Spray a baking pan that fits your air fryer with cooking spray, add quinoa, chicken, black beans, corn, cilantro, kale, green onions, tomato sauce, salsa, chili powder, cumin, garlic powder, jalapenos and mozzarella and toss,
2. Transfer them to your air fryer and cook at 350 °F, for 17 minutes. Slice and serve warm.

Nutrition Facts: Calories: 365; Fat: 12g; Fiber: 6g; Carbs: 22g; Protein: 26g

Meatballs, Tomato Sauce
(Prep + Cook Time: 245 Minutes | Servings: 4)

Ingredients:
- 1 lb. lean beef; ground
- 3 green onions; chopped.
- 2 garlic cloves; minced
- 1 egg yolk
- 1/4 cup bread crumbs
- 1 tbsp. olive oil
- 16 oz. tomato sauce
- 2 tbsp. mustard
- Salt and black pepper to the taste

Instructions:
1. In a bowl; mix beef with onion, garlic, egg yolk, bread crumbs, salt and pepper; stir well and shape medium meatballs out of this mix.
2. Grease meatballs with the oil, place them in your air fryer and cook them at 400 °F, for 10 minutes.

3. In a bowl; mix tomato sauce with mustard, whisk, add over meatballs; toss them and cook at 400 °F, for 5 minutes more. Divide meatballs and sauce on plates and serve.

Nutrition Facts: Calories: 300; Fat: 8g; Fiber: 9g; Carbs: 16g; Protein: 5g

Chicken and kale Recipe

(Prep + Cook Time: 30 Minutes | **Servings:** 6)

Ingredients:
- 1 bunch kale; chopped
- 1 cup chicken; shredded
- 3 carrots; chopped
- 1 cup shiitake mushrooms; roughly sliced
- 1/4 cup chicken stock
- Salt and black pepper to the taste

Instructions:
1. In a blender, mix stock with kale, pulse a few times and pour in a pan that fits your air fryer.
2. Add chicken, mushrooms, carrots, salt and pepper to the taste; toss, close the air fryer basket and cook at 350 °F, for 18 minutes.

Nutrition Facts: Calories: 180; Fat: 7g; Fiber: 2g; Carbs: 10g; Protein: 5g

Meatballs Sandwich Delight

(Prep + Cook Time: 32 Minutes | **Servings:** 4)

Ingredients:
- 3 baguettes; sliced more than halfway through
- 14 oz. beef; ground
- 1 tbsp. olive oil
- 1 tsp. thyme; dried
- 1 tsp. basil; dried
- 7 oz. tomato sauce
- 1 small onion; chopped
- 1 egg; whisked
- 1 tbsp. bread crumbs
- 2 tbsp. cheddar cheese; grated
- 1 tbsp. oregano; chopped
- Salt and black pepper to the taste

Instructions:
1. In a bowl; combine meat with salt, pepper, onion, breadcrumbs, egg, cheese, oregano, thyme and basil; stir, shape medium meatballs and add them to your air fryer after you've greased it with the oil.
2. Cook them at 375 °F, for 12 minutes; flipping them halfway.
3. Add tomato sauce, cook meatballs for 10 minutes more and arrange them on sliced baguettes and serve.

Nutrition Facts: Calories: 380; Fat: 5g; Fiber: 6g; Carbs: 34g; Protein: 20g

Zucchini Casseroles

(Prep + Cook Time: 26 Minutes | **Servings:** 8)

Ingredients:
- 8 zucchinis; cut into medium wedges
- 1 cup veggie stock
- 2 tbsp. olive oil
- 1/4 tsp. thyme; dried
- 1/4 tsp. rosemary; dried
- 4 tbsp. dill; chopped
- 1/2 tsp. basil; chopped
- 2 sweet potatoes; peeled and cut into medium wedges
- 2 yellow onions; chopped
- 1 cup coconut milk
- 1 tbsp. soy sauce
- Salt and black pepper to the taste

Instructions:
1. Heat up a pan that fits your air fryer with the oil over medium heat; add onion, stir and cook for 2 minutes.
2. Add zucchinis, thyme, rosemary, basil, potato, salt, pepper, stock, milk, soy sauce and dill; stir,
3. Place the pan in your air fryer and cook at 360 °F, for 14 minutes, divide among plates and serve right away.

Nutrition Facts: Calories: 133; Fat: 3g; Fiber: 4g; Carbs: 10g; Protein: 5g

Bacon Sandwiches
(**Prep + Cook Time:** 17 Minutes | **Servings:** 4)

Ingredients:
- 8 bacon slices; cooked and cut into thirds
- 1/3 cup bbq sauce
- 1 ¼ cup butter lettuce leaves; torn
- 2 tbsp. honey
- 1 red bell pepper; sliced
- 1 yellow bell pepper; sliced
- 3 pita pockets; halved
- 2 tomatoes; sliced

Instructions:
1. In a bowl, mix BBQ sauce with honey and whisk well.
2. Brush bacon and all bell peppers with some of this mix; place them in your air fryer and cook at 350 °F, for 4 minutes.
3. Shake fryer and cook them for 2 minutes more. Stuff pita pockets with bacon mix, also stuff with tomatoes and lettuce; spread the rest of the BBQ sauce and serve.

Nutrition Facts: Calories: 186; Fat: 6g; Fiber: 9g; Carbs: 14g; Protein: 4g

Chicken and Coconut Casserole
(**Prep + Cook Time:** 35 Minutes | **Servings:** 4)

Ingredients:
- 1 lb. chicken breast; skinless, boneless and cut into thin strips
- 4 lime leaves; torn
- 1 cup veggie stock
- 1 lemongrass stalk; chopped
- 1-inch piece; grated
- 8 oz. mushrooms; chopped.
- 4 Thai chilies; chopped.
- 4 tbsp. fish sauce
- 6 oz. coconut milk
- 1/4 cup lime juice
- 1/4 cup cilantro; chopped
- Salt and black pepper to the taste

Instructions:
1. Pour the stock in a pan that fits your air fryer; bring to a simmer over medium heat, add lemongrass, ginger and lime leaves; stir and cook for 10 minutes.
2. Strain soup, return to pan, add chicken, mushrooms, milk, chilies, fish sauce, lime juice, cilantro, salt and pepper; stir, close the air fryer basket and cook at 360 °F, for 15 minutes. Divide into bowls and serve.

Nutrition Facts: Calories: 150; Fat: 4g; Fiber: 4g; Carbs: 6g; Protein: 7g

Italian Style Eggplant Sandwich
(**Prep + Cook Time:** 26 Minutes | **Servings:** 4)

Ingredients:
- 1 eggplant; sliced
- 2 tsp. parsley; dried
- 1/2 cup breadcrumbs
- 1/2 tsp. Italian seasoning
- 1/2 tsp. garlic powder
- 1/2 tsp. onion powder
- 2 tbsp. milk
- 4 bread slices
- Cooking spray
- 1/2 cup mayonnaise
- 3/4 cup tomato sauce
- 2 cups mozzarella cheese; grated
- Salt and black pepper to the taste

Instructions:
1. Season eggplant slices with salt and pepper, leave aside for 10 minutes and then pat dry them well.
2. In a bowl; mix parsley with breadcrumbs, Italian seasoning, onion and garlic powder, salt and black pepper and stir.
3. In another bowl; mix milk with mayo and whisk well.
4. Brush eggplant slices with mayo mix, dip them in breadcrumbs, place them in your air fryer's basket, spray with cooking oil and cook them at 400 °F, for 15 minutes; flipping them after 8 minutes.
5. Brush each bread slice with olive oil and arrange 2 on a working surface.

6. Add mozzarella and parmesan on each, add baked eggplant slices; spread tomato sauce and basil and top with the other bread slices, greased side down. Divide sandwiches on plates; cut them in halves and serve.

Nutrition Facts: Calories: 324; Fat: 16g; Fiber: 4g; Carbs: 39g; Protein: 12g

Beef Stew
(Prep + Cook Time: 30 Minutes | **Servings:** 4)

Ingredients:
- 2 lbs. beef meat; cut into medium chunks
- 2 carrots; chopped
- 4 potatoes; chopped
- 1-quart veggie stock
- 1/2 tsp. smoked paprika
- A handful thyme; chopped
- Salt and black pepper to the taste

Instructions:
1. In a dish that fits your air fryer; mix beef with carrots, potatoes, stock, salt, pepper, paprika and thyme; stir, place in air fryer's basket and cook at 375 °F, for 20 minutes.
2. Divide into bowls and serve.

Nutrition Facts: Calories: 260; Fat: 5g; Fiber: 8g; Carbs: 20g; Protein: 22g

Stuffed Meatballs
(Prep + Cook Time: 20 Minutes | **Servings:** 4)

Ingredients:
- 1 lb. lean beef; ground
- 20 cheddar cheese cubes
- 1/3 cup bread crumbs
- 1/2 tsp. marjoram; dried
- 3 tbsp. milk
- 1 tbsp. ketchup
- 1 egg
- 1 tbsp. olive oil
- Salt and black pepper to the taste

Instructions:
1. In a bowl; mix bread crumbs with ketchup, milk, marjoram, salt, pepper and egg and whisk well.
2. Add beef; stir and shape 20 meatballs out of this mix.
3. Shape each meatball around a cheese cube, drizzle the oil over them and rub.
4. Place all meatballs in your preheated air fryer and cook at 390 °F, for 10 minutes and serve.

Nutrition Facts: Calories: 200; Fat: 5g; Fiber: 8g; Carbs: 12g; Protein: 5g

Bacon Pudding
(Prep + Cook Time: 40 Minutes | **Servings:** 6)

Ingredients:
- 4 bacon strips; cooked and chopped.
- 1 tbsp. butter; soft
- 2 cups corn
- 3 eggs; whisked
- 3 cups bread; cubed
- 4 tbsp. parmesan; grated
- 1 yellow onion; chopped.
- 1/4 cup celery; chopped.
- 1/2 cup red bell pepper; chopped.
- 1 tsp. thyme; chopped.
- 2 tsp. garlic; minced
- 1/2 cup heavy cream
- 1 ½ cups milk
- Cooking spray
- Salt and black pepper to the taste

Instructions:
1. Grease your air fryer's pan with cooking spray.
2. In a bowl; mix bacon with butter, corn, onion, bell pepper, celery, thyme, garlic, salt, pepper, milk, heavy cream, eggs and bread cubes; toss, pour into greased pan and sprinkle cheese all over
3. Add this to your preheated air fryer at 320 degrees and cook for 30 minutes. Divide among plates and serve warm.

Nutrition Facts: Calories: 276; Fat: 10g; Fiber: 2g; Carbs: 20g; Protein: 10g

Chicken Zucchini

(Prep + Cook Time: 30 Minutes | **Servings:** 4)

Ingredients:
- 1 lb. chicken breasts; skinless, boneless and cubed
- 4 zucchinis; cut with a spiralizer
- 2 garlic cloves; minced

For the pesto:
- 2 cups basil
- 3/4 cup pine nuts
- 1/2 cup olive oil
- 2 cups kale; chopped
- 1 tsp. olive oil
- 2 cups cherry tomatoes; halved
- 1/2 cup almonds; chopped
- Salt and black pepper to the taste

- 1 tbsp. lemon juice
- 1 garlic clove
- A pinch of salt

Instructions:
1. In your food processor, mix basil with kale, lemon juice, garlic, pine nuts, oil and a pinch of salt, pulse really well and leave aside.
2. Heat up a pan that fits your air fryer with the oil over medium heat, add garlic; stir and cook for 1 minute.
3. Add chicken, salt, pepper, stir, almonds, zucchini noodles, garlic, cherry tomatoes and the pesto you've made at the beginning, stir gently; place the pan in a preheated air fryer and cook at 360 °F, for 17 minutes. Divide among plates and serve.

Nutrition Facts: Calories: 344; Fat: 8g; Fiber: 7g; Carbs: 12g; Protein: 16g

Poultry Recipes

Italian Chicken Recipe
(**Prep + Cook Time:** 26 Minutes | **Servings:** 4)

Ingredients:
- 5 chicken thighs
- 1 tbsp. olive oil
- 1/4 cup parmesan; grated
- 1/2 cup sun dried tomatoes
- 2 garlic cloves; minced
- 1 tbsp. thyme; chopped.
- 1/2 cup heavy cream
- 3/4 cup chicken stock
- 1 tsp. red pepper flakes; crushed
- 2 tbsp. basil; chopped
- Salt and black pepper to the taste

Instructions:
1. Season chicken with salt and pepper, rub with half of the oil, place in your preheated air fryer at 350 °F and cook for 4 minutes.
2. Meanwhile; heat up a pan with the rest of the oil over medium high heat, add thyme garlic, pepper flakes, sun dried tomatoes, heavy cream, stock, parmesan, salt and pepper; stir, bring to a simmer, take off heat and transfer to a dish that fits your air fryer.
3. Add chicken thighs on top, close the air fryer basket and cook at 320 °F, for 12 minutes. Divide among plates and serve with basil sprinkled on top.

Nutrition Facts: Calories: 272; Fat: 9g; Fiber: 12g; Carbs: 37g; Protein: 23g

Chicken Cacciatore Recipe
(**Prep + Cook Time:** 30 Minutes | **Servings:** 4)

Ingredients:
- 8 chicken drumsticks; bone-in
- 1/2 cup black olives; pitted and sliced
- 1 bay leaf
- 1 tsp. garlic powder
- 1 yellow onion; chopped
- 28 oz. canned tomatoes and juice; crushed
- 1 tsp. oregano; dried
- Salt and black pepper to the taste

Instructions:
1. In a heat proof dish that fits your air fryer, mix chicken with salt, pepper, garlic powder, bay leaf, onion, tomatoes and juice, oregano and olives; toss, introduce in your preheated air fryer and cook at 365 °F, for 20 minutes. Divide among plates and serve.

Nutrition Facts: Calories: 300; Fat: 12g; Fiber: 8g; Carbs: 20g; Protein: 24g

Fried Japanese Duck Breasts
(**Prep + Cook Time:** 30 Minutes | **Servings:** 6)

Ingredients:
- 20 oz. chicken stock
- 6 duck breasts; boneless
- 4 tbsp. soy sauce
- 1½ tsp. five spice powder
- 2 tbsp. honey
- 4 ginger slices
- 4 tbsp. hoisin sauce
- 1 tsp. sesame oil
- Salt and black pepper to the taste

Instructions:
1. In a bowl, mix five spice powder with soy sauce, salt, pepper and honey, whisk, add duck breasts, toss to coat and leave aside for now.
2. Heat up a pan with the stock over medium high heat, hoisin sauce, ginger and sesame oil; stir well, cook for 2-3 minutes more, take off heat and leave aside.
3. Put the duck breasts in your air fryer and cook them at 400 °F, for 15 minutes. Divide among plates, drizzle hoisin and ginger sauce all over them and serve.

Nutrition Facts: Calories: 336; Fat: 12g; Fiber: 1g; Carbs: 25g; Protein: 33g

Chicken and Asparagus Recipe

(**Prep + Cook Time:** 30 Minutes | **Servings:** 4)

Ingredients:
- 8 chicken wings; halved
- 8 asparagus spears
- 1 tbsp. rosemary; chopped
- 1 tsp. cumin; ground
- Salt and black pepper to the taste

Instructions:
1. Pat dry chicken wings, season with salt, pepper, cumin and rosemary, put them in your air fryer's basket and cook at 360 °F, for 20 minutes.
2. Meanwhile; heat up a pan over medium heat, add asparagus, add water to cover, steam for a few minutes; transfer to a bowl filled with ice water, drain and arrange on plates. Add chicken wings on the side and serve.

Nutrition Facts: Calories: 270; Fat: 8g; Fiber: 12g; Carbs: 24g; Protein: 22g

Chinese Chicken Wings Recipe

(**Prep + Cook Time:** 2 hours 15 Minutes | **Servings:** 6)

Ingredients:
- 16 chicken wings
- 2 tbsp. honey
- 2 tbsp. soy sauce
- Salt and black pepper to the taste
- 1/4 tsp. white pepper
- 3 tbsp. lime juice

Instructions:
1. In a bowl, mix honey with soy sauce, salt, black and white pepper and lime juice, whisk well, add chicken pieces, toss to coat and keep in the fridge for 2 hours.
2. Transfer chicken to your air fryer, cook at 370 °F, for 6 minutes on each side, increase heat to 400 °F and cook for 3 minutes more. Serve hot.

Nutrition Facts: Calories: 372; Fat: 9g; Fiber: 10g; Carbs: 37g; Protein: 24g

Herbed Chicken Recipe

(**Prep + Cook Time:** 70 Minutes | **Servings:** 4)

Ingredients:
- 1 whole chicken
- 1 tsp. garlic powder
- 1 tsp. onion powder
- 1/2 tsp. thyme; dried
- 1 tsp. rosemary; dried
- 1 tbsp. lemon juice
- 2 tbsp. olive oil
- Salt and black pepper to the taste

Instructions:
1. Season chicken with salt and pepper, rub with thyme, rosemary, garlic powder and onion powder, rub with lemon juice and olive oil and leave aside for 30 minutes.
2. Put the chicken in your air fryer and cook at 360 °F, for 20 minutes on each side. Leave chicken aside to cool down, carve and serve.

Nutrition Facts: Calories: 390; Fat: 10g; Fiber: 5g; Carbs: 22g; Protein: 20g

Chicken Thighs and Apple

(**Prep + Cook Time:** 12 hours 30 Minutes | **Servings:** 4)

Ingredients:
- 8 chicken thighs; bone in and skin on
- 1 tbsp. apple cider vinegar
- 3 tbsp. onion; chopped
- 1 tbsp. ginger; grated
- 1/2 tsp. thyme; dried
- 3 apples; cored and cut into quarters
- 3/4 cup apple juice
- 1/2 cup maple syrup
- Salt and black pepper to the taste

Instructions:
1. In a bowl, mix chicken with salt, pepper, vinegar, onion, ginger, thyme, apple juice and maple syrup; toss well, cover and keep in the fridge for 12 hours.
2. Transfer this whole mix to a baking pan that fits your air fryer, add apple pieces, place in your air fryer and cook at 350 °F, for 30 minutes. Divide among plates and serve warm.

Nutrition Facts: Calories: 314; Fat: 8g; Fiber: 11g; Carbs: 34g; Protein: 22g

Coconut Creamy Chicken
(**Prep + Cook Time:** 2 hours 25 Minutes | **Servings:** 4)

Ingredients:
- 4 big chicken legs
- 5 tsp. turmeric powder
- 2 tbsp. ginger; grated
- 4 tbsp. coconut cream
- Salt and black pepper to the taste

Instructions:
1. In a bowl, mix cream with turmeric, ginger, salt and pepper, whisk, add chicken pieces, toss them well and leave aside for 2 hours.
2. Transfer chicken to your preheated air fryer, cook at 370 °F, for 25 minutes; divide among plates and serve.

Nutrition Facts: Calories: 300; Fat: 4g; Fiber: 12g; Carbs: 22g; Protein: 20g

Creamy Chicken, Peas and Rice
(**Prep + Cook Time:** 40 Minutes | **Servings:** 4)

Ingredients:
- 1 lb. chicken breasts; skinless, boneless and cut into quarters
- 1 cup white rice; already cooked
- 1 cup chicken stock
- 1/4 cup parsley; chopped.
- 2 cups peas; frozen
- 1 ½ cups parmesan; grated
- 1 tbsp. olive oil
- 3 garlic cloves; minced
- 1 yellow onion; chopped
- 1/2 cup white wine
- 1/4 cup heavy cream
- Salt and black pepper to the taste

Instructions:
1. Season chicken breasts with salt and pepper, drizzle half of the oil over them, rub well, put the chicken breasts in your air fryer's basket and cook them at 360 °F, for 6 minutes.
2. Heat up a pan with the rest of the oil over medium high heat, add garlic, onion, wine, stock, salt, pepper and heavy cream; stir, bring to a simmer and cook for 9 minutes.
3. Transfer chicken breasts to a heat proof dish that fits your air fryer, add peas, rice and cream mix over them, toss, sprinkle parmesan and parsley all over, place in your air fryer and cook at 420 °F, for 10 minutes. Divide among plates and serve hot.

Nutrition Facts: Calories: 313; Fat: 12g; Fiber: 14g; Carbs: 27g; Protein: 25g

Chicken Salad Recipe
(**Prep + Cook Time:** 20 Minutes | **Servings:** 4)

Ingredients:
- 1 lb. chicken breast; boneless, skinless and halved
- 1/2 cup feta cheese; cubed
- 2 tbsp. lemon juice
- 1½ tsp. mustard
- 1 tbsp. olive oil
- 1 ½ tsp. red wine vinegar
- 1/2 tsp. anchovies; minced
- 3/4 tsp. garlic; minced
- 1 tbsp. water
- 8 cups lettuce leaves; cut into strips
- 4 tbsp. parmesan; grated
- Cooking spray
- Salt and black pepper to the taste

Instructions:
1. Spray chicken breasts with cooking oil, season with salt and pepper, introduce in your air fryer's basket and cook at 370 °F, for 10 minutes; flipping halfway.
2. Transfer chicken beasts to a cutting board, shred using 2 forks, add it to the salad bowl and mix with lettuce leaves.
3. In your blender, mix feta cheese with lemon juice, olive oil, mustard, vinegar, garlic, anchovies, water and half of the parmesan and blend very well. Add this over chicken mix; toss, sprinkle the rest of the parmesan and serve.

Nutrition Facts: Calories: 312; Fat: 6g; Fiber: 16g; Carbs: 22g; Protein: 26g

Chicken Breasts and Tomatoes Sauce

(**Prep + Cook Time:** 30 Minutes | **Servings:** 4)

Ingredients:
- 4 chicken breasts; skinless and boneless
- 1 red onion; chopped
- 1/4 cup balsamic vinegar
- 1/4 cup parmesan; grated
- 1/4 tsp. garlic powder
- 14 oz. canned tomatoes; chopped
- Salt and black pepper to the taste
- Cooking spray

Instructions:
1. Spray the baking pan that fits your air fryer with cooking oil, add chicken, season with salt, pepper, balsamic vinegar, garlic powder, tomatoes and cheese; toss, Transfer this whole mix to your air fryer and cook at 400 °F, for 20 minutes.
2. Divide among plates and serve hot.

Nutrition Facts: Calories: 250; Fat: 12g; Fiber: 12g; Carbs: 19g; Protein: 28g

Chicken and Green Onions Sauce Recipe

(**Prep + Cook Time:** 26 Minutes | **Servings:** 4)

Ingredients:
- 10 chicken drumsticks
- 10 green onions; roughly chopped.
- 1-inch piece ginger root; chopped
- 4 garlic cloves; minced
- 2 tbsp. fish sauce
- 3 tbsp. soy sauce
- 1 tsp. Chinese five spice
- 1 cup coconut milk
- 1 tsp. butter; melted
- 1/4 cup cilantro; chopped.
- 1 tbsp. lime juice
- Salt and black pepper to the taste

Instructions:
1. In your food processor, mix green onions with ginger, garlic, soy sauce, fish sauce, five spice, salt, pepper, butter and coconut milk and pulse well.
2. In a bowl, mix chicken with green onions mix; toss well, transfer everything to a pan that fits your air fryer and cook at 370 °F, for 16 minutes; shake the basket every few minutes to ensure even cooking.
3. Divide among plates, sprinkle cilantro on top, drizzle lime juice and serve with a side salad.

Nutrition Facts: Calories: 321; Fat: 12g; Fiber: 12g; Carbs: 22g; Protein: 20g

Chicken Tenders and Flavored Sauce Recipe

(**Prep + Cook Time:** 20 Minutes | **Servings:** 6)

Ingredients:
- 2 lbs. chicken tenders
- 2 tbsp. cornstarch
- 1 tsp. chili powder
- 2 tsp. garlic powder
- 1 tsp. onion powder
- 1 tsp. sweet paprika
- 2 tbsp. butter
- 2 tbsp. olive oil
- 1/2 cup chicken stock
- 2 cups heavy cream
- 2 tbsp. water
- 2 tbsp. parsley; chopped
- Salt and black pepper to the taste

Instructions:
1. In a bowl, mix garlic powder with onion powder, chili, salt, pepper and paprika; stir, add chicken and toss.
2. Rub chicken tenders with oil, place in your air fryer and cook at 360 °F, for 10 minutes.
3. Meanwhile; heat up a pan with the butter over medium high heat, add cornstarch, stock, cream, water and parsley; stir, cover and cook for 10 minutes. Divide chicken on plates, drizzle sauce all over and serve.

Nutrition Facts: Calories: 351; Fat: 12g; Fiber: 9g; Carbs: 20g; Protein: 17g

Chicken Wings and Mint Sauce Recipe
(**Prep + Cook Time:** 36 Minutes | **Servings:** 6)

Ingredients:
- 18 chicken wings; halved
- 1 tbsp. turmeric powder
- 1 tbsp. cumin; ground
- 2 tbsp. olive oil
- 1 tbsp. ginger; grated
- 1 tbsp. coriander; ground
- 1 tbsp. sweet paprika
- Salt and black pepper to the taste

For the mint sauce:
- 3/4 cup cilantro
- Juice from 1/2 lime
- 1 cup mint leaves
- 1 small ginger piece; chopped
- 1 tbsp. olive oil
- 1 Serrano pepper; chopped
- 1 tbsp. water
- Salt and black pepper to the taste

Instructions:
1. In a bowl, mix 1 tablespoon ginger with cumin, coriander, paprika, turmeric, salt, pepper, cayenne and 2 tablespoon olive oil and stir well.
2. Add chicken wings pieces to this mix; toss to coat well and keep in the fridge for 10 minutes.
3. Transfer chicken to your air fryer's basket and cook at 370 °F, for 16 minutes; flipping them halfway.
4. In your blender, mix mint with cilantro, 1 small ginger pieces, juice from 1/2 lime, 1 tbsp. olive oil, salt, pepper, water and Serrano pepper and blend very well. Divide chicken wings on plates, drizzle mint sauce all over and serve.

Nutrition Facts: Calories: 300; Fat: 15g; Fiber: 11g; Carbs: 27g; Protein: 16g

Chicken Parmesan Recipe
(**Prep + Cook Time:** 25 Minutes | **Servings:** 4)

Ingredients:
- 1 ½ lbs. chicken cutlets; skinless and boneless
- 2 cups panko bread crumbs
- 1/4 cup parmesan; grated
- 1/2 tsp. garlic powder
- 2 cups white flour
- 1 egg; whisked
- 1 cup mozzarella; grated
- 2 cups tomato sauce
- 3 tbsp. basil; chopped.
- Salt and black pepper to the taste

Instructions:
1. In a bowl, mix panko with parmesan and garlic powder and stir.
2. Put the flour in a second bowl and the egg in a third.
3. Season chicken with salt and pepper, dip in flour, then in egg mix and in panko.
4. Put the chicken pieces in your air fryer and cook them at 360 °F, for 3 minutes on each side.
5. Transfer chicken to a baking pan that fits your air fryer, add tomato sauce and top with mozzarella, close the air fryer basket and cook at 375 °F, for 7 minutes. Divide among plates, sprinkle basil on top and serve.

Nutrition Facts: Calories: 304; Fat: 12g; Fiber: 11g; Carbs: 22g; Protein: 15g

Chicken and Coconut Sauce Recipe
(Prep + Cook Time: 22 Minutes | Servings: 6)

Ingredients:
- 3 ½ lbs. chicken breasts
- 1/4 cup coconut milk
- 2 tsp. sweet paprika
- 1 tsp. red pepper flakes
- 2 tbsp. green onions; chopped.
- 1 tbsp. olive oil
- 1 cup chicken stock
- 1 ¼ cups yellow onion; chopped
- 1 tbsp. lime juice
- Salt and black pepper to the taste

Instructions:
1. Heat up a pan that fits your air fryer with the oil over medium high heat, add onions; stir and cook for 4 minutes.
2. Add stock, coconut milk, pepper flakes, paprika, lime juice, salt and pepper and stir well.
3. Add chicken to the pan, add more salt and pepper; toss, close the air fryer basket and cook at 360 °F, for 12 minutes. Divide chicken and sauce on plates and serve.

Nutrition Facts: Calories: 320; Fat: 13g; Fiber: 13g; Carbs: 32g; Protein: 23g

Chicken Thighs Recipe
(Prep + Cook Time: 30 Minutes | Servings: 6)

Ingredients:
- 2 ½ lbs. chicken thighs
- 5 green onions; chopped
- 2 tbsp. sesame oil
- 1 tbsp. sherry wine
- 1/2 tsp. white vinegar
- 1 tbsp. soy sauce
- 1/4 tsp. sugar
- Salt and black pepper to the taste

Instructions:
1. Season chicken with salt and pepper, rub with half of the sesame oil, add to your air fryer and cook at 360 °F, for 20 minutes.
2. Meanwhile; heat up a pan with the rest of the oil over medium high heat, add green onions, sherry wine, vinegar, soy sauce and sugar; toss, cover and cook for 10 minutes.
3. Shred chicken using 2 forks divide among plates, drizzle sauce all over and serve.

Nutrition Facts: Calories: 321; Fat: 8g; Fiber: 12g; Carbs: 36g; Protein: 24g

Chicken and Creamy Mushrooms Recipe
(Prep + Cook Time: 40 Minutes | Servings: 8)

Ingredients:
- 8 chicken thighs
- 1/2 tsp. thyme; dried
- 1/2 tsp. oregano; dried
- 1 tbsp. mustard
- 1/4 cup parmesan; grated
- 8 oz. cremini mushrooms; halved
- 3 garlic cloves; minced
- 3 tbsp. butter; melted
- 1 cup chicken stock
- 1/4 cup heavy cream
- 1/2 tsp. basil; dried
- Salt and black pepper to the taste

Instructions:
1. Rub chicken pieces with 2 tablespoons butter, season with salt and pepper, transfer to your air fryer's basket and cook at 370 °F, for 5 minutes and leave aside in a bowl for now.
2. Meanwhile; heat up a pan with the rest of the butter over medium high heat, add mushrooms and garlic; stir and cook for 5 minutes.
3. Add salt, pepper, stock, oregano, thyme and basil; stir well and transfer to a heat proof dish that fits your air fryer.
4. Add chicken, toss everything, place it in your air fryer and cook at 370 °F, for 20 minutes.
5. Add mustard, parmesan and heavy cream, toss everything again, cook for 5 minutes more, divide among plates and serve.

Nutrition Facts: Calories: 340; Fat: 10g; Fiber: 13g; Carbs: 22g; Protein: 12g

Turkey Quarters and Veggies Recipe

(Prep + Cook Time: 44 Minutes | **Servings:** 4)

Ingredients:
- 2 lbs. turkey quarters
- 1/2 tsp. rosemary; dried
- 1/2 tsp. sage; dried
- 1/2 tsp. thyme; dried
- 1 yellow onion; chopped
- 1 carrot; chopped
- 3 garlic cloves; minced
- 1 celery stalk; chopped
- 1 cup chicken stock
- 2 tbsp. olive oil
- 2 bay leaves
- Salt and black pepper to the taste

Instructions:
1. Rub turkey quarters with salt, pepper, half of the oil, thyme, sage, rosemary and thyme, place the turkey quarters in your air fryer and cook at 360 °F, for 20 minutes.
2. In a pan that fits your air fryer, mix onion with carrot, garlic, celery, the rest of the oil, stock, bay leaves, salt and pepper and toss.
3. Add turkey, introduce everything in your air fryer and cook at 360 °F, for 14 minutes more. Divide everything on plates and serve.

Nutrition Facts: Calories: 362; Fat: 12g; Fiber: 16g; Carbs: 22g; Protein: 17g

Chinese Duck Legs Recipe

(Prep + Cook Time: 46 Minutes | **Servings:** 2)

Ingredients:
- 2 duck legs
- 2 dried chilies; chopped.
- 1 tbsp. olive oil
- 2-star anise
- 1 bunch spring onions; chopped
- 4 ginger slices
- 1 tbsp. oyster sauce
- 1 tbsp. soy sauce
- 1 tsp. sesame oil
- 14 oz. water
- 1 tbsp. rice wine

Instructions:
1. Heat up a pan with the oil over medium high heat, add chili, star anise, sesame oil, rice wine, ginger, oyster sauce, soy sauce and water; stir and cook for 6 minutes.
2. Add spring onions and duck legs, toss to coat, transfer to a pan that fits your air fryer and cook at 370 °F, for 30 minutes. Divide among plates and serve.

Nutrition Facts: Calories: 300; Fat: 12g; Fiber: 12g; Carbs: 26g; Protein: 18g

Chicken & Parsley Sauce

(Prep + Cook Time: 55 Minutes | **Servings:** 6)

Ingredients:
- 12 chicken thighs
- 1 cup parsley; chopped.
- 1 tsp. oregano; dried
- 1/2 cup olive oil
- 1/4 cup red wine
- 4 garlic cloves
- A pinch of salt
- A drizzle of maple syrup

Instructions:
1. In your food processor, mix parsley with oregano, garlic, salt, oil, wine and maple syrup and pulse really well.
2. In a bowl, mix chicken with parsley sauce; toss well and keep in the fridge for 30 minutes.
3. Drain chicken, transfer to your air fryer's basket and cook at 380 °F, for 25 minutes; flipping chicken once. Divide chicken on plates, drizzle parsley sauce all over and serve.

Nutrition Facts: Calories: 354; Fat: 10g; Fiber: 12g; Carbs: 22g; Protein: 17g

Mexican Chicken Recipe

(Prep + Cook Time: 30 Minutes | **Servings:** 4)

Ingredients:
- 1 lb. chicken breast; boneless and skinless
- 16 oz. salsa verde
- 1 tbsp. olive oil
- 1½ cup Monterey Jack cheese; grated
- 1/4 cup cilantro; chopped
- 1 tsp. garlic powder
- Salt and black pepper to the taste

Instructions:
1. Pour salsa verde in a baking pan that fits your air fryer, season chicken with salt, pepper, garlic powder, brush with olive oil and place it over your salsa verde.
2. Close the air fryer basket and cook at 380 °F, for 20 minutes.
3. Sprinkle cheese on top and cook for 2 minutes more. Divide among plates and serve hot.

Nutrition Facts: Calories: 340; Fat: 18g; Fiber: 14g; Carbs: 32g; Protein: 18g

Chinese Stuffed Chicken Recipe

(Prep + Cook Time: 45 Minutes | **Servings:** 8)

Ingredients:
- 1 whole chicken
- 10 wolfberries
- 2 red chilies; chopped
- 4 ginger slices
- 1 yam; cubed
- 1 tsp. soy sauce
- 3 tsp. sesame oil
- Salt and white pepper to the taste

Instructions:
1. Season chicken with salt, pepper, rub with soy sauce and sesame oil and stuff with wolfberries, yam cubes, chilies and ginger.
2. Place the mix in your air fryer, cook at 400 °F, for 20 minutes and then at 360 °F, for 15 minutes. Carve chicken, divide among plates and serve.

Nutrition Facts: Calories: 320; Fat: 12g; Fiber: 17g; Carbs: 22g; Protein: 12g

Duck Breasts Recipe

(Prep + Cook Time: 50 Minutes | **Servings:** 6)

Ingredients:
- 6 duck breasts; halved
- 3 tbsp. flour
- 6 tbsp. butter; melted
- 2 cups chicken stock
- 1/2 cup white wine
- 1/4 cup parsley; chopped
- 2 cups mushrooms; chopped.
- Salt and black pepper to the taste

Instructions:
1. Season duck breasts with salt and pepper, place them in a bowl, add melted butter; toss and transfer to another bowl.
2. Combine melted butter with flour, wine, salt, pepper and chicken stock and stir well.
3. Arrange duck breasts in a baking pan that fits your air fryer, pour the sauce over them, add parsley and mushrooms, close the air fryer basket and cook at 350 °F, for 40 minutes. Divide among plates and serve.

Nutrition Facts: Calories: 320; Fat: 28g; Fiber: 12g; Carbs: 12g; Protein: 22g

Chicken and Lentils Casserole Recipe

(Prep + Cook Time: 1 hour 10 Minutes | **Servings:** 8)

Ingredients:
- 2 lb. chicken breasts; skinless, boneless and chopped
- 1 ½ cups green lentils
- 3 cups chicken stock
- 3 tsp. cumin; ground
- 5 garlic cloves; minced
- 1 yellow onion; chopped
- 2 red bell peppers; chopped
- 14 oz. canned tomatoes; chopped.
- 2 cups corn
- 2 cups Cheddar cheese; shredded
- 2 tbsp. jalapeno pepper; chopped.
- 1 tbsp. garlic powder
- 1 cup cilantro; chopped
- Cooking spray
- Salt and cayenne pepper to the taste

Instructions:
1. Put the stock in a pot, add some salt, add lentils; stir, bring to a boil over medium heat, cover and simmer for 35 minutes.
2. Meanwhile; spray chicken pieces with some cooking spray, season with salt, cayenne pepper and 1 tsp. cumin, put them in your air fryer's basket and cook them at 370 degrees for 6 minutes. flipping half way.
3. Transfer chicken to a heat proof dish that fits your air fryer, add bell peppers, garlic, tomatoes, onion, salt, cayenne and 1 tsp. cumin.
4. Drain lentils and add them to the chicken mix as well.
5. Add jalapeno pepper, garlic powder, the rest of the cumin, corn, half of the cheese and half of the cilantro, close the air fryer basket and cook at 320 °F, for 25 minutes.
6. Sprinkle the rest of the cheese and the remaining cilantro, divide chicken casserole on plates and serve.

Nutrition Facts: Calories: 344; Fat: 11g; Fiber: 12g; Carbs: 22g; Protein: 33g

Honey Duck Breasts Recipe

(Prep + Cook Time: 32 Minutes | **Servings:** 2)

Ingredients:
- 1 smoked duck breast; halved
- 1 tsp. honey
- 1 tsp. tomato paste
- 1 tbsp. mustard
- 1/2 tsp. apple vinegar

Instructions:
1. In a bowl, mix honey with tomato paste, mustard and vinegar, whisk well, add duck breast pieces, toss to coat well, transfer to your air fryer and cook at 370 °F, for 15 minutes.
2. Take duck breast out of the fryer, add to honey mix, toss again, return to air fryer and cook at 370 °F, for 6 minutes more. Divide among plates and serve with a side salad.

Nutrition Facts: Calories: 274; Fat: 11g; Fiber: 13g; Carbs: 22g; Protein: 13g

Pepperoni Chicken Recipe

(Prep + Cook Time: 32 Minutes | **Servings:** 6)

Ingredients:
- 4 medium chicken breasts; skinless and boneless
- 14 oz. tomato paste
- 1 tbsp. olive oil
- 1 tsp. oregano; dried
- 6 oz. mozzarella; sliced
- 1 tsp. garlic powder
- 2 oz. pepperoni; sliced
- Salt and black pepper to the taste

Instructions:
1. In a bowl, mix chicken with salt, pepper, garlic powder and oregano and toss.
2. Put the chicken in your air fryer, cook at 350 °F, for 6 minutes and transfer to a pan that fits your air fryer.

3. Add mozzarella slices on top, spread tomato paste, top with pepperoni slices, close the air fryer basket and cook at 350 °F, for 15 minutes more. Divide among plates and serve.

Nutrition Facts: Calories: 320; Fat: 10g; Fiber: 16g; Carbs: 23g; Protein: 27g

Fall Fried Chicken

(Prep + Cook Time: 30 Minutes | **Servings:** 8)

Ingredients:
- 3 lbs. chicken breasts; skinless and boneless
- 1 yellow onion; chopped.
- 1 garlic clove; minced
- 10 white mushrooms; halved
- 1 tbsp. olive oil
- 1 red bell pepper; chopped
- 1 green bell pepper
- 2 tbsp. mozzarella cheese; shredded
- Salt and black pepper to the taste
- Cooking spray

Instructions:
1. Season chicken with salt and pepper, rub with garlic, spray with cooking spray, place in your preheated air fryer and cook at 390 °F, for 12 minutes.
2. Meanwhile; heat up a pan with the oil over medium heat, add onion; stir and sauté for 2 minutes.
3. Add mushrooms, garlic and bell peppers; stir and cook for 8 minutes.
4. Divide chicken on plates, add mushroom mix on the side, sprinkle cheese while chicken is still hot and serve right away.

Nutrition Facts: Calories: 305; Fat: 12g; Fiber: 11g; Carbs: 26g; Protein: 22g

Duck and Plum Sauce Recipe

(Prep + Cook Time: 42 Minutes | **Servings:** 2)

Ingredients:
- 2 duck breasts
- 9 oz. red plumps; stoned; cut into small wedges
- 2 tbsp. sugar
- 2 tbsp. red wine
- 1 tbsp. butter; melted
- 1-star anise
- 1 tbsp. olive oil
- 1 shallot; chopped
- 1 cup beef stock

Instructions:
1. Heat up the pan with the olive oil over medium heat, add shallot; stir and cook for 5 minutes.
2. Add sugar and plums; stir and cook until sugar dissolves.
3. Add stock and wine; stir, cook for 15 minutes; take off heat and keep warm for now.
4. Score duck breasts, season with salt and pepper, rub with melted butter, transfer to a heat proof dish that fits your air fryer, add star anise and plum sauce, close the air fryer basket and cook at 360 °F, for 12 minutes. Divide everything on plates and serve.

Nutrition Facts: Calories: 400; Fat: 25g; Fiber: 12g; Carbs: 29g; Protein: 25g

Cheese Crusted Chicken Recipe

(Prep + Cook Time: 25 Minutes | **Servings:** 4)

Ingredients:
- 4 bacon slices; cooked and crumbled
- 4 chicken breasts; skinless and boneless
- 1 tbsp. water
- 1/2 cup avocado oil
- 1 egg; whisked
- 1 cup asiago cheese; shredded
- 1/4 tsp. garlic powder
- 1 cup parmesan cheese; grated
- Salt and black pepper to the taste

Instructions:
1. In a bowl, mix parmesan with garlic, salt and pepper and stir.
2. In another bowl, mix egg with water and whisk well.
3. Season chicken with salt and pepper and dip each pieces into egg and then into cheese mix.

4. Add chicken to your air fryer and cook at 320 °F, for 15 minutes. Divide chicken on plates, sprinkle bacon and asiago cheese on top and serve.

Nutrition Facts: Calories: 400; Fat: 22g; Fiber: 12g; Carbs: 32g; Protein: 47g

Lemony Chicken
(Prep + Cook Time: 40 Minutes | Servings: 6)

Ingredients:
- 1 whole chicken; cut into medium pieces
- 1 tbsp. olive oil
- Juice from 2 lemons
- Zest from 2 lemons; grated
- Salt and black pepper to the taste

Instructions:
1. Season chicken with salt, pepper, rub with oil and lemon zest, drizzle lemon juice, place the chicken in your air fryer and cook at 350 °F, for 30 minutes; flipping chicken pieces halfway. Divide among plates and serve with a side salad.

Nutrition Facts: Calories: 334; Fat: 24g; Fiber: 12g; Carbs: 26g; Protein: 20g

Turkey, Mushrooms and Peas Casserole
(Prep + Cook Time: 30 Minutes | Servings: 4)

Ingredients:
- 2 lbs. turkey breasts; skinless, boneless
- 1 yellow onion; chopped
- 1 celery stalk; chopped.
- 1/2 cup peas
- 1 cup chicken stock
- 1 cup cream of mushrooms soup
- 1 cup bread cubes
- Salt and black pepper to the taste

Instructions:
1. In a pan that fits your air fryer, mix turkey with salt, pepper, onion, celery, peas and stock, close the air fryer basket and cook at 360 °F, for 15 minutes.
2. Add bread cubes and cream of mushroom soup; stir toss and cook at 360 °F, for 5 minutes more. Divide among plates and serve hot.

Nutrition Facts: Calories: 271; Fat: 9g; Fiber: 9g; Carbs: 16g; Protein: 7g

Duck Breast with Fig Sauce Recipe
(Prep + Cook Time: 30 Minutes | Servings: 4)

Ingredients:
- 2 duck breasts; skin on, halved
- 1 tbsp. white flour
- 1 tbsp. olive oil
- 1/2 tsp. thyme; chopped
- 1/2 cup port wine
- 1/2 tsp. garlic powder
- 1/4 tsp. sweet paprika
- 1 cup beef stock
- 3 tbsp. butter; melted
- 1 shallot; chopped
- 4 tbsp. fig preserves
- Salt and black pepper to the taste

Instructions:
1. Season duck breasts with salt and pepper, drizzle half of the melted butter, rub well, place the duck breasts in your air fryer's basket and cook at 350 °F, for 5 minutes on each side.
2. Meanwhile; heat up a pan with the olive oil and the rest of the butter over medium high heat, add shallot; stir and cook for 2 minutes.
3. Add thyme, garlic powder, paprika, stock, salt, pepper, wine and figs; stir and cook for 7-8 minutes.
4. Add flour; stir well, cook until sauce thickens a bit and take off heat.
5. Divide duck breasts on plates, drizzle figs sauce all over and serve.

Nutrition Facts: Calories: 246; Fat: 12g; Fiber: 4g; Carbs: 22g; Protein: 3g

Chicken Thighs and Baby Potatoes

(**Prep + Cook Time:** 40 Minutes | **Servings:** 4)

Ingredients:
- 8 chicken thighs
- 2 tbsp. olive oil
- 1 lb. baby potatoes; halved
- 2 tsp. oregano; dried
- 2 tsp. rosemary; dried
- 2 garlic cloves; minced
- 1 red onion; chopped
- 2 tsp. thyme; chopped.
- 1/2 tsp. sweet paprika
- Salt and black pepper to the taste

Instructions:
1. In a bowl, mix chicken thighs with potatoes, salt, pepper, thyme, paprika, onion, rosemary, garlic, oregano and oil.
2. Toss to coat, spread everything in a heat proof dish that fits your air fryer and cook at 400 °F, for 30 minutes, shake the basket every few minutes to ensure even cooking. Divide among plates and serve.

Nutrition Facts: Calories: 364; Fat: 14g; Fiber: 13g; Carbs: 21g; Protein: 34g

Chicken and Apricot Sauce Recipe

(**Prep + Cook Time:** 30 Minutes | **Servings:** 4)

Ingredients:
- 1 whole chicken; cut into medium pieces
- 2 tbsp. honey
- 1 tbsp. olive oil
- 1/2 tsp. smoked paprika
- 1/4 cup white wine
- 2 tbsp. white vinegar
- 1/4 cup apricot preserves
- 1 ½ tsp. ginger; grated
- 1/2 tsp. marjoram; dried
- 1/4 cup chicken stock
- Salt and black pepper to the taste

Instructions:
1. Season chicken with salt, pepper, marjoram and paprika; toss to coat, add oil, rub well, place in your air fryer and cook at 360 °F, for 10 minutes.
2. Transfer chicken to a pan that fits your air fryer, add stock, wine, vinegar, ginger, apricot preserves and honey; toss, put it in your air fryer and cook at 360 °F, for 10 minutes more. Divide chicken and apricot sauce on plates and serve.

Nutrition Facts: Calories: 200; Fat: 7g; Fiber: 19g; Carbs: 20g; Protein: 14g

Creamy Chicken Casserole Recipe

(**Prep + Cook Time:** 22 Minutes | **Servings:** 4)

Ingredients:
- 2 cup chicken breasts; skinless, boneless and cubed
- 10 oz. spinach; chopped
- 1/2 cup parmesan; grated
- 1/2 cup heavy cream
- 4 tbsp. butter
- 3 tbsp. flour
- 1 ½ cups milk
- 1 cup bread crumbs
- Salt and black pepper to the taste

Instructions:
1. Heat up a pan with the butter over medium heat, add flour and stir well.
2. Add milk, heavy cream and parmesan; stir well, cook for 1-2 minutes more and take off heat.
3. In a pan that fits your air fryer basket, spread chicken and spinach.
4. Add salt and pepper and toss.
5. Add cream mix and spread, sprinkle bread crumbs on top, close the air fryer basket and cook at 350 for 12 minutes. Divide chicken and spinach mix on plates and serve.

Nutrition Facts: Calories: 321; Fat: 9g; Fiber: 12g; Carbs: 22g; Protein: 17g

Chicken and Garlic Sauce Recipe
(Prep + Cook Time: 30 Minutes | **Servings:** 4)

Ingredients:
- 4 chicken breasts; skin on and bone-in
- 1 tbsp. butter; melted
- 40 garlic cloves; peeled and chopped.
- 2 thyme springs
- 1/4 cup chicken stock
- 2 tbsp. parsley; chopped
- 1/4 cup dry white wine
- 1 tbsp. olive oil
- Salt and black pepper to the taste

Instructions:
1. Season chicken breasts with salt and pepper, rub with the oil, place in your air fryer, cook at 360 °F, for 4 minutes on each side and transfer to a heat proof dish that fits your air fryer.
2. Add melted butter, garlic, thyme, stock, wine and parsley; toss, close the air fryer basket and cook at 350 °F, for 15 minutes more. Divide everything on plates and serve.

Nutrition Facts: Calories: 227; Fat: 9g; Fiber: 13g; Carbs: 22g; Protein: 12g

Duck and Veggies Recipe
(Prep + Cook Time: 30 Minutes | **Servings:** 8)

Ingredients:
- 1 duck; chopped in medium pieces
- 1 cup chicken stock
- 1 small ginger piece; grated
- 3 cucumbers; chopped.
- 3 tbsp. white wine
- 2 carrots; chopped
- Salt and black pepper to the taste

Instructions:
1. In a pan that fits your air fryer, mix duck pieces with cucumbers, wine, carrots, ginger, stock, salt and pepper; toss, close the air fryer basket and cook at 370 °F, for 20 minutes. Divide everything on plates and serve.

Nutrition Facts: Calories: 200; Fat: 10g; Fiber: 8g; Carbs: 20g; Protein: 22g

Chicken and Cauliflower Rice Mix Recipe
(Prep + Cook Time: 30 Minutes | **Servings:** 6)

Ingredients:
- 3 lbs. chicken thighs; boneless and skinless
- 3 bacon slices; chopped
- 3 carrots; chopped
- 2 bay leaves
- 1/4 cup red wine vinegar
- 4 garlic cloves; minced
- 4 tbsp. olive oil
- 1 tbsp. garlic powder
- 1 tbsp. Italian seasoning
- 24 oz. cauliflower rice
- 1 tsp. turmeric powder
- 1 cup beef stock
- Salt and black pepper to the taste

Instructions:
1. Heat up a pan that fits your air fryer over medium high heat, add bacon, carrots, onion and garlic; stir and cook for 8 minutes.
2. Add chicken, oil, vinegar, turmeric, garlic powder, Italian seasoning and bay leaves; stir, close the air fryer basket and cook at 360 °F, for 12 minutes. Add cauliflower rice and stock; stir, cook for 6 minutes more, divide among plates and serve.

Nutrition Facts: Calories: 340; Fat: 12g; Fiber: 12g; Carbs: 16g; Protein: 8g

Greek Chicken Recipe

(Prep + Cook Time: 25 Minutes | **Servings:** 4)

Ingredients:
- 1 lb. chicken thighs
- 2 tbsp. olive oil
- Juice from 1 lemon
- 1 tsp. oregano; dried
- 3 garlic cloves; minced
- 1/2 lb. asparagus; trimmed
- 1 zucchini; roughly chopped.
- 1 lemon sliced
- Salt and black pepper to the taste

Instructions:
1. In a heat proof dish that fits your air fryer, mix chicken pieces with oil, lemon juice, oregano, garlic, salt, pepper, asparagus, zucchini and lemon slices; toss, introduce in preheated air fryer and cook at 380 °F, for 15 minutes. Divide everything on plates and serve.

Nutrition Facts: Calories: 300; Fat: 8g; Fiber: 12g; Carbs: 20g; Protein: 18g

Marinated Duck Breasts Recipe

(Prep + Cook Time: 1 day 15 Minutes | **Servings:** 2)

Ingredients:
- 2 duck breasts
- 2 garlic cloves; minced
- 6 tarragon springs
- 1 tbsp. butter
- 1/4 cup sherry wine
- 1 cup white wine
- 1/4 cup soy sauce
- Salt and black pepper to the taste

Instructions:
1. In a bowl, mix duck breasts with white wine, soy sauce, garlic, tarragon, salt and pepper; toss well and keep in the fridge for 1 day.
2. Transfer duck breasts to your preheated air fryer at 350 °F and cook for 10 minutes; flipping halfway.
3. Meanwhile; pour the marinade in a pan, heat up over medium heat, add butter and sherry; stir, bring to a simmer, cook for 5 minutes and take off heat. Divide duck breasts on plates, drizzle sauce all over and serve.

Nutrition Facts: Calories: 475; Fat: 12g; Fiber: 3g; Carbs: 10g; Protein: 48g

Chicken Breasts with Passion Fruit Sauce

(Prep + Cook Time: 20 Minutes | **Servings:** 4)

Ingredients:
- 4 chicken breasts
- 4 passion fruits; halved, deseeded and pulp reserved

1 tbsp. whiskey
- 2-star anise
- 2 oz. maple syrup
- 1 bunch chives; chopped
- Salt and black pepper to the taste

Instructions:
1. Heat up a pan with the passion fruit pulp over medium heat, add whiskey, star anise, maple syrup and chives; stir well, simmer for 5-6 minutes and take off heat.
2. Season chicken with salt and pepper, place the chicken in the preheated air fryer and cook at 360 °F, for 10 minutes; flipping halfway. Divide chicken on plates, heat up the sauce a bit, drizzle it over chicken and serve.

Nutrition Facts: Calories: 374; Fat: 8g; Fiber: 22g; Carbs: 34g; Protein: 37g

Duck Breasts and Mango Mix Recipe

(Prep + Cook Time: 1 hour 10 Minutes | **Servings:** 4)

Ingredients:
- 4 duck breasts
- 3 garlic cloves; minced
- 2 tbsp. olive oil

For the mango mix:
- 1 mango; peeled and chopped
- 1 ½ tbsp. lemon juice
- 1 tbsp. coriander; chopped
- 1 red onion; chopped
- 1½ tbsp. lemongrass; chopped.
- 3 tbsp. lemon juice
- Salt and black pepper to the taste
- 1 tsp. ginger; grated
- 3/4 tsp. sugar
- 1 tbsp. sweet chili sauce

Instructions:
1. In a bowl, mix duck breasts with salt, pepper, lemongrass, 3 tbsp. lemon juice, olive oil and garlic; toss well, keep in the fridge for 1 hour, transfer to your air fryer and cook at 360 °F, for 10 minutes; flipping once.
2. Meanwhile; in a bowl, mix mango with coriander, onion, chili sauce, lemon juice, ginger and sugar and toss well.
3. Divide duck on plates, add mango mix on the side and serve.

Nutrition Facts: Calories: 465; Fat: 11g; Fiber: 4g; Carbs: 29g; Protein: 38g

Chicken and Chestnuts Mix Recipe

(Prep + Cook Time: 22 Minutes | **Servings:** 2)

Ingredients:
- 1/2 lb. chicken pieces
- 1 small yellow onion; chopped
- 2 tsp. garlic; minced
- 2 tbsp. soy sauce
- 4 tbsp. water chestnuts
- 2 tbsp. chicken stock
- 2 tbsp. balsamic vinegar
- 2 tortillas for serving
- A pinch of ginger; grated
- A pinch of allspice; ground

Instructions:
1. In a pan that fits your air fryer, mix chicken meat with onion, garlic, ginger, allspice, chestnuts, soy sauce, stock and vinegar; stir, transfer to your air fryer and cook at 360 °F, for 12 minutes. Divide everything on plates and serve.

Nutrition Facts: Calories: 301; Fat: 12g; Fiber: 7g; Carbs: 24g; Protein: 12g

Duck and Cherries Recipe

(Prep + Cook Time: 30 Minutes | **Servings:** 4)

Ingredients:
- 4 duck breasts; boneless, skin on and scored
- 1 tbsp. ginger; grated
- 1 tsp. cumin; ground
- 1/2 tsp. clove; ground
- 2 cups cherries; pitted
- 1/2 cup sugar
- 1/4 cup honey
- 1/3 cup balsamic vinegar
- 1/2 cup yellow onion; chopped
- 1/2 tsp. cinnamon powder
- 4 sage leaves; chopped
- 1 tsp. garlic; minced
- 1 jalapeno; chopped
- 2 cups rhubarb; sliced
- Salt and black pepper to the taste

Instructions:
1. Season duck breast with salt and pepper, place the duck breasts in your air fryer and cook at 350 °F, for 5 minutes on each side.
2. Meanwhile; heat up a pan over medium heat, add sugar, honey, vinegar, garlic, ginger, cumin, clove, cinnamon, sage, jalapeno, rhubarb, onion and cherries; stir, bring to a simmer and cook for 10 minutes.
3. Add duck breasts; toss well, divide everything on plates and serve.

Nutrition Facts: Calories: 456; Fat: 13g; Fiber: 4g; Carbs: 64g; Protein: 31g

Chicken Breasts and BBQ Chili Sauce Recipe

(Prep + Cook Time: 30 Minutes | **Servings:** 6)

Ingredients:
- 6 chicken breasts; skinless and boneless
- 2 cups chili sauce
- 2 cups ketchup
- 1 cup pear jelly
- 1/4 cup honey
- 1 tsp. garlic powder
- 1/2 tsp. liquid smoke
- 1 tsp. chili powder
- 1 tsp. mustard powder
- 1 tsp. sweet paprika
- Salt and black pepper to the taste

Instructions:
1. Season chicken breasts with salt and pepper, put the chicken in your preheated air fryer and cook at 350 °F, for 10 minutes.
2. Meanwhile; heat up a pan with the chili sauce over medium heat, add ketchup, pear jelly, honey, liquid smoke, chili powder, mustard powder, sweet paprika, salt, pepper and the garlic powder; stir, bring to a simmer and cook for 10 minutes. Add air fried chicken breasts; toss well, divide among plates and serve.

Nutrition Facts: Calories: 473; Fat: 13g; Fiber: 7g; Carbs: 39g; Protein: 33g

Tea Glazed Chicken Recipe

(Prep + Cook Time: 40 Minutes | **Servings:** 6)

Ingredients:
- 6 chicken legs
- 6 black tea bags
- 1/4 tsp. red pepper flakes
- 1 tbsp. olive oil
- 1/2 cup pineapple preserves
- 1/2 cup apricot preserves
- 1 cup hot water
- 1 tbsp. soy sauce
- 1 onion; chopped
- Salt and black pepper to the taste

Instructions:
1. Put the hot water in a bowl, add tea bags, leave aside covered for 10 minutes; discard bags at the end and transfer tea to another bowl.
2. Add soy sauce, pepper flakes, apricot and pineapple preserves, whisk really well and take off heat.
3. Season chicken with salt and pepper, rub with oil, put it in your air fryer and cook at 350 °F, for 5 minutes.
4. Spread onion on the bottom of a baking pan that fits your air fryer, add chicken pieces, drizzle the tea glaze on top, close the air fryer basket and cook at 320 °F, for 25 minutes. Divide everything on plates and serve.

Nutrition Facts: Calories: 298; Fat: 14g; Fiber: 1g; Carbs: 14g; Protein: 21g

Cider Glazed Chicken Recipe

(Prep + Cook Time: 24 Minutes | **Servings:** 4)

Ingredients:
- 6 chicken thighs; bone in and skin on
- 1 sweet potato; cubed
- 2 apples; cored and sliced
- 1 tbsp. olive oil
- 1 tbsp. rosemary; chopped.
- 2/3 cup apple cider
- 1 tbsp. mustard
- 2 tbsp. honey
- 1 tbsp. butter
- Salt and black pepper to the taste

Instructions:
1. Heat up a pan that fits your air fryer with half of the oil over medium high heat, add cider, honey, butter and mustard, whisk well, bring to a simmer, take off heat, add chicken and toss really well.
2. In a bowl, mix potato cubes with rosemary, apples, salt, pepper and the rest of the oil; toss well and add to chicken mix.
3. Place pan in your air fryer and cook at 390 °F, for 14 minutes. Divide everything on plates and serve.

Nutrition Facts: Calories: 241; Fat: 7g; Fiber: 12g; Carbs: 28g; Protein: 22g

Duck Breasts with Red Wine and Orange Sauce Recipe

(**Prep + Cook Time:** 45 Minutes | **Servings:** 4)

Ingredients:
- 2 duck breasts; skin on and halved
- 2 cups chicken stock
- 2 cups orange juice
- 2 tsp. pumpkin pie spice
- 2 tbsp. olive oil
- 2 tbsp. butter
- 1/2 cup honey
- 2 tbsp. sherry vinegar
- 4 cups red wine
- Salt and black pepper to the taste

Instructions:
1. Heat up a pan with the orange juice over medium heat, add honey; stir well and cook for 10 minutes.
2. Add wine, vinegar, stock, pie spice and butter; stir well, cook for 10 minutes more and take off heat.
3. Season duck breasts with salt and pepper, rub with olive oil, place in preheated air fryer at 370 °F and cook for 7 minutes on each side.
4. Divide duck breasts on plates, drizzle wine and orange juice all over and serve right away.

Nutrition Facts: Calories: 300; Fat: 8g; Fiber: 12g; Carbs: 24g; Protein: 11g

Veggie Stuffed Chicken Breasts Recipe

(**Prep + Cook Time:** 25 Minutes | **Servings:** 4)

Ingredients:
- 4 chicken breasts; skinless and boneless
- 2 tbsp. olive oil
- 3 tomatoes; chopped
- 1 red onion; chopped
- 1 zucchini; chopped
- 1 tsp. Italian seasoning
- 2 yellow bell peppers; chopped
- 1 cup mozzarella; shredded
- Salt and black pepper to the taste

Instructions:
1. Mix a slit on each chicken breast creating a pocket, season with salt and pepper and rub them with olive oil.
2. In a bowl, mix zucchini with Italian seasoning, bell peppers, tomatoes and onion and stir.
3. Stuff chicken breasts with this mix, sprinkle mozzarella over them, place them in your air fryer's basket and cook at 350 °F, for 15 minutes. Divide among plates and serve.

Nutrition Facts: Calories: 300; Fat: 12g; Fiber: 7g; Carbs: 22g; Protein: 18g

Duck and Tea Sauce Recipe

(**Prep + Cook Time:** 30 Minutes | **Servings:** 4)

Ingredients:
- 2 duck breast halves; boneless
- 3/4 cup shallot; chopped
- 2 ¼ cup chicken stock
- 1 ½ cup orange juice
- 3 tsp. earl gray tea leaves
- 3 tbsp. butter; melted
- 1 tbsp. honey
- Salt and black pepper to the taste

Instructions:
1. Season duck breast halves with salt and pepper, put the duck breast in a preheated air fryer and cook at 360 °F, for 10 minutes.
2. Meanwhile; heat up a pan with the butter over medium heat, add shallot; stir and cook for 2-3 minutes.
3. Add stock; stir and cook for another minute.
4. Add orange juice, tea leaves and honey; stir, cook for 2-3 minutes more and strain into a bowl.
5. Divide duck on plates, drizzle tea sauce all over and serve.

Nutrition Facts: Calories: 228; Fat: 11g; Fiber: 2g; Carbs: 20g; Protein: 12g

Chicken and Peaches Recipe

(Prep + Cook Time: 40 Minutes | **Servings:** 6)

Ingredients:
- 1 whole chicken; cut into medium pieces
- 3/4 cup water
- 1/3 cup honey
- 1/4 cup olive oil
- 4 peaches; halved
- Salt and black pepper to the taste

Instructions:
1. Pour the water in a pot, bring to a simmer over medium heat, add honey, whisk really well and leave aside.
2. Rub chicken pieces with the oil, season with salt and pepper, place in your air fryer's basket and cook at 350 °F, for 10 minutes.
3. Brush chicken with some of the honey mix, cook for 6 minutes more, flip again, brush one more time with the honey mix and cook for 7 minutes more.
4. Divide chicken pieces on plates and keep warm.
5. Brush peaches with what's left of the honey marinade, place them in your air fryer and cook them for 3 minutes. Divide among plates next to chicken pieces and serve.

Nutrition Facts: Calories: 430; Fat: 14g; Fiber: 3g; Carbs: 15g; Protein: 20g

Chicken and Creamy Veggie Mix Recipe

(Prep + Cook Time: 40 Minutes | **Servings:** 6)

Ingredients:
- 29 oz. chicken stock
- 2 cups whipping cream
- 40 oz. chicken pieces; boneless and skinless
- 3 tbsp. butter; melted
- 1/2 cup yellow onion; chopped.
- 3/4 cup red peppers; chopped
- 1 bay leaf
- 8 oz. mushrooms; chopped
- 17 oz. asparagus; trimmed
- 3 tsp. thyme; chopped.
- Salt and black pepper to the taste

Instructions:
1. Heat up a pan with the butter over medium heat, add onion and peppers; stir and cook for 3 minutes.
2. Add stock, bay leaf, salt and pepper, bring to a boil and simmer for 10 minutes.
3. Add asparagus, mushrooms, chicken, cream, thyme, salt and pepper to the taste; stir, close the air fryer basket and cook at 360 °F, for 15 minutes. Divide chicken and veggie mix on plates and serve.

Nutrition Facts: Calories: 360; Fat: 27g; Fiber: 13g; Carbs: 24g; Protein: 47g

Duck Breasts Recipe

(Prep + Cook Time: 25 Minutes | **Servings:** 4)

Ingredients:
- 4 duck breasts; skinless and boneless
- 4 garlic heads; peeled, tops cut off and quartered
- 2 tbsp. lemon juice
- 1/2 tsp. lemon pepper
- 1 ½ tbsp. olive oil
- Salt and black pepper to the taste

Instructions:
1. In a bowl, mix duck breasts with garlic, lemon juice, salt, pepper, lemon pepper and olive oil and toss everything.
2. Transfer duck and garlic to your air fryer and cook at 350 °F, for 15 minutes. Divide duck breasts and garlic on plates and serve.

Nutrition Facts: Calories: 200; Fat: 7g; Fiber: 1g; Carbs: 11g; Protein: 17g

Chicken and Spinach Salad Recipe
(**Prep + Cook Time:** 22 Minutes | **Servings:** 2)

Ingredients:
- 2 chicken breasts; skinless and boneless
- 2 tsp. parsley; dried
- 1/2 tsp. onion powder
- 1 avocado; pitted, peeled and chopped
- 1/4 cup olive oil
- 1 tbsp. tarragon; chopped.
- 2 tsp. sweet paprika
- 1/2 cup lemon juice
- 5 cups baby spinach
- 8 strawberries; sliced
- 1 small red onion; sliced
- 2 tbsp. balsamic vinegar
- Salt and black pepper to the taste

Instructions:
1. Put the chicken in a bowl, add lemon juice, parsley, onion powder and paprika and toss.
2. Transfer chicken to your air fryer and cook at 360 °F, for 12 minutes.
3. In a bowl, mix spinach, onion, strawberries and avocado and toss.
4. In another bowl, mix oil with vinegar, salt, pepper and tarragon, whisk well, add to the salad and toss. Divide chicken on plates, add spinach salad on the side and serve.

Nutrition Facts: Calories: 240; Fat: 5g; Fiber: 13g; Carbs: 25g; Protein: 22g

Duck Breasts with Endives Recipe
(**Prep + Cook Time:** 35 Minutes | **Servings:** 4)

Ingredients:
- 2 duck breasts
- 1 tbsp. sugar
- 1 tbsp. olive oil
- 6 endives; julienned
- 2 tbsp. cranberries
- 8 oz. white wine
- 1 tbsp. garlic; minced
- 2 tbsp. heavy cream
- Salt and black pepper to the taste

Instructions:
1. Score duck breasts and season them with salt and pepper, put the duck breast in a preheated air fryer and cook at 350 °F, for 20 minutes; flipping them halfway.
2. Meanwhile; heat up a pan with the oil over medium heat, add sugar and endives; stir and cook for 2 minutes.
3. Add salt, pepper, wine, garlic, cream and cranberries; stir and cook for 3 minutes. Divide duck breasts on plates, drizzle the endives sauce all over and serve.

Nutrition Facts: Calories: 400; Fat: 12g; Fiber: 32g; Carbs: 29g; Protein: 28g

Chicken and Capers Recipe
(**Prep + Cook Time:** 30 Minutes | **Servings:** 2)

Ingredients:
- 4 chicken thighs
- 3 tbsp. capers
- 4 garlic cloves; minced
- 1/2 cup chicken stock
- 1 lemon; sliced
- 4 green onions; chopped
- 3 tbsp. butter; melted
- Salt and black pepper to the taste

Instructions:
1. Brush chicken with butter, sprinkle salt and pepper to the taste, place them in a baking pan that fits your air fryer.
2. Also add capers, garlic, chicken stock and lemon slices, toss to coat, close the air fryer basket and cook at 370 °F, for 20 minutes, shake the basket every few minutes to ensure even cooking. Sprinkle green onions, divide among plates and serve.

Nutrition Facts: Calories: 200; Fat: 9g; Fiber: 10g; Carbs: 17g; Protein: 7g

Chicken and Black Olives Sauce Recipe

(**Prep + Cook Time:** 18 Minutes | **Servings:** 2)

Ingredients:
- 1 chicken breast cut into 4 pieces
- 2 tbsp. olive oil

For the sauce:
- 1 cup black olives; pitted
- 2 tbsp. olive oil
- 1/4 cup parsley; chopped
- 3 garlic cloves; minced
- 1 tbsp. lemon juice
- Salt and black pepper to the taste

Instructions:
1. In your food processor, mix olives with salt, pepper, 2 tbsp. olive oil, lemon juice and parsley, blend very well and transfer to a bowl.
2. Season chicken with salt and pepper, rub with the oil and garlic, place in your preheated air fryer and cook at 370 °F, for 8 minutes. Divide chicken on plates, top with olives sauce and serve.

Nutrition Facts: Calories: 270; Fat: 12g; Fiber: 12g; Carbs: 23g; Protein: 22g

Fish and Seafood Recipes

Asian Style Salmon
(Prep + Cook Time: 1 hour 15 Minutes | Servings: 2)

Ingredients:
- 2 medium salmon fillets
- 6 tbsp. light soy sauce
- 1 tsp. water
- 6 tbsp. honey
- 3 tsp. mirin

Instructions:
1. In a bowl; mix soy sauce with honey, water and mirin, whisk well, add salmon, rub well and leave aside in the fridge for 1 hour.
2. Transfer salmon to your air fryer and cook at 360 °F, for 15 minutes; flipping them after 7 minutes.
3. Meanwhile; put the soy marinade in a pan, heat up over medium heat; whisk well, cook for 2 minutes and take off heat. Divide salmon on plates, drizzle marinade all over and serve.

Nutrition Facts: Calories: 300; Fat: 12g; Fiber: 8g; Carbs: 13g; Protein: 24g

Trout Fillet & Orange Sauce
(Prep + Cook Time: 20 Minutes | Servings: 4)

Ingredients:
- 4 trout fillets; skinless and boneless
- 4 spring onions; chopped
- 1 tbsp. olive oil
- 1 tbsp. ginger; minced
- Salt and black pepper to the taste
- Juice and zest from 1 orange

Instructions:
1. Season trout fillets with salt, pepper, rub them with the olive oil, place in a pan that fits your air fryer, add ginger, green onions, orange zest and juice; toss well, place in your air fryer and cook at 360 °F, for 10 minutes. Divide fish and sauce on plates and serve right away.

Nutrition Facts: Calories: 239; Fat: 10g; Fiber: 7g; Carbs: 18g; Protein: 23g

Cod Fillets with Grapes and Fennel Salad
(Prep + Cook Time: 25 Minutes | Servings: 2)

Ingredients:
- 2 black cod fillets; boneless
- 1 tbsp. olive oil
- 1 fennel bulb; thinly sliced
- 1 cup grapes; halved
- 1/2 cup pecans
- Salt and black pepper to the taste

Instructions:
1. Drizzle half of the oil over fish fillets; season with salt and pepper, rub well, place fillets in your air fryer's basket; cook for 10 minutes at 400 °F and transfer to a plate.
2. In a bowl; mix pecans with grapes, fennel, the rest of the oil, salt and pepper; toss to coat, add to a pan that fits your air fryer and cook at 400 °F, for 5 minutes. Divide cod on plates; add fennel and grapes mix on the side and serve.

Nutrition Facts: Calories: 300; Fat: 4g; Fiber: 2g; Carbs: 32g; Protein: 22g

Shrimp and Cauliflower Recipe

(Prep + Cook Time: 22 Minutes | **Servings:** 2)

Ingredients:
- 1 lb. shrimp; peeled and deveined
- 1 cauliflower head; riced
- 2 garlic cloves; minced
- 4 bacon slices; cooked and crumbled
- 1/4 cup heavy cream
- 8 oz. mushrooms; roughly chopped
- A pinch of red pepper flakes
- Salt and black pepper to the taste
- 1/2 cup beef stock
- 1 tbsp. butter
- Cooking spray
- 1 tbsp. parsley; finely chopped.
- 1 tbsp. chives; chopped

Instructions:
1. Season shrimp with salt and pepper, spray with cooking oil, place in your air fryer and cook at 360 °F, for 7 minutes.
2. Meanwhile; heat up a pan with the butter over medium heat, add mushrooms; stir and cook for 3-4 minutes.
3. Add garlic, cauliflower rice, pepper flakes, stock, cream, chives, parsley, salt and pepper; stir, cook for a few minutes and take off heat. Divide shrimp on plates, add cauliflower mix on the side, sprinkle bacon on top and serve.

Nutrition Facts: Calories: 245; Fat: 7g; Fiber: 4g; Carbs: 6g; Protein: 20g

Vinaigrette and Cod

(Prep + Cook Time: 25 Minutes | **Servings:** 4)

Ingredients:
- 4 cod fillets; skinless and boneless
- 12 cherry tomatoes; halved
- 2 tbsp. olive oil
- 8 black olives; pitted and roughly chopped
- 2 tbsp. lemon juice
- Salt and black pepper to the taste
- Cooking spray
- 1 bunch basil; chopped

Instructions:
1. Season cod with salt and pepper to the taste; place in your air fryer's basket and cook at 360 °F, for 10 minutes; flipping after 5 minutes.
2. Meanwhile; heat up a pan with the oil over medium heat, add tomatoes, olives and lemon juice; stir, bring to a simmer, add basil, salt and pepper; stir well and take off heat. Divide fish on plates and serve with the vinaigrette drizzled on top.

Nutrition Facts: Calories: 300; Fat: 5g; Fiber: 8g; Carbs: 12g; Protein: 8g

Tangy Saba Fish

(Prep + Cook Time: 18 Minutes | **Servings:** 1)

Ingredients:
- 4 Saba fish fillet; boneless
- 3 red chili pepper; chopped
- 2 tbsp. lemon juice
- 2 tbsp. olive oil
- 2 tbsp. garlic; minced
- Salt and black pepper to the taste

Instructions:
1. Season fish fillets with salt and pepper and add lemon juice, oil, chili and garlic toss to coat, transfer fish to your air fryer and cook at 360 °F, for 8 minutes; flipping halfway. Divide among plates and serve with some fries.

Nutrition Facts: Calories: 300; Fat: 4g; Fiber: 8g; Carbs: 15g; Protein: 15g

Cod with Pearl Onions Recipe

(Prep + Cook Time: 25 Minutes | **Servings:** 2)

Ingredients:
- 14 oz. pearl onions
- 8 oz. mushrooms; sliced
- 2 medium cod fillets
- 1 tbsp. parsley; dried
- 1 tsp. thyme; dried
- Black pepper to the taste

Instructions:
1. Put the fish in a heat proof dish that fits your air fryer; add onions, parsley, mushrooms, thyme and black pepper; toss well, put it in your air fryer and cook at 350 °F and cook for 15 minutes. Divide everything on plates and serve.

Nutrition Facts: Calories: 270; Fat: 14g; Fiber: 8g; Carbs: 14g; Protein: 22g

Salmon Thyme and Parsley

(Prep + Cook Time: 25 Minutes | **Servings:** 4)

Ingredients:
- 4 salmon fillets; boneless
- 4 thyme springs
- 4 parsley springs
- 3 tbsp. extra virgin olive oil
- Juice from 1 lemon
- 1 yellow onion; chopped
- 3 tomatoes; sliced
- Salt and black pepper to the taste

Instructions:
1. Drizzle 1 tbsp. oil in a pan that fits your air fryer; add a layer of tomatoes, salt and pepper, drizzle 1 more tbsp. oil, add fish, season them with salt and pepper, drizzle the rest of the oil, add thyme and parsley springs, onions, lemon juice, salt and pepper.
2. Place in your air fryer's basket and cook at 360 °F, for 12 minutes, shake the basket every few minutes to ensure even cooking. Divide everything on plates and serve right away.

Nutrition Facts: Calories: 242; Fat: 9g; Fiber: 12g; Carbs: 20g; Protein: 31g

East Trout and Butter Sauce

(Prep + Cook Time: 20 Minutes | **Servings:** 4)

Ingredients:
- 4 trout fillets; boneless
- 6 tbsp. butter
- 2 tbsp. olive oil
- 2 tsp. lemon juice
- Salt and black pepper to the taste
- 3 tsp. lemon zest; grated
- 3 tbsp. chives; chopped

Instructions:
1. Season trout with salt and pepper, drizzle the olive oil, rub, transfer to your air fryer and cook at 360 °F, for 10 minutes; flipping once.
2. Meanwhile; heat up a pan with the butter over medium heat, add salt, pepper, chives, lemon juice and zest, whisk well; cook for 1-2 minutes and take off heat. Divide fish fillets on plates, drizzle butter sauce all over and serve.

Nutrition Facts: Calories: 300; Fat: 12g; Fiber: 9g; Carbs: 27g; Protein: 24g

Flavored Fried Salmon
(**Prep + Cook Time:** 1 hour 8 Minutes | **Servings:** 2)

Ingredients:
- 2 salmon fillets
- 2 tbsp. lemon juice
- 1/3 cup soy sauce
- 3 scallions; chopped
- 1/3 cup brown sugar
- 1/2 tsp. garlic powder
- 1/3 cup water
- 2 tbsp. olive oil
- Salt and black pepper to the taste

Instructions:
1. In a bowl; mix sugar with water, soy sauce, garlic powder, salt, pepper, oil and lemon juice, whisk well, add salmon fillets; toss to coat and leave aside in the fridge for 1 hour.
2. Transfer salmon fillets to the fryer's basket and cook at 360 °F, for 8 minutes flipping them halfway. Divide salmon on plates; sprinkle scallions on top and serve right away.

Nutrition Facts: Calories: 300; Fat: 12g; Fiber: 10g; Carbs: 23g; Protein: 20g

Pollock Recipe
(**Prep + Cook Time:** 25 Minutes | **Servings:** 6)

Ingredients:
- 4 Pollock fillets; boneless
- 1/2 cup sour cream
- 1/4 cup parmesan; grated
- 2 tbsp. butter; melted
- Salt and black pepper to the taste
- Cooking spray

Instructions:
1. In a bowl, mix sour cream with butter, parmesan, salt and pepper and whisk well.
2. Spray fish with cooking spray and season with salt and pepper.
3. Spread sour cream mix on one side of each Pollock fillet, arrange them in your preheated air fryer at 320 °F and cook them for 15 minutes. Divide Pollock fillets on plates and serve with a tasty side salad.

Nutrition Facts: Calories: 300; Fat: 13g; Fiber: 3g; Carbs: 14g; Protein: 25g

Oriental Fish Recipe
(**Prep + Cook Time:** 22 Minutes | **Servings:** 4)

Ingredients:
- 2 lbs. red snapper fillets; boneless
- 3 garlic cloves; minced
- 2 tbsp. water
- 1/2 tsp. cumin; ground
- 1 tbsp. lemon juice
- 1 yellow onion; chopped
- 1 tbsp. tamarind paste
- 1 tbsp. oriental sesame oil
- 1 tbsp. ginger; grated
- 3 tbsp. mint; chopped
- Salt and black pepper to the taste

Instructions:
1. In your food processor, mix garlic with onion, salt, pepper, tamarind paste, sesame oil, ginger, water and cumin, pulse well and rub fish with this mix.
2. Place fish in your preheated air fryer at 320 °F and cook for 12 minutes; flipping fish halfway. Divide fish on plates, drizzle lemon juice all over, sprinkle mint and serve right away.

Nutrition Facts: Calories: 241; Fat: 8g; Fiber: 16g; Carbs: 17g; Protein: 12g

Peas and Cod Fillets

(Prep + Cook Time: 20 Minutes | **Servings:** 4)

Ingredients:
- 4 cod fillets; boneless
- 1/2 tsp. oregano; dried
- 1/2 tsp. sweet paprika
- 2 tbsp. parsley; chopped.
- 2 cups peas
- 4 tbsp. wine
- 2 garlic cloves; minced
- Salt and pepper to the taste

Instructions:
1. In your food processor mix garlic with parsley, salt, pepper, oregano, paprika and wine and blend well.
2. Rub fish with half of this mix, place in your air fryer and cook at 360 °F, for 10 minutes.
3. Meanwhile; put the peas in a pot, add water to cover, add salt, bring to a boil over medium high heat, cook for 10 minutes; drain and divide among plates. Also divide fish on plates, spread the rest of the herb dressing all over and serve.

Nutrition Facts: Calories: 261; Fat: 8g; Fiber: 12g; Carbs: 20g; Protein: 22g

Shrimp and Crab Recipe

(Prep + Cook Time: 35 Minutes | **Servings:** 4)

Ingredients:
- 1/2 cup yellow onion; chopped
- 1 cup green bell pepper; chopped.
- 1 cup celery; chopped
- 2 tbsp. breadcrumbs
- 1 tbsp. butter; melted
- 1 tsp. sweet paprika
- 1 lb. shrimp; peeled and deveined
- 1 cup crabmeat; flaked
- 1 cup mayonnaise
- 1 tsp. Worcestershire sauce
- Salt and black pepper to the taste

Instructions:
1. In a bowl; mix shrimp with crab meat, bell pepper, onion, mayo, celery, salt, pepper and Worcestershire sauce; toss well and transfer to a pan that fits your air fryer.
2. Sprinkle bread crumbs and paprika, add melted butter, place in your air fryer and cook at 320 °F, for 25 minutes, shake the basket every few minutes to ensure even cooking. Divide among plates and serve right away.

Nutrition Facts: Calories: 200; Fat: 13g; Fiber: 9g; Carbs: 17g; Protein: 19g

Asian Style Halibut

(Prep + Cook Time: 40 Minutes | **Servings:** 3)

Ingredients:
- 1 lb. halibut steaks
- 2/3 cup soy sauce
- 1/4 tsp. red pepper flakes; crushed
- 1/4 cup orange juice
- 1/4 tsp. ginger; grated
- 1/4 cup sugar
- 2 tbsp. lime juice
- 1/2 cup mirin
- 1 garlic clove; minced

Instructions:
1. Pour soy sauce in a pan; heat up over medium heat, add mirin, sugar, lime and orange juice, pepper flakes, ginger and garlic; stir well, bring to a boil and take off heat.
2. Transfer half of the marinade to a bowl, add halibut, toss to coat and leave aside in the fridge for 30 minutes.
3. Transfer halibut to your air fryer and cook at 390 °F, for 10 minutes; flipping once. Divide halibut steaks on plates; drizzle the rest of the marinade all over and serve hot.

Nutrition Facts: Calories: 286; Fat: 5g; Fiber: 12g; Carbs: 14g; Protein: 23g

Salmon with Mash and Capers

(**Prep + Cook Time:** 30 Minutes | **Servings:** 4)

Ingredients:
- 4 salmon fillets; skinless and boneless
- Juice from 1 lemon
- 2 tsp. olive oil
- 1 tbsp. capers; drained
- Salt and black pepper to the taste

For the potato mash:
- 1 lb. potatoes; chopped.
- 1/2 cup milk
- 2 tbsp. olive oil
- 1 tbsp. dill; dried

Instructions:
1. Put the potatoes in a pot, add water to cover, add some salt, bring to a boil over medium high heat, cook for 15 minutes; drain, transfer to a bowl; mash with a potato masher, add 2 tbsp. oil, dill, salt, pepper and milk, whisk well and leave aside for now.
2. Season salmon with salt and pepper, drizzle 2 tsp. oil over them, rub, transfer to your air fryer's basket, add capers on top, cook at 360 °F and cook for 8 minutes. Divide salmon and capers on plates; add mashed potatoes on the side, drizzle lemon juice all over and serve.

Nutrition Facts: Calories: 300; Fat: 17g; Fiber: 8g; Carbs: 12g; Protein: 18g

Tabasco Shrimp Recipe

(**Prep + Cook Time:** 20 Minutes | **Servings:** 4)

Ingredients:
- 1 lb. shrimp; peeled and deveined
- 1/2 tsp. parsley; dried
- 1 tsp. red pepper flakes
- 2 tbsp. olive oil
- 1 tsp. Tabasco sauce
- 2 tbsp. water
- 1 tsp. oregano; dried
- 1/2 tsp. smoked paprika
- Salt and black pepper to the taste

Instructions:
1. In a bowl; mix oil with water, Tabasco sauce, pepper flakes, oregano, parsley, salt, pepper, paprika and shrimp and toss well to coat.
2. Transfer shrimp to your preheated air fryer at 370 °F and cook for 10 minutes, (shake the basket after 5 minutes). Divide shrimp on plates and serve with a side salad.

Nutrition Facts: Calories: 200; Fat: 5g; Fiber: 6g; Carbs: 13g; Protein: 8g

Salmon and Avocado Salsa

(**Prep + Cook Time:** 40 Minutes | **Servings:** 4)

Ingredients:
- 4 salmon fillets
- 1 tbsp. olive oil
- 1 tsp. cumin; ground
- 1 tsp. sweet paprika
- 1/2 tsp. chili powder
- 1 tsp. garlic powder
- Salt and black pepper to the taste

For the salsa:
- 1 small red onion; chopped
- 1 avocado; pitted, peeled and chopped.
- 2 tbsp. cilantro; chopped
- Juice from 2 limes
- Salt and black pepper to the taste

Instructions:
1. In a bowl; mix salt, pepper, chili powder, onion powder, paprika and cumin; stir, rub salmon with this mix, drizzle the oil, rub again, transfer to your air fryer and cook at 350 °F, for 5 minutes on each side.
2. Meanwhile; in a bowl, mix avocado with red onion, salt, pepper, cilantro and lime juice and stir. Divide fillets on plates, top with avocado salsa and serve.

Nutrition Facts: Calories: 300; Fat: 14g; Fiber: 4g; Carbs: 18g; Protein: 16g

Air Fried Cod

(Prep + Cook Time: 22 Minutes | Servings: 4)

Ingredients:
- 2 cod fish; 7 oz. each
- A drizzle of sesame oil
- 4 ginger slices
- 3 spring onions; chopped.
- 2 tbsp. coriander; chopped
- 1 cup water
- 1 tsp. dark soy sauce
- 4 tbsp. light soy sauce
- 1 tbsp. sugar
- 3 tbsp. olive oil
- Salt and black pepper to the taste

Instructions:
1. Season fish with salt, pepper, drizzle sesame oil, rub well and leave aside for 10 minutes.
2. Add fish to your air fryer and cook at 356 °F, for 12 minutes.
3. Meanwhile; heat up a pot with the water over medium heat, add dark and light soy sauce and sugar; stir, bring to a simmer and take off heat.
4. Heat up a pan with the olive oil over medium heat, add ginger and green onions; stir, cook for a few minutes and take off heat. Divide fish on plates, top with ginger and green onions, drizzle soy sauce mix, sprinkle coriander and serve right away.

Nutrition Facts: Calories: 300; Fat: 17g; Fiber: 8g; Carbs: 20g; Protein: 22g

Roasted Cod & Prosciutto

(Prep + Cook Time: 20 Minutes | Servings: 4)

Ingredients:
- 4 medium cod filets
- 1 tbsp. parsley; chopped
- 1/4 cup butter; melted
- 2 garlic cloves; minced
- 2 tbsp. lemon juice
- 3 tbsp. prosciutto; chopped.
- 1 tsp. Dijon mustard
- 1 shallot; chopped
- Salt and black pepper to the taste

Instructions:
1. In a bowl; mix mustard with butter, garlic, parsley, shallot, lemon juice, prosciutto, salt and pepper and whisk well.
2. Season fish with salt and pepper; spread prosciutto mix all over, put it in your air fryer and cook at 390 °F, for 10 minutes. Divide among plates and serve.

Nutrition Facts: Calories: 200; Fat: 4g; Fiber: 7g; Carbs: 12g; Protein: 6g

Cod Steaks with Plum Sauce

(Prep + Cook Time: 30 Minutes | Servings: 2)

Ingredients:
- 2 big cod steaks
- 1/2 tsp. garlic powder
- 1/2 tsp. ginger powder
- 1/4 tsp. turmeric powder
- Salt and black pepper to the taste
- 1 tbsp. plum sauce
- Cooking spray

Instructions:
1. Season cod steaks with salt and pepper, spray them with cooking oil, add garlic powder, ginger powder and turmeric powder and rub well.
2. Place cod steaks in your air fryer and cook at 360 °F, for 15 minutes; flipping them after 7 minutes.
3. Heat up a pan over medium heat, add plum sauce; stir and cook for 2 minutes. Divide cod steaks on plates, drizzle plum sauce all over and serve.

Nutrition Facts: Calories: 250; Fat: 7g; Fiber: 1g; Carbs: 14g; Protein: 12g

Tuna and Chimichurri Sauce

(**Prep + Cook Time:** 18 Minutes | **Servings:** 4)

Ingredients:
- 1 lb. sushi tuna steak
- 1 tsp. red pepper flakes
- 1 tsp. thyme; chopped
- 3 garlic cloves; minced
- 3 tbsp. balsamic vinegar
- 2 tbsp. parsley; chopped.
- 2 tbsp. basil; chopped
- 2 avocados; pitted, peeled and sliced
- 1/2 cup cilantro; chopped
- 1/3 cup olive oil+ 2 tbsp.
- 1 small red onion; chopped.
- 1 jalapeno pepper; chopped
- 6 oz. baby arugula
- Salt and black pepper to the taste

Instructions:
1. In a bowl; mix ⅓ cup oil with jalapeno, vinegar, onion, cilantro, basil, garlic, parsley, pepper flakes, thyme, salt and pepper; whisk well and leave aside for now.
2. Season tuna with salt and pepper, rub with the rest of the oil; place in your air fryer and cook at 360 °F, for 3 minutes on each side.
3. Mix arugula with half of the chimichuri mix you've made and toss to coat. Divide arugula on plates, slice tuna and also divide among plates; top with the rest of the chimichuri and serve.

Nutrition Facts: Calories: 276; Fat: 3g; Fiber: 1g; Carbs: 14g; Protein: 20g

Creamy-Shrimp and Veggies

(**Prep + Cook Time:** 40 Minutes | **Servings:** 4)

Ingredients:
- 8 oz. mushrooms; chopped
- 1 asparagus bunch; cut into medium pieces
- 1 lb. shrimp; peeled and deveined
- 1 tsp. red pepper flakes; crushed
- 1/4 cup butter; melted
- 1 cup parmesan cheese; grated
- 1 spaghetti squash; cut into halves
- 2 tbsp. olive oil
- 2 tsp. Italian seasoning
- 1 yellow onion; chopped.
- 2 garlic cloves; minced
- 1 cup heavy cream
- Salt and black pepper to the taste

Instructions:
1. Place squash halves in you air fryer's basket; cook at 390 °F, for 17 minutes; transfer to a cutting board, scoop insides and transfer to a bowl.
2. Put water in a pot, add some salt, bring to a boil over medium heat, add asparagus, steam for a couple of minutes; transfer to a bowl filled with ice water, drain and leave aside as well.
3. Heat up a pan that fits your air fryer with the oil over medium heat, add onions and mushrooms; stir and cook for 7 minutes.
4. Add pepper flakes, Italian seasoning, salt, pepper, squash, asparagus, shrimp, melted butter, cream, parmesan and garlic; toss and cook in your air fryer at 360 °F, for 6 minutes. Divide everything on plates and serve.

Nutrition Facts: Calories: 325; Fat: 6g; Fiber: 5g; Carbs: 14g; Protein: 13g

Coconut Tilapia Recipe

(Prep + Cook Time: 20 Minutes | **Servings:** 4)

Ingredients:
- 4 medium tilapia fillets
- 1/2 cup coconut milk
- 1 tsp. ginger; grated
- 1/2 cup cilantro; chopped
- 2 garlic cloves; chopped
- 1/2 tsp. garam masala
- Salt and black pepper to the taste
- Cooking spray
- 1/2 jalapeno; chopped.

Instructions:
1. In your food processor, mix coconut milk with salt, pepper, cilantro, ginger, garlic, jalapeno and garam masala and pulse really well.
2. Spray fish with cooking spray, spread coconut mix all over, rub well, transfer to your air fryer's basket and cook at 400 °F, for 10 minutes. Divide among plates and serve hot.

Nutrition Facts: Calories: 200; Fat: 5g; Fiber: 6g; Carbs: 25g; Protein: 26g

Mustard Salmon Recipe

(Prep + Cook Time: 20 Minutes | **Servings:** 1)

Ingredients:
- 1 big salmon fillet; boneless
- 2 tbsp. mustard
- 1 tbsp. coconut oil
- 1 tbsp. maple extract
- Salt and black pepper to the taste

Instructions:
1. In a bowl; mix maple extract with mustard, whisk well, season salmon with salt and pepper and brush salmon with this mix.
2. Spray some cooking spray over fish; place in your air fryer and cook at 370 °F, for 10 minutes; flipping halfway. Serve with a tasty side salad.

Nutrition Facts: Calories: 300; Fat: 7g; Fiber: 14g; Carbs: 16g; Protein: 20g

Squid and Guacamole

(Prep + Cook Time: 16 Minutes | **Servings:** 2)

Ingredients:
- 2 medium squids; tentacles separated and tubes scored lengthwise
- Juice from 1 lime
- 1 tbsp. olive oil
- Salt and black pepper to the taste

For the guacamole:
- 1 tomato; chopped
- 1 red onion; chopped
- 2 avocados; pitted, peeled and chopped.
- 1 tbsp. coriander; chopped
- 2 red chilies; chopped
- Juice from 2 limes

Instructions:
1. Season squid and squid tentacles with salt, pepper, drizzle the olive oil all over. Put it in your air fryer's basket and cook at 360 °F, for 3 minutes on each side.
2. Transfer squid to a bowl; drizzle lime juice all over and toss.
3. Meanwhile; put avocado in a bowl, mash with a fork, add coriander, chilies, tomato, onion and juice from 2 limes and toss. Divide squid on plates, top with guacamole and serve.

Nutrition Facts: Calories: 500; Fat: 43g; Fiber: 6g; Carbs: 7g; Protein: 20g

Salmon and Lemon Relish Recipe

(**Prep + Cook Time:** 40 Minutes | **Servings:** 2)

Ingredients:
- 2 salmon fillets; boneless
- 1 tbsp. olive oil

For the relish:
- 1 Meyer lemon; cut in wedges and then sliced
- 2 tbsp. parsley; chopped
- Salt and black pepper to the taste
- 1 tbsp. lemon juice
- 1 shallot; chopped.
- 1/4 cup olive oil

Instructions:
1. Season salmon with salt and pepper, rub with 1 tbsp. oil, place in your air fryer's basket and cook at 320 °F, for 20 minutes; flipping the fish halfway.
2. Meanwhile; in a bowl, mix shallot with the lemon juice, a pinch of salt and black pepper; stir and leave aside for 10 minutes.
3. In a separate bowl; mix marinated shallot with lemon slices, salt, pepper, parsley and 1/4 cup oil and whisk well. Divide salmon on plates, top with lemon relish and serve.

Nutrition Facts: Calories: 200; Fat: 3g; Fiber: 3g; Carbs: 23g; Protein: 19g

Chinese Style Cod

(**Prep + Cook Time:** 20 Minutes | **Servings:** 2)

Ingredients:
- 2 medium cod fillets; boneless
- 1 tbsp. light soy sauce
- 1/2 tsp. ginger; grated
- 1 tsp. peanuts; crushed
- 2 tsp. garlic powder

Instructions:
1. Put the fish fillets in a heat proof dish that fits your air fryer, add garlic powder, soy sauce and ginger; toss well.
2. Put it in your air fryer and cook at 350 °F, for 10 minutes. Divide fish on plates, sprinkle peanuts on top and serve.

Nutrition Facts: Calories: 254; Fat: 10g; Fiber: 11g; Carbs: 14g; Protein: 23g

Catfish Fillets Recipe

(**Prep + Cook Time:** 22 Minutes | **Servings:** 4)

Ingredients:
- 2 catfish fillets
- 1 tsp. mustard
- 1 tbsp. balsamic vinegar
- 3/4 cup catsup
- 1/2 tsp. garlic; minced
- 2 oz. butter
- 4 oz. Worcestershire sauce
- 1/2 tsp. jerk seasoning
- Salt and black pepper to the taste
- 1 tbsp. parsley; chopped

Instructions:
1. Heat up a pan with the butter over medium heat, add Worcestershire sauce, garlic, jerk seasoning, mustard, catsup, vinegar, salt and pepper; stir well, take off heat and add fish fillets.
2. Toss well, leave aside for 10 minutes; drain fillets, transfer them to your preheated air fryer's basket at 350 °F and cook for 8 minutes; flipping fillets halfway. Divide among plates, sprinkle parsley on top and serve right away.

Nutrition Facts: Calories: 351; Fat: 8g; Fiber: 16g; Carbs: 27g; Protein: 17g

Halibut and Sun Dried Tomatoes

(Prep + Cook Time: 20 Minutes | **Servings:** 2)

Ingredients:
- 2 medium halibut fillets
- 2 garlic cloves; minced
- 2 tsp. olive oil
- 6 sun dried tomatoes; chopped
- 2 small red onions; sliced
- 1 fennel bulb; sliced
- 9 black olives; pitted and sliced
- 4 rosemary springs; chopped.
- 1/2 tsp. red pepper flakes; crushed
- Salt and black pepper to the taste

Instructions:
1. Season fish with salt, pepper, rub with garlic and oil and put it in a heat proof dish that fits your air fryer.
2. Add onion slices, sun dried tomatoes, fennel, olives, rosemary and sprinkle pepper flakes, transfer to your air fryer and cook at 380 °F, for 10 minutes. Divide fish and veggies on plates and serve.

Nutrition Facts: Calories: 300; Fat: 12g; Fiber: 9g; Carbs: 18g; Protein: 21g

Salmon & Chives Vinaigrette

(Prep + Cook Time: 22 Minutes | **Servings:** 4)

Ingredients:
- 4 salmon fillets; boneless
- 2 tbsp. dill; chopped.
- 1 tbsp. olive oil
- 3 tbsp. balsamic vinegar
- 2 tbsp. chives; chopped
- 1/3 cup maple syrup
- Salt and black pepper to the taste

Instructions:
1. Season fish with salt and pepper, rub with the oil, place in your air fryer and cook at 350 °F, for 8 minutes; flipping once.
2. Heat up a small pot with the vinegar over medium heat, add maple syrup, chives and dill; stir and cook for 3 minutes. Divide fish on plates and serve with chives vinaigrette on top.

Nutrition Facts: Calories: 270; Fat: 3g; Fiber: 13g; Carbs: 25g; Protein: 10g

Italian Barramundi Fillets

(Prep + Cook Time: 18 Minutes | **Servings:** 4)

Ingredients:
- 2 barramundi fillets; boneless
- 1 tbsp. olive oil+ 2 tsp.
- 2 tsp. Italian seasoning
- 1/4 cup green olives; pitted and chopped
- 1/4 cup cherry tomatoes; chopped
- 1/4 cup black olives; chopped.
- 2 tbsp. parsley; chopped
- 1 tbsp. lemon zest
- 2 tbsp. lemon zest
- Salt and black pepper to the taste

Instructions:
1. Rub fish with salt, pepper, Italian seasoning and 2 tsp. olive oil, transfer to your air fryer and cook at 360 °F, for 8 minutes; flipping them halfway.
2. In a bowl; mix tomatoes with black olives, green olives, salt, pepper, lemon zest and lemon juice, parsley and 1 tbsp. olive oil and toss well. Divide fish on plates; add tomato salsa on top and serve.

Nutrition Facts: Calories: 270; Fat: 4g; Fiber: 2g; Carbs: 18g; Protein: 27g

Marinated Salmon Recipe

(**Prep + Cook Time:** 1 hour 20 Minutes | **Servings:** 6)

Ingredients:
- 1 whole salmon
- 1 tbsp. dill; chopped.
- 1 tbsp. tarragon; chopped
- 1 tbsp. garlic; minced
- Juice from 2 lemons
- 1 lemon; sliced
- A pinch of salt and black pepper

Instructions:
1. In a large fish, mix fish with salt, pepper and lemon juice; toss well and keep in the fridge for 1 hour.
2. Stuff salmon with garlic and lemon slices, place in your air fryer's basket and cook at 320 °F, for 25 minutes. Divide among plates and serve with a tasty coleslaw on the side.

Nutrition Facts: Calories: 300; Fat: 8g; Fiber: 9g; Carbs: 19g; Protein: 27g

Buttery Shrimp Skewers

(**Prep + Cook Time:** 16 Minutes | **Servings:** 2)

Ingredients:
- 8 shrimps; peeled and deveined
- 8 green bell pepper slices
- 1 tbsp. rosemary; chopped.
- 1 tbsp. butter; melted
- 4 garlic cloves; minced
- Salt and black pepper to the taste

Instructions:
1. In a bowl; mix shrimp with garlic, butter, salt, pepper, rosemary and bell pepper slices; toss to coat and leave aside for 10 minutes.
2. Arrange 2 shrimp and 2 bell pepper slices on a skewer and repeat with the rest of the shrimp and bell pepper pieces.
3. Place them all in your air fryer's basket and cook at 360 °F, for 6 minutes. Divide among plates and serve right away.

Nutrition Facts: Calories: 140; Fat: 1g; Fiber: 12g; Carbs: 15g; Protein: 7g

Fish and Couscous Recipe

(**Prep + Cook Time:** 25 Minutes | **Servings:** 4)

Ingredients:
- 2½ lbs. sea bass; gutted
- 5 tsp. fennel seeds
- 3/4 cup whole wheat couscous; cooked
- 2 red onions; chopped
- Cooking spray
- 2 small fennel bulbs; cored and sliced
- 1/4 cup almonds; toasted and sliced
- Salt and black pepper to the taste

Instructions:
1. Season fish with salt and pepper, spray with cooking spray; place in your air fryer and cook at 350 °F, for 10 minutes.
2. Meanwhile; spray a pan with some cooking oil and heat it up over medium heat.
3. Add fennel seeds to this pan; stir and toast them for 1 minute.
4. Add onion, salt, pepper, fennel bulbs, almonds and couscous; stir, cook for 2-3 minutes and divide among plates. Add fish next to couscous mix and serve right away.

Nutrition Facts: Calories: 354; Fat: 7g; Fiber: 10g; Carbs: 20g; Protein: 22g

Delightful French Cod

(Prep + Cook Time: 32 Minutes **| Servings:** 4)

Ingredients:
- 2 lbs. cod; boneless
- 14 oz. canned tomatoes; stewed
- 1 yellow onion; chopped
- 1/2 cup white wine
- 2 garlic cloves; minced
- 3 tbsp. parsley; chopped.
- Salt and black pepper to the taste
- 2 tbsp. olive oil
- 2 tbsp. butter

Instructions:
1. Heat up a pan with the oil over medium heat, add garlic and onion; stir and cook for 5 minutes.
2. Add wine; stir and cook for 1 minute more.
3. Add tomatoes; stir, bring to a boil, cook for 2 minutes; add parsley; stir again and take off heat.
4. Pour this mix into a heat proof dish that fits your air fryer, add fish, season it with salt and pepper and cook in your fryer at 350 °F, for 14 minutes. Divide fish and tomatoes mix on plates and serve.

Nutrition Facts: Calories: 231; Fat: 8g; Fiber: 12g; Carbs: 26g; Protein: 14g

Hawaiian Salmon Recipe

(Prep + Cook Time: 20 Minutes **| Servings:** 2)

Ingredients:
- 20 oz. canned pineapple pieces and juice
- 2 medium salmon fillets; boneless
- 1/2 tsp. ginger; grated
- 2 tsp. garlic powder
- 1 tsp. onion powder
- 1 tbsp. balsamic vinegar
- Salt and black pepper to the taste

Instructions:
1. Season salmon with garlic powder, onion powder, salt and black pepper, rub well, transfer to a heat proof dish that fits your air fryer, add ginger and pineapple chunks and toss them really gently.
2. Drizzle the vinegar all over. Put it in your air fryer and cook at 350 °F, for 10 minutes. Divide everything on plates and serve.

Nutrition Facts: Calories: 200; Fat: 8g; Fiber: 12g; Carbs: 17g; Protein: 20g

Salmon and Avocado Sauce Recipe

(Prep + Cook Time: 20 Minutes **| Servings:** 4)

Ingredients:
- 4 salmon fillets; boneless
- 1 avocado; pitted, peeled and chopped
- 1/4 cup cilantro; chopped
- 1/3 cup coconut milk
- 1 tbsp. lime juice
- 1 tbsp. lime zest; grated
- 1 tsp. onion powder
- 1 tsp. garlic powder
- Salt and black pepper to the taste

Instructions:
1. Season salmon fillets with salt, black pepper and lime zest, rub well. Place the salmon fillets in your air fryer, cook at 350 °F, for 9 minutes; flipping once and divide among plates.
2. In your food processor, mix avocado with cilantro, garlic powder, onion powder, lime juice, salt, pepper and coconut milk; blend well, drizzle over salmon and serve right away.

Nutrition Facts: Calories: 260; Fat: 7g; Fiber: 20g; Carbs: 28g; Protein: 18g

Tasty Catfish

(Prep + Cook Time: 30 Minutes | **Servings:** 4)

Ingredients:
- 4 cat fish fillets
- A pinch of sweet paprika
- 1 tbsp. parsley; chopped
- 1 tbsp. lemon juice
- 1 tbsp. olive oil
- Salt and black pepper to the taste

Instructions:
1. Season catfish fillets with salt, pepper, paprika, drizzle oil, rub well, place in your air fryer's basket and cook at 400 °F, for 20 minutes; flipping the fish after 10 minutes. Divide fish on plates, drizzle lemon juice all over, sprinkle parsley and serve.

Nutrition Facts: Calories: 253; Fat: 6g; Fiber: 12g; Carbs: 26g; Protein: 22g

Salmon and Orange Marmalade Recipe

(Prep + Cook Time: 25 Minutes | **Servings:** 4)

Ingredients:
- 1 lb. wild salmon; skinless, boneless and cubed
- 2 lemons; sliced
- 1/4 cup orange juice
- 1/3 cup orange marmalade
- 1/4 cup balsamic vinegar
- A pinch of salt and black pepper

Instructions:
1. Heat up a pot with the vinegar over medium heat; add marmalade and orange juice; stir, bring to a simmer, cook for 1 minute and take off heat.
2. Thread salmon cubes and lemon slices on skewers, season with salt and black pepper, brush them with half of the orange marmalade mix, arrange in your air fryer's basket and cook at 360 °F, for 3 minutes on each side. Brush skewers with the rest of the vinegar mix; divide among plates and serve right away with a side salad.

Nutrition Facts: Calories: 240; Fat: 9g; Fiber: 12g; Carbs: 14g; Protein: 10g

Salmon & Blackberry Glaze

(Prep + Cook Time: 43 Minutes | **Servings:** 4)

Ingredients:
- 4 medium salmon fillets; skinless
- 1 cup water
- 1-inch ginger piece; grated
- Juice from 1/2 lemon
- 12 oz. blackberries
- 1 tbsp. olive oil
- 1/4 cup sugar
- Salt and black pepper to the taste

Instructions:
1. Heat up a pot with the water over medium high heat, add ginger, lemon juice and blackberries; stir, bring to a boil, cook for 4-5 minutes; take off heat, strain into a bowl, return to pan and combine with sugar.
2. Stir this mix, bring to a simmer over medium low heat and cook for 20 minutes.
3. Leave blackberry sauce to cool down, brush salmon with it, season with salt and pepper, drizzle olive oil all over and rub fish well.
4. Place fish in your preheated air fryer at 350 °F and cook for 10 minutes; flipping fish fillets once. Divide among plates, drizzle some of the remaining blackberry sauce all over and serve.

Nutrition Facts: Calories: 312; Fat: 4g; Fiber: 9g; Carbs: 19g; Protein: 14g

Stuffed Salmon Delight

(**Prep + Cook Time:** 30 Minutes | **Servings:** 2)

Ingredients:
- 2 salmon fillets; skinless and boneless
- 5 oz. tiger shrimp; peeled, deveined and chopped
- 1 tbsp. olive oil
- 6 mushrooms; chopped.
- 3 green onions; chopped
- 2 cups spinach; torn
- 1/4 cup macadamia nuts; toasted and chopped
- Salt and black pepper to the taste

Instructions:
1. Heat up a pan with half of the oil over medium high heat, add mushrooms, onions, salt and pepper; stir and cook for 4 minutes.
2. Add macadamia nuts, spinach and shrimp; stir, cook for 3 minutes and take off heat.
3. Make an incision lengthwise in each salmon fillet, season with salt and pepper, divide spinach and shrimp mix into incisions and rub with the rest of the olive oil.
4. Place in your air fryer's basket and cook at 360 °F and cook for 10 minutes; flipping halfway. Divide stuffed salmon on plates and serve.

Nutrition Facts: Calories: 290; Fat: 15g; Fiber: 3g; Carbs: 12g; Protein: 31g

Honey Sea Bass Recipe

(**Prep + Cook Time:** 20 Minutes | **Servings:** 2)

Ingredients:
- 2 sea bass fillets
- Zest from 1/2 orange; grated
- Juice from 1/2 orange
- 2 tbsp. mustard
- 2 tsp. honey
- 2 tbsp. olive oil
- 1/2 lb. canned lentils; drained
- A small bunch of dill; chopped
- 2 oz. watercress
- A small bunch of parsley; chopped
- A pinch of salt and black pepper

Instructions:
1. Season fish fillets with salt and pepper, add orange zest and juice, rub with 1 tbsp. oil, with honey and mustard, rub, transfer to your air fryer and cook at 350 °F, for 10 minutes; flipping halfway.
2. Meanwhile; put the lentils in a small pot, warm it up over medium heat, add the rest of the oil, watercress, dill and parsley; stir well and divide among plates. Add fish fillets and serve right away.

Nutrition Facts: Calories: 212; Fat: 8g; Fiber: 12g; Carbs: 9g; Protein: 17g

Snapper Fillets and Veggies Recipe

(**Prep + Cook Time:** 24 Minutes | **Servings:** 2)

Ingredients:
- 2 red snapper fillets; boneless
- 1 tbsp. olive oil
- 1/2 cup red bell pepper; chopped.
- 1/2 cup green bell pepper; chopped
- 1/2 cup leeks; chopped.
- 1 tsp. tarragon; dried
- A splash of white wine
- Salt and black pepper to the taste

Instructions:
1. In a heat proof dish that fits your air fryer; mix fish fillets with salt, pepper, oil, green bell pepper, red bell pepper, leeks, tarragon and wine; toss well.
2. Transfer everything in preheated air fryer at 350 °F and cook for 14 minutes; flipping fish fillets halfway. Divide fish and veggies on plates and serve warm.

Nutrition Facts: Calories: 300; Fat: 12g; Fiber: 8g; Carbs: 29g; Protein: 12g

Black Cod & Plum Sauce
(Prep + Cook Time: 25 Minutes | **Servings:** 2)

Ingredients:
- 2 medium black cod fillets; skinless and boneless
- 1 red plum; pitted and chopped
- 2 tsp. raw honey
- 1/4 tsp. black peppercorns; crushed
- 1 egg white
- 1/2 cup red quinoa; already cooked
- 2 tsp. whole wheat flour
- 4 tsp. lemon juice
- 1/2 tsp. smoked paprika
- 1 tsp. olive oil
- 2 tsp. parsley
- 1/4 cup water

Instructions:
1. In a bowl; mix 1 tsp. lemon juice with egg white, flour and 1/4 tsp. paprika and whisk well.
2. Put the quinoa in a bowl and mix it with ⅓ of egg white mix.
3. Put the fish into the bowl with the remaining egg white mix and toss to coat.
4. Dip fish in quinoa mix; coat well and leave aside for 10 minutes.
5. Heat up a pan with 1 tsp. oil over medium heat; add peppercorns, honey and plum; stir, bring to a simmer and cook for 1 minute.
6. Add the rest of the lemon juice, the rest of the paprika and the water; stir well and simmer for 5 minutes.
7. Add parsley; stir, take sauce off heat and leave aside for now.
8. Put the fish in your air fryer and cook at 380 °F, for 10 minute. Arrange fish on plates, drizzle plum sauce on top and serve.

Nutrition Facts: Calories: 324; Fat: 14g; Fiber: 22g; Carbs: 27g; Protein: 22g

Creamy Salmon Recipe
(Prep + Cook Time: 20 Minutes | **Servings:** 4)

Ingredients:
- 4 salmon fillets; boneless
- 1/3 cup cheddar cheese; grated
- 1 ½ tsp. mustard
- 1/2 cup coconut cream
- 1 tbsp. olive oil
- Salt and black pepper to the taste

Instructions:
1. Season salmon with salt and pepper, drizzle the oil and rub well.
2. In a bowl; mix coconut cream with cheddar, mustard, salt and pepper and stir well.
3. Transfer salmon to a pan that fits your air fryer; add coconut cream mix, close the air fryer basket and cook at 320 °F, for 10 minutes. Divide among plates and serve.

Nutrition Facts: Calories: 200; Fat: 6g; Fiber: 14g; Carbs: 17g; Protein: 20g

Spanish Salmon Recipe
(Prep + Cook Time: 25 Minutes | **Servings:** 6)

Ingredients:
- 2 cups bread croutons
- 3 red onions; cut into medium wedges
- 5 tbsp. olive oil
- 6 medium salmon fillets; skinless and boneless
- 2 tbsp. parsley; chopped
- 3/4 cup green olives; pitted
- 3 red bell peppers; cut into medium wedges
- 1/2 tsp. smoked paprika
- Salt and black pepper to the taste

Instructions:
1. In a heat proof dish that fits your air fryer, mix bread croutons with onion wedges, bell pepper ones, olives, salt, pepper, paprika and 3 tbsp. olive oil; toss well, place in your air fryer and cook at 356 °F, for 7 minutes.

2. Rub salmon with the rest of the oil; add over veggies and cook at 360 °F, for 8 minutes. Divide fish and veggie mix on plates, sprinkle parsley all over and serve.

Nutrition Facts: Calories: 321; Fat: 8g; Fiber: 14g; Carbs: 27g; Protein: 22g

Flavored Jamaican Salmon Recipe

(**Prep + Cook Time:** 20 Minutes | **Servings:** 4)

Ingredients:
- 4 cups baby arugula
- 2 cups radish; julienned
- 2 tsp. sriracha sauce
- 4 tsp. sugar
- 3 scallions; chopped
- 2 cups cabbage; shredded
- 1 ½ tsp. Jamaican jerk seasoning
- 1/4 cup pepitas; toasted
- 2 tsp. olive oil
- 4 tsp. apple cider vinegar
- 3 tsp. avocado oil
- 4 medium salmon fillets; boneless
- Salt and black pepper to the taste

Instructions:
1. In a bowl; mix sriracha with sugar, whisk and transfer 2 tsp. to another bowl.
2. Combine 2 tsp. sriracha mix with the avocado oil, olive oil, vinegar, salt and pepper and whisk well.
3. Sprinkle jerk seasoning over salmon, rub with sriracha and sugar mix and season with salt and pepper.
4. Transfer to your air fryer and cook at 360 °F, for 10 minutes; flipping once.
5. In a bowl; mix radishes with cabbage, arugula, salt, pepper, sriracha and vinegar mix and toss well. Divide salmon and radish mix on plates, sprinkle pepitas and scallions on top and serve.

Nutrition Facts: Calories: 290; Fat: 6g; Fiber: 12g; Carbs: 17g; Protein: 10g

Fried Branzino

(**Prep + Cook Time:** 20 Minutes | **Servings:** 4)

Ingredients:
- 4 medium branzino fillets; boneless
- 1/2 cup parsley; chopped
- 2 tbsp. olive oil
- A pinch of red pepper flakes; crushed
- Zest from 1 lemon; grated
- Zest from 1 orange; grated
- Juice from 1/2 lemon
- Juice from 1/2 orange
- Salt and black pepper to the taste

Instructions:
1. In a large bowl; mix fish fillets with lemon zest, orange zest, lemon juice, orange juice, salt, pepper, oil and pepper flakes; toss really well, transfer fillets to your preheated air fryer at 350 °F and bake for 10 minutes; flipping fillets once. Divide fish on plates, sprinkle with parsley and serve right away.

Nutrition Facts: Calories: 261; Fat: 8g; Fiber: 12g; Carbs: 21g; Protein: 12g

Crusted Salmon Recipe

(**Prep + Cook Time:** 20 Minutes | **Servings:** 4)

Ingredients:
- 1 cup pistachios; chopped.
- 4 salmon fillets
- 1/4 cup lemon juice
- 2 tbsp. honey
- 1 tbsp. mustard
- 1 tsp. dill; chopped
- Salt and black pepper to the taste

Instructions:
1. In a bowl; mix pistachios with mustard, honey, lemon juice, salt, black pepper and dill; whisk and spread over salmon.
2. Put it in your air fryer and cook at 350 °F, for 10 minutes. Divide among plates and serve with a side salad.

Nutrition Facts: Calories: 300; Fat: 17g; Fiber: 12g; Carbs: 20g; Protein: 22g

Lemon Sole & Swiss Chard

(Prep + Cook Time: 24 Minutes | **Servings:** 4)

Ingredients:
- 2 bunches Swiss chard; chopped
- 4 tbsp. butter
- 1/4 cup lemon juice
- 3 tbsp. capers
- 2 garlic cloves; minced
- 1 tsp. lemon zest; grated
- 4 white bread slices; quartered
- 1/4 cup walnuts; chopped.
- 1/4 cup parmesan; grated
- 4 tbsp. olive oil
- 4 sole fillets; boneless
- Salt and black pepper to the taste

Instructions:
1. In your food processor, mix bread with walnuts, cheese and lemon zest and pulse well.
2. Add half of the olive oil, pulse really well again and leave aside for now.
3. Heat up a pan with the butter over medium heat, add lemon juice, salt, pepper and capers; stir well, add fish and toss it.
4. Transfer fish to your preheated air fryer's basket, top with bread mix you've made at the beginning and cook at 350 °F, for 14 minutes.
5. Meanwhile; heat up another pan with the rest of the oil, add garlic, Swiss chard, salt and pepper; stir gently, cook for 2 minutes and take off heat. Divide fish on plates and serve with sautéed chard on the side.

Nutrition Facts: Calories: 321; Fat: 7g; Fiber: 18g; Carbs: 27g; Protein: 12g

Stuffed Calamari Recipe

(Prep + Cook Time: 35 Minutes | **Servings:** 4)

Ingredients:
- 4 big calamari; tentacles separated and chopped and tubes reserved
- 2 tbsp. parsley; chopped.
- 2 oz. canned tomato puree
- 1 yellow onion; chopped
- 5 oz. kale; chopped
- 2 garlic cloves; minced
- 1 red bell pepper; chopped
- 1 tbsp. olive oil
- Salt and black pepper to the taste

Instructions:
1. Heat up a pan with the oil over medium heat; add onion and garlic; stir and cook for 2 minutes.
2. Add bell pepper, tomato puree, calamari tentacles, kale, salt and pepper; stir, cook for 10 minutes and take off heat. stir and cook for 3 minutes.
3. Stuff calamari tubes with this mix, secure with toothpicks, put it in your air fryer and cook at 360 °F, for 20 minutes. Divide calamari on plates; sprinkle parsley all over and serve.

Nutrition Facts: Calories: 322; Fat: 10g; Fiber: 14g; Carbs: 14g; Protein: 22g

Swordfish and Mango Salsa

(Prep + Cook Time: 16 Minutes | **Servings:** 2)

Ingredients:
- 2 medium swordfish steaks
- 2 tsp. avocado oil
- 1 tbsp. cilantro; chopped.
- 1 mango; chopped
- 1 avocado; pitted, peeled and chopped
- A pinch of cumin
- A pinch of onion powder
- A pinch of garlic powder
- 1 orange; peeled and sliced
- 1/2 tbsp. balsamic vinegar
- Salt and black pepper to the taste

Instructions:
1. Season fish steaks with salt, pepper, garlic powder, onion powder and cumin and rub with half of the oil; place in your air fryer and cook at 360 °F, for 6 minutes; flipping halfway.

2. Meanwhile; in a bowl, mix avocado with mango, cilantro, balsamic vinegar, salt, pepper and the rest of the oil and stir well. Divide fish on plates; top with mango salsa and serve with orange slices on the side.

Nutrition Facts: Calories: 200; Fat: 7g; Fiber: 2g; Carbs: 14g; Protein: 14g

Red Snapper Recipe

(**Prep + Cook Time:** 45 Minutes | **Servings:** 4)

Ingredients:
- 1 big red snapper; cleaned and scored
- 3 garlic cloves; minced
- 1 jalapeno; chopped
- 1/4 lb. okra; chopped.
- 1 tbsp. butter
- 2 tbsp. olive oil
- 1 red bell pepper; chopped
- 2 tbsp. white wine
- 2 tbsp. parsley; chopped
- Salt and black pepper to the taste

Instructions:
1. In a bowl; mix jalapeno, wine with garlic; stir well and rub snapper with this mix.
2. Season fish with salt and pepper and leave it aside for 30 minutes.
3. Meanwhile; heat up a pan with 1 tbsp. butter over medium heat, add bell pepper and okra; stir and cook for 5 minutes.
4. Stuff red snapper's belly with this mix; also add parsley and rub with the olive oil.
5. Place in preheated air fryer and cook at 400 °F, for 15 minutes; flipping the fish halfway. Divide among plates and serve.

Nutrition Facts: Calories: 261; Fat: 7g; Fiber: 18g; Carbs: 28g; Protein: 18g

Tilapia & Chives Sauce

(**Prep + Cook Time:** 18 Minutes | **Servings:** 4)

Ingredients:
- 4 medium tilapia fillets
- 2 tsp. honey
- 1/4 cup Greek yogurt
- Juice from 1 lemon
- 2 tbsp. chives; chopped
- Cooking spray
- Salt and black pepper to the taste

Instructions:
1. Season fish with salt and pepper, spray with cooking spray, place in preheated air fryer 350 °F and cook for 8 minutes; flipping halfway.
2. Meanwhile; in a bowl, mix yogurt with honey, salt, pepper, chives and lemon juice and whisk really well. Divide air fryer fish on plates, drizzle yogurt sauce all over and serve right away.

Nutrition Facts: Calories: 261; Fat: 8g; Fiber: 18g; Carbs: 24g; Protein: 21g

Chili Salmon Recipe

(**Prep + Cook Time:** 25 Minutes | **Servings:** 12)

Ingredients:
- 1 lb. salmon; cubed
- 1¼ cups coconut; shredded
- 1/3 cup flour
- 4 red chilies; chopped
- 3 garlic cloves; minced
- 1/4 cup balsamic vinegar
- 1 egg
- 2 tbsp. olive oil
- 1/4 cup water
- 1/2 cup honey
- A pinch of salt and black pepper

Instructions:
1. In a bowl; mix flour with a pinch of salt and stir.
2. In another bowl; mix egg with black pepper and whisk.
3. Put the coconut in a third bowl.

4. Dip salmon cubes in flour, egg and coconut, put them in your air fryer's basket, cook at 370 °F, for 8 minutes; (Shake the basket after 4 minutes of cooking time) and divide among plates.
5. Heat up a pan with the water over medium high heat, add chilies, cloves, vinegar and honey; stir very well, bring to a boil, simmer for a couple of minutes; drizzle over salmon and serve.

Nutrition Facts: Calories: 220; Fat: 12g; Fiber: 2g; Carbs: 14g; Protein: 13g

Salmon and Avocado Salad Recipe

(**Prep + Cook Time:** 30 Minutes | **Servings:** 4)

Ingredients:
- 2 medium salmon fillets
- 1/4 cup melted butter
- 1 jalapeno pepper; chopped.
- 5 cilantro springs; chopped
- 2 tbsp. white wine vinegar
- 4 oz. mushrooms; sliced
- Sea salt and black pepper to the taste
- 12 cherry tomatoes; halved
- 2 tbsp. olive oil
- 8 oz. lettuce leaves; torn
- 1 avocado; pitted, peeled and cubed
- 1 oz. feta cheese; crumbled

Instructions:
1. Place salmon on a lined baking pan, brush with 2 tbsp. melted butter, season with salt and pepper; broil for 15 minutes over medium heat and then keep warm.
2. Meanwhile; heat up a pan with the rest of the butter over medium heat, add mushrooms; stir and cook for a few minutes.
3. Put the tomatoes in a bowl, add salt, pepper and 1 tbsp. olive oil and toss to coat.
4. In a salad bowl; mix salmon with mushrooms, lettuce, avocado, tomatoes, jalapeno and cilantro. Add the rest of the oil, vinegar, salt and pepper, sprinkle cheese on top and serve.

Nutrition Facts: Calories: 235; Fat: 6g; Fiber: 8g; Carbs: 19g; Protein: 5g

Salmon and Greek Yogurt Sauce Recipe

(**Prep + Cook Time:** 30 Minutes | **Servings:** 2)

Ingredients:
- 2 medium salmon fillets
- 1 tbsp. basil; chopped
- 6 lemon slices
- 1 cup Greek yogurt
- 2 tsp. curry powder
- A pinch of cayenne pepper
- 1 garlic clove; minced
- 1/2 tsp. mint; chopped.
- 1/2 tsp. cilantro; chopped
- Sea salt and black pepper to the taste

Instructions:
1. Place each salmon fillet on a parchment paper piece, make 3 splits in each and stuff them with basil.
2. Season with salt and pepper, top each fillet with 3 lemon slices, fold parchment, seal edges, bake in the oven at 400 °F for 20 minutes.
3. Meanwhile; in a bowl, mix yogurt with cayenne pepper, salt to the taste, garlic, curry, mint and cilantro and whisk well. Transfer fish to plates, drizzle the yogurt sauce you've just prepared on top and serve right away!

Nutrition Facts: Calories: 242; Fat: 1g; Fiber: 2g; Carbs: 3g; Protein: 3g

Meat Recipes

Marinated Pork Chops and Onions Recipe
(Prep + Cook Time: 24 hours 25 Minutes | **Servings:** 6)

Ingredients:
- 2 pork chops
- 1/2 tsp. oregano; dried
- 1/2 tsp. thyme; dried
- 1/4 cup olive oil
- 2 yellow onions; sliced
- 2 garlic cloves; minced
- 2 tsp. mustard
- 1 tsp. sweet paprika
- A pinch of cayenne pepper
- Salt and black pepper to the taste

Instructions:
1. In a bowl; mix oil with garlic, mustard, paprika, black pepper, oregano, thyme and cayenne and whisk well.
2. Combine onions with meat and mustard mix, toss to coat, cover and keep in the fridge for 1 day.
3. Transfer meat and onions mix to a pan that fits your air fryer and cook at 360 °F, for 25 minutes.
4. Divide everything on plates and serve.

Nutrition Facts: Calories: 384; Fat: 4g; Fiber: 4g; Carbs: 17g; Protein: 25g

Beef and Cabbage Mix Recipe
(Prep + Cook Time: 50 Minutes | **Servings:** 6)

Ingredients:
- 2 ½ lbs. beef brisket
- 1 cup beef stock
- 3 garlic cloves; chopped
- 4 carrots; chopped
- 2 bay leaves
- 1 cabbage head; cut into medium wedges
- 3 turnips; cut into quarters
- Salt and black pepper to the taste

Instructions:
1. Put the beef brisket and stock in a large pan that fits your air fryer, season beef with salt and pepper, add garlic and bay leaves, carrots, cabbage, potatoes and turnips, toss, close the air fryer basket and cook at 360 °F and cook for 40 minutes. Divide among plates and serve.

Nutrition Facts: Calories: 353; Fat: 16g; Fiber: 7g; Carbs: 20g; Protein: 24g

Lamb and Lemon Sauce Recipe
(Prep + Cook Time: 40 Minutes | **Servings:** 4)

Ingredients:
- 2 lamb shanks
- 2 garlic cloves; minced
- 4 tbsp. olive oil
- Juice from 1/2 lemon
- Zest from 1/2 lemon
- 1/2 tsp. oregano; dried
- Salt and black pepper to the taste

Instructions:
1. Season lamb with salt, pepper, rub with garlic, put the lamb in your air fryer and cook at 350 °F, for 30 minutes.
2. Meanwhile; in a bowl, mix lemon juice with lemon zest, some salt and pepper, the olive oil and oregano and whisk very well. Shred lamb, discard bone, divide among plates, drizzle the lemon dressing all over and serve.

Nutrition Facts: Calories: 260; Fat: 7g; Fiber: 3g; Carbs: 15g; Protein: 12g

Lamb Shanks and Carrots Recipe

(**Prep + Cook Time:** 55 Minutes | **Servings:** 4)

Ingredients:
- 4 lamb shanks
- 2 tbsp. olive oil
- 1 yellow onion; finely chopped.
- 1 tsp. oregano; dried
- 1 tomato; roughly chopped.
- 2 tbsp. water
- 4 oz. red wine
- 6 carrots; roughly chopped.
- 2 garlic cloves; minced
- 2 tbsp. tomato paste
- Salt and black pepper to the taste

Instructions:
1. Season lamb with salt and pepper, rub with oil, put the lamb in your air fryer and cook at 360 °F, for 10 minutes.
2. In a pan that fits your air fryer, mix onion with carrots, garlic, tomato paste, tomato, oregano, wine and water and toss.
3. Add lamb, toss, close the air fryer basket and cook at 370 °F, for 35 minutes. Divide everything on plates and serve.

Nutrition Facts: Calories: 432; Fat: 17g; Fiber: 8g; Carbs: 17g; Protein: 25g

Chinese Steak and Broccoli Recipe

(**Prep + Cook Time:** 57 Minutes | **Servings:** 4)

Ingredients:
- 3/4 lb. round steak; cut into strips
- 1 lb. broccoli florets
- 1 tsp. sugar
- 1/3 cup sherry
- 1/3 cup oyster sauce
- 1 tbsp. olive oil
- 1 garlic clove; minced
- 2 tsp. sesame oil
- 1 tsp. soy sauce

Instructions:
1. In a bowl; mix sesame oil with oyster sauce, soy sauce, sherry and sugar; stir well, add beef, toss and leave aside for 30 minutes.
2. Transfer beef to a pan that fits your air fryer, also add broccoli, garlic and oil, toss everything and cook at 380 °F, for 12 minutes. Divide among plates and serve.

Nutrition Facts: Calories: 330; Fat: 12g; Fiber: 7g; Carbs: 23g; Protein: 23g

Beef Roast and Wine Sauce Recipe

(**Prep + Cook Time:** 55 Minutes | **Servings:** 6)

Ingredients:
- 3 lbs. beef roast
- 17 oz. beef stock
- 4 garlic cloves; minced
- 3 carrots; chopped
- 5 potatoes; chopped
- 3 oz. red wine
- 1/2 tsp. chicken salt
- Salt and black pepper to the taste
- 1/2 tsp. smoked paprika
- 1 yellow onion; chopped

Instructions:
1. In a bowl; mix salt, pepper, chicken salt and paprika; stir, rub beef with this mix and put it in a big pan that fits your air fryer.
2. Add onion, garlic, stock, wine, potatoes and carrots, close the air fryer basket and cook at 360 °F, for 45 minutes. Divide everything on plates and serve.

Nutrition Facts: Calories: 304; Fat: 20g; Fiber: 7g; Carbs: 20g; Protein: 32g

Braised Pork Recipe

(Prep + Cook Time: 1 hour 20 Minutes | **Servings:** 4)

Ingredients:
- 2 lbs. pork loin roast; boneless and cubed
- 4 tbsp. butter; melted
- 2 cups chicken stock
- 1/2 lb. red grapes
- 1 bay leaf
- 1/2 yellow onion; chopped.
- 1/2 cup dry white wine
- 2 garlic cloves; minced
- 1 tsp. thyme; chopped
- 1 thyme spring
- 2 tbsp. white flour
- Salt and black pepper to the taste

Instructions:
1. Season pork cubes with salt and pepper, rub with 2 tbsp. melted butter, put it in your air fryer and cook at 370 °F, for 8 minutes.
2. Meanwhile; heat up a pan that fits your air fryer with 2 tbsp. butter over medium high heat, add garlic and onion; stir and cook for 2 minutes.
3. Add wine, stock, salt, pepper, thyme, flour and bay leaf; stir well, bring to a simmer and take off heat.
4. Add pork cubes and grapes, toss, close the air fryer basket and cook at 360 °F, for 30 minutes more.
5. Divide everything on plates and serve.

Nutrition Facts: Calories: 320; Fat: 4g; Fiber: 5g; Carbs: 29g; Protein: 38g

Beef Fillets with Garlic Mayo Recipe

(Prep + Cook Time: 50 Minutes | **Servings:** 8)

Ingredients:
- 3 lbs. beef fillet
- 1 cup mayonnaise
- 1/3 cup sour cream
- 2 tbsp. chives; chopped
- 2 tbsp. mustard
- 2 tbsp. mustard
- 1/4 cup tarragon; chopped
- 2 garlic cloves; minced
- Salt and black pepper to the taste

Instructions:
1. Season beef with salt and pepper to the taste, place in your air fryer, cook at 370 °F, for 20 minutes; transfer to a plate and leave aside for a few minutes.
2. In a bowl; mix garlic with sour cream, chives, mayo, some salt and pepper, whisk and leave aside.
3. In another bowl, mix mustard with Dijon mustard and tarragon, whisk, add beef, toss, return to your air fryer and cook at 350 °F, for 20 minutes more. Divide beef on plates, spread garlic mayo on top and serve.

Nutrition Facts: Calories: 400; Fat: 12g; Fiber: 2g; Carbs: 27g; Protein: 19g

Fennel Flavored Pork Roast Recipe

(Prep + Cook Time: 1 hour 10 Minutes | **Servings:** 10)

Ingredients:
- 5 ½ lbs. pork loin roast; trimmed
- 1 tbsp. fennel seeds
- 2 tsp. red pepper; crushed
- 1/4 cup olive oil
- 3 garlic cloves; minced
- 2 tbsp. rosemary; chopped.
- 1 tsp. fennel; ground
- Salt and black pepper to the taste

Instructions:
1. In your food processor mix garlic with fennel seeds, fennel, rosemary, red pepper, some black pepper and the olive oil and blend until you obtain a paste.
2. Spread 2 tablespoons of garlic paste on pork loin, rub well, season with salt and pepper, place in your preheated air fryer and cook at 350 °F, for 30 minutes.
3. Reduce heat to 300 °F and cook for 15 minutes more. Slice pork, divide among plates and serve.

Nutrition Facts: Calories: 300; Fat: 14g; Fiber: 9g; Carbs: 26g; Protein: 22g

Coffee Flavored Steaks Recipe

(Prep + Cook Time: 25 Minutes | **Servings:** 4)

Ingredients:
- 1 ½ tbsp. coffee; ground
- 4 rib eye steaks
- 2 tsp. onion powder
- 1/4 tsp. ginger; ground
- 1/4 teaspoon; coriander, ground
- 1/2 tbsp. sweet paprika
- 2 tbsp. chili powder
- 2 tsp. garlic powder
- A pinch of cayenne pepper
- Black pepper to the taste

Instructions:
1. In a bowl; mix coffee with paprika, chili powder, garlic powder, onion powder, ginger, coriander, cayenne and black pepper; stir, rub steaks with this mix, put it in a preheated air fryer and cook at 360 °F, for 15 minutes. Divide steaks on plates and serve with a side salad.

Nutrition Facts: Calories: 160; Fat: 10g; Fiber: 8g; Carbs: 14g; Protein: 12g

Provencal Pork Recipe

(Prep + Cook Time: 25 Minutes | **Servings:** 2)

Ingredients:
- 7 oz. pork tenderloin
- 1 red onion; sliced
- 1 yellow bell pepper; cut into strips
- 2 tsp. Provencal herbs
- 1/2 tbsp. mustard
- 1 tbsp. olive oil
- 1 green bell pepper; cut into strips
- Salt and black pepper to the taste

Instructions:
1. In a baking pan that fits your air fryer, mix yellow bell pepper with green bell pepper, onion, salt, pepper, Provencal herbs and half of the oil and toss well.
2. Season pork with salt, pepper, mustard and the rest of the oil, toss well and add to veggies. Transfer everything in to your air fryer,
3. Cook at 370 °F, for 15 minutes; divide among plates and serve.

Nutrition Facts: Calories: 300; Fat: 8g; Fiber: 7g; Carbs: 21g; Protein: 23g

Creamy Pork Recipe

(Prep + Cook Time: 32 Minutes | **Servings:** 6)

Ingredients:
- 2 lbs. pork meat; boneless and cubed
- 2 yellow onions; chopped.
- 2 tbsp. dill; chopped.
- 2 tbsp. sweet paprika
- 1 tbsp. olive oil
- 1 garlic clove; minced
- 3 cups chicken stock
- 2 tbsp. white flour
- 1 ½ cups sour cream
- Salt and black pepper to the taste

Instructions:
1. In a pan that fits your air fryer, mix pork with salt, pepper and oil, toss, close the air fryer basket and cook at 360 °F, for 7 minutes.
2. Add onion, garlic, stock, paprika, flour, sour cream and dill, toss and cook at 370 °F, for 15 minutes more. Divide everything on plates and serve right away.

Nutrition Facts: Calories: 300; Fat: 4g; Fiber: 10g; Carbs: 26g; Protein: 34g

Lamb Roast and Potatoes Recipe

(Prep + Cook Time: 55 Minutes | **Servings:** 6)

Ingredients:
- 4 lbs. lamb roast
- 4 bay leaves
- 3 garlic cloves; minced
- 1 spring rosemary
- 6 potatoes; halved
- 1/2 cup lamb stock
- Salt and black pepper to the taste

Instructions:
1. Put the potatoes in a dish that fits your air fryer, add lamb, garlic, rosemary spring, salt, pepper, bay leaves and stock, toss, close the air fryer basket and cook at 360 °F, for 45 minutes. Slice lamb, divide among plates and serve with potatoes and cooking juices.

Nutrition Facts: Calories: 273; Fat: 4g; Fiber: 12g; Carbs: 25g; Protein: 29g

Lemony Lamb Leg Recipe

(Prep + Cook Time: 1 hour 10 Minutes | **Servings:** 6)

Ingredients:
- 4 lbs. lamb leg
- 2 tbsp. olive oil
- 2 springs rosemary; chopped.
- 2 tbsp. lemon juice
- 2 lbs. baby potatoes
- 1 cup beef stock
- 2 tbsp. parsley; chopped
- 2 tbsp. oregano; chopped
- 1 tbsp. lemon rind; grated
- 3 garlic cloves; minced
- Salt and black pepper to the taste

Instructions:
1. Make small cuts all over lamb, insert rosemary springs and season with salt and pepper.
2. In a bowl; mix 1 tbsp. oil with oregano, parsley, garlic, lemon juice and rind; stir and rub lamb with this mix.
3. Heat up a pan that fits your air fryer with the rest of the oil over medium high heat, add potatoes; stir and cook for 3 minutes.
4. Add lamb and stock; stir, close the air fryer basket and cook at 360 °F, for 1 hour. Divide everything on plates and serve.

Nutrition Facts: Calories: 264; Fat: 4g; Fiber: 12g; Carbs: 27g; Protein: 32g

Oriental Fried Lamb Recipe

(Prep + Cook Time: 52 Minutes | **Servings:** 8)

Ingredients:
- 2 ½ lbs. lamb shoulder; chopped.
- 3 tbsp. honey
- 3 oz. almonds; peeled and chopped.
- 9 oz. plumps; pitted
- 8 oz. veggie stock
- 2 yellow onions; chopped
- 2 garlic cloves; minced
- 1 tsp. cumin powder
- 1 tsp. turmeric powder
- 1 tsp. ginger powder
- 1 tsp. cinnamon powder
- Salt and black pepper to the tastes
- 3 tbsp. olive oil

Instructions:
1. In a bowl; mix cinnamon powder with ginger, cumin, turmeric, garlic, olive oil and lamb, toss to coat, place in your preheated air fryer and cook at 350 °F, for 8 minutes.
2. Transfer meat to a dish that fits your air fryer, add onions, stock, honey and plums; stir, close the air fryer basket and cook at 350 °F, for 35 minutes. Divide everything on plates and serve with almond sprinkled on top.

Nutrition Facts: Calories: 432; Fat: 23g; Fiber: 6g; Carbs: 18g; Protein: 20g

Greek Beef Meatballs Salad Recipe

(**Prep + Cook Time:** 20 Minutes | **Servings:** 6)

Ingredients:
- 17 oz. beef; ground
- 1 yellow onion; grated
- 5 bread slices; cubed
- 2 garlic cloves; minced
- 1/4 cup mint; chopped.
- 2 ½ tsp. oregano; dried
- 1/4 cup milk
- 1 egg; whisked
- 1/4 cup parsley; chopped.
- Salt and black pepper to the taste
- 1 tbsp. olive oil
- 7 oz. cherry tomatoes; halved
- 1 cup baby spinach
- 1 ½ tbsp. lemon juice
- 7 oz. Greek yogurt
- Cooking spray

Instructions:
1. Put torn bread In a bowl; add milk, soak for a few minutes; squeeze and transfer to another bowl.
2. Add beef, egg, salt, pepper, oregano, mint, parsley, garlic and onion; stir and shape medium meatballs out of this mix.
3. Spray them with cooking spray, place them in your air fryer and cook at 370 °F, for 10 minutes.
4. In a salad bowl, mix spinach with cucumber and tomato. Add meatballs, the oil, some salt, pepper, lemon juice and yogurt, toss and serve.

Nutrition Facts: Calories: 200; Fat: 4g; Fiber: 8g; Carbs: 13g; Protein: 27g

Beef Brisket and Onion Sauce Recipe

(**Prep + Cook Time:** 2 hours 10 Minutes | **Servings:** 6)

Ingredients:
- 1 lb. yellow onion; chopped
- 4 lbs. beef brisket
- 8 earl grey tea bags
- 1/2 lb. celery; chopped.
- 1 lb. carrot; chopped
- Salt and black pepper to the taste
- 4 cups water

For the sauce:
- 16 oz. canned tomatoes; chopped
- 1 lb. sweet onion; chopped
- 1 cup brown sugar
- 8 earl grey tea bags
- 1/2 lb. celery; chopped
- 1 oz. garlic; minced
- 4 oz. vegetable oil
- 1 cup white vinegar

Instructions:
1. Pour the water in a heat proof dish that fits your air fryer, add 1 lb. onion, 1 lb. carrot, 1/2 lb. celery, salt and pepper; stir and bring to a simmer over medium high heat.
2. Add beef brisket and 8 tea bags; stir, transfer to your air fryer and cook at 300 °F, for 1 hour and 30 minutes.
3. Meanwhile; heat up a pan with the vegetable oil over medium high heat, add 1 lb. onion; stir and sauté for 10 minutes.
4. Add garlic, 1/2 lb. celery, tomatoes, sugar, vinegar, salt, pepper and 8 tea bags; stir, bring to a simmer, cook for 10 minutes and discard tea bags. Transfer beef brisket to a cutting board, slice, divide among plates, drizzle onion sauce all over and serve.

Nutrition Facts: Calories: 400; Fat: 12g; Fiber: 4g; Carbs: 38g; Protein: 34g

Pork with Couscous Recipe
(**Prep + Cook Time:** 45 Minutes | **Servings:** 6)

Ingredients:
- 2 ½ lbs. pork loin; boneless and trimmed
- 2 ¼ tsp. sage; dried
- 3/4 cup chicken stock
- 1/2 tbsp. sweet paprika
- 1/2 tbsp. garlic powder
- 1/4 tsp. marjoram; dried
- 1/4 tsp. rosemary; dried
- 1 tsp. basil; dried
- 2 tbsp. olive oil
- 2 cups couscous; cooked
- 1 tsp. oregano; dried
- Salt and black pepper to the taste

Instructions:
1. In a bowl; mix oil with stock, paprika, garlic powder, sage, rosemary, thyme, marjoram, oregano, salt and pepper to the taste, whisk well, add pork loin, toss well and leave aside for 1 hour.
2. Transfer everything to a pan that fits your air fryer and cook at 370 °F, for 35 minutes. Divide among plates and serve with couscous on the side.

Nutrition Facts: Calories: 310; Fat: 4g; Fiber: 6g; Carbs: 37g; Protein: 34g

Lamb Ribs Recipe
(**Prep + Cook Time:** 55 Minutes | **Servings:** 8)

Ingredients:
- 8 lamb ribs
- 4 garlic cloves; minced
- 2 carrots; chopped
- 3 tbsp. white flour
- 2 cups veggie stock
- 1 tbsp. rosemary; chopped
- 2 tbsp. extra virgin olive oil
- Salt and black pepper to the taste

Instructions:
1. Season lamb ribs with salt and pepper, rub with oil and garlic, put it in a preheated air fryer and cook at 360 °F, for 10 minutes.
2. In a heat proof dish that fits your fryer, mix stock with flour and whisk well.
3. Add rosemary, carrots and lamb ribs, place in your air fryer and cook at 350 °F, for 30 minutes. Divide lamb mix on plates and serve hot.

Nutrition Facts: Calories: 302; Fat: 7g; Fiber: 2g; Carbs: 22g; Protein: 27g

Rib Eye Steak Recipe
(**Prep + Cook Time:** 30 Minutes | **Servings:** 4)

Ingredients:
- 2 lbs. rib eye steak
- Salt and black pepper to the taste
- 1 tbsp. olive oil

For the rub:
- 3 tbsp. sweet paprika
- 1 tbsp. brown sugar
- 1 tbsp. cumin; ground
- 2 tbsp. onion powder
- 2 tbsp. oregano; dried
- 2 tbsp. garlic powder
- 1 tbsp. rosemary; dried

Instructions:
1. In a bowl; mix paprika with onion and garlic powder, sugar, oregano, rosemary, salt, pepper and cumin; stir and rub steak with this mix.
2. Season steak with salt and pepper, rub again with the oil. Put it in your air fryer and cook at 400 °F, for 20 minutes; flipping them halfway. Transfer steak to a cutting board, slice and serve with a side salad.

Nutrition Facts: Calories: 320; Fat: 8g; Fiber: 7g; Carbs: 22g; Protein: 21g

Garlic and Bell Pepper Beef Recipe

(**Prep + Cook Time:** 60 Minutes | **Servings:** 4)

Ingredients:
- 11 oz. steak fillets; sliced
- 4 garlic cloves; minced
- 2 tbsp. olive oil
- 1 tbsp. sugar
- 2 tbsp. fish sauce
- 2 tsp. corn flour
- 1/2 cup beef stock
- 1 red bell pepper; cut into strips
- Black pepper to the taste
- 4 green onions; sliced

Instructions:
1. In a pan that fits your air fryer mix beef with oil, garlic, black pepper and bell pepper; stir, cover and keep in the fridge for 30 minutes.
2. Put the pan in your preheated air fryer and cook at 360 °F, for 14 minutes.
3. In a bowl; mix sugar with fish sauce; stir well, pour over beef and cook at 360 °F, for 7 minutes more.
4. Add stock mixed with corn flour and green onions, toss and cook at 370 °F, for 7 minutes more. Divide everything on plates and serve.

Nutrition Facts: Calories: 343; Fat: 3g; Fiber: 12g; Carbs: 26g; Protein: 38g

Beef Strips with Snow Peas and Mushrooms Recipe

(**Prep + Cook Time:** 32 Minutes | **Servings:** 2)

Ingredients:
- 2 beef steaks; cut into strips
- 7 oz. snow peas
- 2 tbsp. soy sauce
- 8 oz. white mushrooms; halved
- 1 yellow onion; cut into rings
- 1 tsp. olive oil
- Salt and black pepper to the taste

Instructions:
1. In a bowl; mix olive oil with soy sauce, whisk, add beef strips and toss.
2. In another bowl, mix snow peas, onion and mushrooms with salt, pepper and the oil, toss well, put it in a pan that fits your air fryer and cook at 350 °F, for 16 minutes.
3. Add beef strips to the pan as well and cook at 400 °F, for 6 minutes more.
4. Divide everything on plates and serve.

Nutrition Facts: Calories: 235; Fat: 8g; Fiber: 2g; Carbs: 22g; Protein: 24g

Beef and Green Onions Marinade Recipe

(**Prep + Cook Time:** 30 Minutes | **Servings:** 4)

Ingredients:
- 1 lb. lean beef
- 1 cup green onion; chopped
- 1 cup soy sauce
- 1/2 cup water
- 1/4 cup sesame seeds
- 5 garlic cloves; minced
- 1 tsp. black pepper
- 1/4 cup brown sugar

Instructions:
1. In a bowl; mix onion with soy sauce, water, sugar, garlic, sesame seeds and pepper, whisk, add meat, toss and leave aside for 10 minutes.
2. Drain beef, transfer to your preheated air fryer and cook at 390 °F, for 20 minutes. Slice, divide among plates and serve with a side salad.

Nutrition Facts: Calories: 329; Fat: 8g; Fiber: 12g; Carbs: 26g; Protein: 22g

Crispy Lamb Recipe

(Prep + Cook Time: 40 Minutes | **Servings:** 4)

Ingredients:
- 28 oz. rack of lamb
- 1 tbsp. bread crumbs
- 1 garlic clove; minced
- 2 tbsp. macadamia nuts; toasted and crushed
- 1 tbsp. olive oil
- 1 egg;
- 1 tbsp. rosemary; chopped.
- Salt and black pepper to the taste

Instructions:
1. In a bowl; mix oil with garlic and stir well.
2. Season lamb with salt, pepper and brush with the oil.
3. In another bowl, mix nuts with breadcrumbs and rosemary.
4. Put the egg in a separate bowl and whisk well.
5. Dip lamb in egg, then in macadamia mix, place them in your air fryer's basket, cook at 360 °F and cook for 25 minutes; increase heat to 400 °F and cook for 5 minutes more. Divide among plates and serve right away.

Nutrition Facts: Calories: 230; Fat: 2g; Fiber: 2g; Carbs: 10g; Protein: 12g

Ham and Cauliflower Mix Recipe

(Prep + Cook Time: 4 hours 10 Minutes | **Servings:** 6)

Ingredients:
- 4 cups ham; cubed
- 16 oz. cauliflower florets
- 8 oz. cheddar cheese; grated
- 4 garlic cloves; minced
- 1/4 cup heavy cream
- 14 oz. chicken stock
- 1/2 tsp. garlic powder
- 1/2 tsp. onion powder
- Salt and black pepper to the taste

Instructions:
1. In a pan that fits your air fryer, mix ham with stock, cheese, cauliflower, garlic powder, onion powder, salt, pepper, garlic and heavy cream; stir, put it in your air fryer and cook at 300 °F, for 1 hour. Divide into bowls and serve.

Nutrition Facts: Calories: 320; Fat: 20g; Fiber: 3g; Carbs: 16g; Protein: 23g

Pork Chops and Green Beans Recipe

(Prep + Cook Time: 25 Minutes | **Servings:** 4)

Ingredients:
- 4 pork chops; bone in
- 2 tbsp. olive oil
- 16 oz. green beans
- 3 garlic cloves; minced
- 2 tbsp. parsley; chopped
- 1 tbsp. sage; chopped
- Salt and black pepper to the taste

Instructions:
1. In a pan that fits your air fryer, mix pork chops with olive oil, sage, salt, pepper, green beans, garlic and parsley, toss, close the air fryer basket and cook at 360 °F, for 15 minutes
2. Divide everything on plates and serve

Nutrition Facts: Calories: 261; Fat: 7g; Fiber: 9g; Carbs: 14g; Protein: 20g

Asian Pork Recipe

(Prep + Cook Time: 45 Minutes | **Servings:** 4)

Ingredients:
- 14 oz. pork chops; cubed
- 1 tsp. ginger powder
- 2 tsp. chili paste
- 2 garlic cloves; minced
- 2 tbsp. olive oil
- 3 oz. peanuts; ground
- 3 tbsp. soy sauce
- 1 shallot; chopped
- 1 tsp. coriander; ground
- 7 oz. coconut milk
- Salt and black pepper to the taste

Instructions:
1. In a bowl; mix ginger with 1 tsp. chili paste, half of the garlic, half of the soy sauce and half of the oil, whisk, add meat, toss and leave aside for 10 minutes.
2. Transfer meat to your air fryer's basket and cook at 400 °F, for 12 minutes; turning halfway.
3. Meanwhile; heat up a pan with the rest of the oil over medium high heat, add shallot, the rest of the garlic, coriander, coconut milk, the rest of the peanuts, the rest of the chili paste and the rest of the soy sauce; stir and cook for 5 minutes. Divide pork on plates, spread coconut mix on top and serve.

Nutrition Facts: Calories: 423; Fat: 11g; Fiber: 4g; Carbs: 42g; Protein: 18g

Beef Medallions Mix Recipe

(Prep + Cook Time: 2 hours 10 Minutes | **Servings:** 4)

Ingredients:
- 4 beef medallions
- 2 tsp. chili powder
- 1 cup tomatoes; crushed
- 2 tsp. onion powder
- 2 tbsp. soy sauce
- 1 tbsp. hot pepper
- 2 tbsp. lime juice
- Salt and black pepper to the taste

Instructions:
1. In a bowl; mix tomatoes with hot pepper, soy sauce, chili powder, onion powder, a pinch of salt, black pepper and lime juice and whisk well
2. Arrange beef medallions in a dish, pour sauce over them, toss and leave them aside for 2 hours.
3. Discard tomato marinade, put the beef in your preheated air fryer and cook at 360 °F, for 10 minutes. Divide steaks on plates and serve with a side salad

Nutrition Facts: Calories: 230; Fat: 4g; Fiber: 1g; Carbs: 13g; Protein: 14g

Fried Pork Shoulder Recipe

(Prep + Cook Time: 1 hour and 50 minutes | **Servings:** 6)

Ingredients:
- 4 lbs. pork shoulder
- 3 tbsp. garlic; minced
- 3 tbsp. olive oil
- Salt and black pepper to the taste

Instructions:
1. In a bowl; mix olive oil with salt, pepper and oil, whisk well and brush pork shoulder with this mix.
2. Place in preheated air fryer and cook at 390 °F, for 10 minutes.
3. Reduce heat to 300 °F and roast pork for 1 hour and 10 minutes. Slice pork shoulder, divide among plates and serve with a side salad.

Nutrition Facts: Calories: 221; Fat: 4g; Fiber: 4g; Carbs: 7g; Protein: 10g

Mexican Beef Mix Recipe

(Prep + Cook Time: 1 hour and 20 minutes | **Servings:** 8)

Ingredients:
- 2 lbs. beef roast; cubed
- 2 yellow onions; chopped.
- 2 tbsp. olive oil
- 2 tbsp. cilantro; chopped.
- 6 garlic cloves; minced
- 2 green bell peppers; chopped.
- 1 habanero pepper; chopped.
- 4 jalapenos; chopped.
- 14 oz. canned tomatoes; chopped.
- 1/2 cup water
- 1 ½ tsp. cumin; ground
- 1/2 cup black olives; pitted and chopped.
- 1 tsp. oregano; dried
- Salt and black pepper to the taste

Instructions:
1. In a pan that fits your air fryer, combine beef with oil, green bell peppers, onions, jalapenos, habanero pepper, tomatoes, garlic, water, cilantro, oregano, cumin, salt and pepper; stir.
2. Put it in your air fryer and cook at 300 °F, for 1 hour and 10 minutes. Add olives; stir, divide into bowls and serve.

Nutrition Facts: Calories: 305; Fat: 14g; Fiber: 4g; Carbs: 18g; Protein: 25g

Garlic Lamb Chops Recipe

(Prep + Cook Time: 20 Minutes | **Servings:** 4)

Ingredients:
- 8 lamb chops
- 3 tbsp. olive oil
- 4 garlic cloves; minced
- 1 tbsp. oregano; chopped.
- 1 tbsp. coriander; chopped.
- Salt and black pepper to the taste

Instructions:
1. In a bowl; mix oregano with salt, pepper, oil, garlic and lamb chops and toss to coat.
2. Transfer lamb chops to your air fryer and cook at 400 °F, for 10 minutes. Divide lamb chops on plates and serve with a side salad.

Nutrition Facts: Calories: 231; Fat: 7g; Fiber: 5g; Carbs: 14g; Protein: 23g

Sausage and Kale Recipe

(Prep + Cook Time: 30 Minutes | **Servings:** 4)

Ingredients:
- 1 ½ lb. Italian pork sausage; sliced
- 1 cup yellow onion; chopped
- 1/2 cup red bell pepper; chopped.
- 1/4 cup red hot chili pepper; chopped.
- 1 cup water
- Salt and black pepper to the taste
- 5 lbs. kale; chopped
- 1 tsp. garlic; minced

Instructions:
1. In a pan that fits your air fryer, mix sausage with onion, bell pepper, salt, pepper, kale, garlic, water and chili pepper, toss well. Put it in the preheated air fryer and cook at 300 °F, for 20 minutes. Divide everything on plates and serve.

Nutrition Facts: Calories: 150; Fat: 4g; Fiber: 1g; Carbs: 12g; Protein: 14g

Lamb and Spinach Mix Recipe

(Prep + Cook Time: 45 Minutes | **Servings:** 6)

Ingredients:
- 1 lb. lamb meat; cubed
- 2 tbsp. ginger; grated
- 2 garlic cloves; minced
- 2 tsp. cardamom; ground
- 1/2 tsp. chili powder
- 1 tsp. turmeric
- 2 tsp. coriander; ground
- 1 lb. spinach
- 1 red onion; chopped
- 2 tsp. cumin powder
- 1 tsp. garam masala
- 14 oz. canned tomatoes; chopped.

Instructions:
1. In a heat proof dish that fits your air fryer, mix lamb with spinach, tomatoes, ginger, garlic, onion, cardamom, cloves, cumin, garam masala, chili, turmeric and coriander; stir.
2. Transfer to the preheated air fryer and cook at 360 °F, for 35 minutes Divide into bowls and serve.

Nutrition Facts: Calories: 160; Fat: 6g; Fiber: 3g; Carbs: 17g; Protein: 20g

Short Ribs and Beer Sauce Recipe
(Prep + Cook Time: 60 Minutes | **Servings:** 6)

Ingredients:
- 4 lbs. short ribs; cut into small pieces
- 1 yellow onion; chopped.
- 1 cup chicken stock
- 1 bay leaf
- 6 thyme springs; chopped
- Salt and black pepper to the taste
- 1/4 cup tomato paste
- 1 cup dark beer
- 1 Portobello mushroom; dried

Instructions:
1. Heat up a pan that fits your air fryer over medium heat, add tomato paste, onion, stock, beer, mushroom, bay leaves and thyme and bring to a simmer.
2. Add ribs, close the air fryer basket and cook at 350 °F, for 40 minutes. Divide everything on plates and serve.

Nutrition Facts: Calories: 300; Fat: 7g; Fiber: 8g; Carbs: 18g; Protein: 23g

Beef Stuffed Squash Recipe
(Prep + Cook Time: 50 Minutes | **Servings:** 2)

Ingredients:
- 1 lb. beef; ground
- 1 spaghetti squash; pricked
- Salt and black pepper to the taste
- 3 garlic cloves; minced
- 1 yellow onion; chopped
- 1 Portobello mushroom; sliced
- 28 oz. canned tomatoes; chopped.
- 1 tsp. oregano; dried
- 1/4 tsp. cayenne pepper
- 1/2 tsp. thyme; dried
- 1 green bell pepper; chopped

Instructions:
1. Put the spaghetti squash in your air fryer, cook at 350 °F, for 20 minutes; transfer to a cutting board, and cut into halves and discard seeds.
2. Heat up a pan over medium high heat, add meat, garlic, onion and mushroom; stir and cook until meat browns.
3. Add salt, pepper, thyme, oregano, cayenne, tomatoes and green pepper; stir and cook for 10 minutes.
4. Stuff squash with the beef mix and close the air fryer basket and cook at 360 °F, for 10 minutes. Divide among plates and serve.

Nutrition Facts: Calories: 260; Fat: 7g; Fiber: 2g; Carbs: 14g; Protein: 10g

Burgundy Beef Mix Recipe
(Prep + Cook Time: 1 hour 10 Minutes | **Servings:** 7)

Ingredients:
- 2 lbs. beef chuck roast; cubed
- 15 oz. canned tomatoes; chopped
- 4 carrots; chopped.
- 1/2 lbs. mushrooms; sliced
- 2 celery ribs; chopped
- 2 yellow onions; chopped
- 1/2 tsp. mustard powder
- 3 tbsp. almond flour
- 1 tbsp. thyme; chopped
- 1 cup water
- 1 cup beef stock
- Salt and black pepper to the taste

Instructions:
1. Heat up a heat proof pot that fits your air fryer over medium high heat, add beef; stir and brown them for a couple of minutes.
2. Add tomatoes, mushrooms, onions, carrots, celery, salt, pepper mustard, stock and thyme and stir.
3. In a bowl mix water with flour; stir well, add this to the pot, toss, close the air fryer basket and cook at 300 °F, for 1 hour. Divide into bowls and serve.

Nutrition Facts: Calories: 275; Fat: 13g; Fiber: 4g; Carbs: 17g; Protein: 28g

Beef Curry Recipe

(Prep + Cook Time: 55 Minutes | **Servings:** 4)

Ingredients:
- 2 lbs. beef steak; cubed
- 2 yellow onions; chopped
- 2 garlic cloves; minced
- 10 oz. canned coconut milk
- 2 tbsp. tomato sauce
- 2 tbsp. olive oil
- 3 potatoes; cubed
- 1 tbsp. wine mustard
- 2 ½ tbsp. curry powder
- Salt and black pepper to the taste

Instructions:
1. Heat up a pan that fits your air fryer with the oil over medium high heat, add onions and garlic; stir and cook for 4 minutes.
2. Add potatoes and mustard; stir and cook for 1 minute.
3. Add beef, curry powder, salt, pepper, coconut milk and tomato sauce; stir, transfer to your air fryer and cook at 360 °F, for 40 minutes. Divide into bowls and serve.

Nutrition Facts: Calories: 432; Fat: 16g; Fiber: 4g; Carbs: 20g; Protein: 27g

Pork Chops and Roasted Peppers Recipe

(Prep + Cook Time: 26 Minutes | **Servings:** 4)

Ingredients:
- 4 pork chops; bone in
- 3 tbsp. lemon juice
- 1 tbsp. smoked paprika
- 2 roasted bell peppers; chopped.
- 2 tbsp. thyme; chopped
- 3 garlic cloves; minced
- 3 tbsp. olive oil
- Salt and black pepper to the taste

Instructions:
1. In a pan that fits your air fryer, mix pork chops with oil, lemon juice, smoked paprika, thyme, garlic, bell peppers, salt and pepper, toss well, close the air fryer basket and cook at 400 °F, for 16 minutes
2. Divide pork chops and peppers mix on plates and serve right away.

Nutrition Facts: Calories: 321; Fat: 6g; Fiber: 8g; Carbs: 14g; Protein: 17g

Lamb and Creamy Brussels Sprouts Recipe

(Prep + Cook Time: 1 hour and 20 minutes | **Servings:** 4)

Ingredients:
- 2 lbs. leg of lamb; scored
- 1 ½ lbs. Brussels sprouts; trimmed
- 2 tbsp. olive oil
- 1 tbsp. rosemary; chopped
- 1 tbsp. lemon thyme; chopped.
- 1 tbsp. butter; melted
- 1/2 cup sour cream
- 1 garlic clove; minced
- Salt and black pepper to the taste

Instructions:
1. Season leg of lamb with salt, pepper, thyme and rosemary, brush with oil, place in your air fryer's basket, cook at 300 °F, for 1 hour, transfer to a plate and keep warm.
2. In a pan that fits your air fryer, mix Brussels sprouts with salt, pepper, garlic, butter and sour cream, toss, put it in your air fryer and cook at 400 °F, for 10 minutes. Divide lamb on plates, add Brussels sprouts on the side and serve.

Nutrition Facts: Calories: 440; Fat: 23g; Fiber: 0g; Carbs: 2g; Protein: 25g

Mustard Marinated Beef Recipe

(**Prep + Cook Time:** 55 Minutes | **Servings:** 6)

Ingredients:
- 6 bacon strips
- 3/4 cup red wine
- 3 garlic cloves; minced
- 2 tbsp. butter
- 1 tbsp. horseradish
- 1 tbsp. mustard
- 3 lbs. beef roast
- 1 ¾ cup beef stock
- Salt and black pepper to the taste

Instructions:
1. In a bowl; mix butter with mustard, garlic, salt, pepper and horseradish, whisk and rub beef with this mix.
2. Arrange bacon strips on a cutting board, place beef on top, fold bacon around beef, transfer to the air fryer's basket, cook at 400 °F, for 15 minutes and transfer to a pan that fits your fryer.
3. Add stock and wine to beef, close the air fryer basket and cook at 360 °F, for 30 minutes more.
4. Carve beef, divide among plates and serve with a side salad.

Nutrition Facts: Calories: 500; Fat: 9g; Fiber: 4g; Carbs: 29g; Protein: 36g

Tasty Ham and Greens Recipe

(**Prep + Cook Time:** 26 Minutes | **Servings:** 8)

Ingredients:
- 4 cups ham; chopped
- 16 oz. collard greens; chopped
- 14 oz. canned black eyed peas; drained
- 2 tbsp. olive oil
- 2 tbsp. flour
- 3 cups chicken stock
- 5 oz. onion; chopped
- 1/2 tsp. red pepper; crushed

Instructions:
1. Drizzle the oil in a pan that fits your air fryer, add ham, stock and flour and whisk
2. Also add onion, black eyed peas, red pepper and collard greens, close the air fryer basket and cook at 390 °F, for 16 minutes. Divide everything on plates and serve.

Nutrition Facts: Calories: 322; Fat: 6g; Fiber: 8g; Carbs: 12g; Protein: 5g

Sirloin Steaks and Pico De Gallo Recipe

(**Prep + Cook Time:** 20 Minutes | **Servings:** 4)

Ingredients:
- 4 medium sirloin steaks
- 2 tbsp. chili powder
- 1 tsp. onion powder
- 1 tsp. garlic powder
- 1 tsp. cumin; ground
- 1/2 tbsp. sweet paprika
- Salt and black pepper to the taste

For the Pico de gallo:
- 1 small red onion; chopped
- 1 small green bell pepper; chopped.
- 1 jalapeno; chopped.
- 2 tomatoes; chopped
- 2 garlic cloves; minced
- 2 tbsp. lime juice
- 1/4 cup cilantro; chopped
- 1/4 tsp. cumin; ground

Instructions:
1. In a bowl; mix chili powder with a pinch of salt, black pepper, onion powder, garlic powder, paprika and 1 tsp. cumin; stir well, season steaks with this mix, put them in your air fryer and cook at 360 °F, for 10 minutes.
2. In a bowl; mix red onion with tomatoes, garlic, lime juice, bell pepper, jalapeno, cilantro, black pepper to the taste and 1/4 tsp. cumin and toss. Top steaks with this mix and serve right away

Nutrition Facts: Calories: 200; Fat: 12g; Fiber: 4g; Carbs: 15g; Protein: 18g

Pork Chops and Mushrooms Mix Recipe

(Prep + Cook Time: 50 Minutes | **Servings:** 3)

Ingredients:
- 3 pork chops; boneless
- 8 oz. mushrooms; sliced
- 1 tsp. nutmeg
- 1 tbsp. balsamic vinegar
- 1 tsp. garlic powder
- 1 yellow onion; chopped.
- 1 cup mayonnaise
- 1/2 cup olive oil

Instructions:
1. Heat up a pan that fits your air fryer with the oil over medium heat, add mushrooms and onions; stir and cook for 4 minutes.
2. Add pork chops, nutmeg and garlic powder and brown on both sides.
3. Place the pan in your air fryer's basket and cook at 330 °F and cook for 30 minutes. Add vinegar and mayo; stir, divide everything on plates and serve.

Nutrition Facts: Calories: 600; Fat: 10g; Fiber: 1g; Carbs: 8g; Protein: 22g

Beef Kabobs Recipe

(Prep + Cook Time: 20 Minutes | **Servings:** 4)

Ingredients:
- 2 lbs. sirloin steak; cut into medium pieces
- 2 red bell peppers; chopped
- 1/2 tbsp. cumin; ground
- 1/4 cup olive oil
- 1/4 cup salsa
- 1 red onion; chopped
- 1 zucchini; sliced
- Juice form 1 lime
- 2 tbsp. chili powder
- 2 tbsp. hot sauce
- Salt and black pepper to the taste

Instructions:
1. In a bowl; mix salsa with lime juice, oil, hot sauce, chili powder, cumin, salt and black pepper and whisk well.
2. Divide meat bell peppers, zucchini and onion on skewers, brush kabobs with the salsa mix you made earlier, put them in your preheated air fryer and cook them for 10 minutes at 370 °F, flipping kabobs halfway. Divide among plates and serve with a side salad.

Nutrition Facts: Calories: 170; Fat: 5g; Fiber: 2g; Carbs: 13g; Protein: 16g

Creamy Lamb Recipe

(Prep + Cook Time: 1 day 1 hour | **Servings:** 8)

Ingredients:
- 5 lbs. leg of lamb
- 2 cups low fat buttermilk
- 2 tbsp. mustard
- 1/2 cup butter
- 2 tbsp. basil; chopped
- 2 tbsp. tomato paste
- 2 garlic cloves; minced
- Salt and black pepper to the taste
- 1 cup white wine
- 1 tbsp. cornstarch mixed with 1 tbsp. water
- 1/2 cup sour cream

Instructions:
1. Put the lamb roast in a big dish, add buttermilk, toss to coat, cover and keep in the fridge for 24 hours.
2. Pat dry lamb and put it in a pan that fits your air fryer.
3. In a bowl; mix butter with tomato paste, mustard, basil, rosemary, salt, pepper and garlic, whisk well, spread over lamb, transfer everything into your air fryer and cook at 300 °F, for 1 hour.
4. Slice lamb, divide among plates, leave aside for now and heat up cooking juices from the pan on your stove. Add wine, cornstarch mix, salt, pepper and sour cream; stir, take off heat, drizzle this sauce over lamb and serve.

Nutrition Facts: Calories: 287; Fat: 4g; Fiber: 7g; Carbs: 19g; Protein: 25g

Beef Casserole Recipe

(Prep + Cook Time: 65 Minutes | **Servings:** 12)

Ingredients:
- 2 lbs. beef; ground
- 2 cups eggplant; chopped.
- 2 tsp. gluten free Worcestershire sauce
- 28 oz. canned tomatoes; chopped.
- 2 cups mozzarella; grated
- 16 oz. tomato sauce
- 2 tsp. mustard
- 2 tbsp. parsley; chopped.
- 1 tsp. oregano; dried
- 1 tbsp. olive oil
- Salt and black pepper to the taste

Instructions:
1. In a bowl; mix eggplant with salt, pepper and oil and toss to coat.
2. In another bowl, mix beef with salt, pepper, mustard and Worcestershire sauce; stir well and spread on the bottom of a pan that fits your air fryer.
3. Add eggplant mix, tomatoes, tomato sauce, parsley, oregano and sprinkle mozzarella at the end.
4. Close the air fryer basket and cook at 360 °F, for 35 minutes Divide among plates and serve hot.

Nutrition Facts: Calories: 200; Fat: 12g; Fiber: 2g; Carbs: 16g; Protein: 15g

Ham and Veggie Air Fried Mix Recipe

(Prep + Cook Time: 30 Minutes | **Servings:** 6)

Ingredients:
- 2 cups ham; chopped
- 1/4 cup butter
- 1/4 cup flour
- 6 oz. sweet peas
- 4 oz. mushrooms; halved
- 3 cups milk
- 1/2 tsp. thyme; dried
- 1 cup baby carrots

Instructions:
1. Heat up a pan that fits your air fryer with the butter over medium heat, melt it, add flour and whisk well
2. Add milk and, well again and take off heat
3. Add thyme, ham, peas, mushrooms and baby carrots, toss, put it in your air fryer and cook at 360 °F, for 20 minutes. Divide everything on plates and serve.

Nutrition Facts: Calories: 311; Fat: 6g; Fiber: 8g; Carbs: 12g; Protein: 7g

Lamb Shanks Recipe

(Prep + Cook Time: 55 Minutes | **Servings:** 4)

Ingredients:
- 4 lamb shanks
- 1 yellow onion; chopped
- 1 tbsp. olive oil
- 2 tsp. honey
- 5 oz. dry sherry
- 2 ½ cups chicken stock
- 4 tsp. coriander seeds; crushed
- 2 tbsp. white flour
- 4 bay leaves
- Salt and pepper to the taste

Instructions:
1. Season lamb shanks with salt and pepper, rub with half of the oil, put the lamb shanks in your air fryer and cook at 360 °F, for 10 minutes.
2. Heat up a pan that fits your air fryer with the rest of the oil over medium high heat, add onion and coriander; stir and cook for 5 minutes.
3. Add flour, sherry, stock, honey and bay leaves, salt and pepper; stir, bring to a simmer, add lamb.
4. Place the pan in your air fryer and cook at 360 °F, for 30 minutes. Divide everything on plates and serve.

Nutrition Facts: Calories: 283; Fat: 4g; Fiber: 2g; Carbs: 17g; Protein: 26g

Lamb and Green Pesto Recipe

(Prep + Cook Time: 1 hour 45 Minutes | **Servings:** 4)

Ingredients:
- 2 lbs. lamb riblets
- 1 cup parsley
- 1 cup mint
- 1 small yellow onion; roughly chopped
- 1/3 cup pistachios; chopped.
- 1 tsp. lemon zest; grated
- 5 tbsp. olive oil
- 1/2 onion; chopped.
- 5 garlic cloves; minced
- Juice from 1 orange
- Salt and black pepper to the taste

Instructions:
1. In your food processor, mix parsley with mint, onion, pistachios, lemon zest, salt, pepper and oil and blend very well.
2. Rub lamb with this mix, place in a bowl; cover and leave in the fridge for 1 hour.
3. Transfer lamb to a baking pan that fits your air fryer, also add garlic, drizzle orange juice and cook in your air fryer at 300 °F, for 45 minutes.

Nutrition Facts: Calories: 200; Fat: 4g; Fiber: 6g; Carbs: 15g; Protein: 7g

Stuffed Pork Steaks Recipe

(Prep + Cook Time: 30 Minutes | **Servings:** 4)

Ingredients:
- 4 pork loin steaks
- 2 pickles; chopped
- 4 ham slices
- 6 Swiss cheese slices
- Zest from 2 limes; grated
- Zest from 1 orange; grated
- Juice from 1 orange
- Juice from 2 limes
- 4 tsp. garlic; minced
- 3/4 cup olive oil
- 1 cup cilantro; chopped.
- 1 cup mint; chopped
- 1 tsp. oregano; dried
- 2 tsp. cumin; ground
- 2 tbsp. mustard
- Salt and black pepper to the taste

Instructions:
1. In your food processor, mix lime zest and juice with orange zest and juice, garlic, oil, cilantro, mint, oregano, cumin, salt and pepper and blend well.
2. Season steaks with salt and pepper, place them into a bowl, add marinade and toss to coat.
3. Place steaks on a working surface, divide pickles, cheese, mustard and ham on them, roll and secure with toothpicks.
4. Put the stuffed pork steaks in your air fryer and cook at 340 °F, for 20 minutes. Divide among plates and serve with a side salad.

Nutrition Facts: Calories: 270; Fat: 7g; Fiber: 2g; Carbs: 13g; Protein: 20g

Mediterranean Steaks and Scallops Recipe

(Prep + Cook Time: 24 Minutes | **Servings:** 2)

Ingredients:
- 2 beef steaks
- 10 sea scallops
- 1 tsp. lemon zest
- 1/4 cup butter
- 1/4 cup veggie stock
- 4 garlic cloves; minced
- 1 shallot; chopped
- 2 tbsp. lemon juice
- 2 tbsp. parsley; chopped.
- 2 tbsp. basil; chopped
- Salt and black pepper to the taste

Instructions:
1. Season steaks with salt and pepper, put them in your air fryer, cook at 360 °F, for 10 minutes and transfer to a pan that fits the fryer.

2. Add shallot, garlic, butter, stock, basil, lemon juice, parsley, lemon zest and scallops, toss everything gently and cook at 360 °F, for 4 minutes more. Divide steaks and scallops on plates and serve.

Nutrition Facts: Calories: 150; Fat: 2g; Fiber: 2g; Carbs: 14g; Protein: 17g

Filet Mignon and Mushrooms Sauce Recipe

(Prep + Cook Time: 35 Minutes | **Servings:** 4)

Ingredients:
- 12 mushrooms; sliced
- 4 fillet mignons
- 1/4 cup Dijon mustard
- 1/4 cup wine
- 1¼ cup coconut cream
- 1 shallot; chopped
- 2 tbsp. parsley; chopped.
- 2 garlic cloves; minced
- 2 tbsp. olive oil
- Salt and black pepper to the taste

Instructions:
1. Heat up a pan with the oil over medium high heat, add garlic and shallots; stir and cook for 3 minutes.
2. Add mushrooms; stir and cook for 4 minutes more.
3. Add wine; stir and cook until it evaporates.
4. Add coconut cream, mustard, parsley, a pinch of salt and black pepper to the taste; stir, cook for 6 minutes more and take off heat.
5. Season fillets with salt and pepper, put them in your air fryer and cook at 360 °F, for 10 minutes. Divide fillets on plates and serve with the mushroom sauce on top.

Nutrition Facts: Calories: 340; Fat: 12g; Fiber: 1g; Carbs: 14g; Protein: 23g

Fried Sausage and Mushrooms Recipe

(Prep + Cook Time: 50 Minutes | **Servings:** 6)

Ingredients:
- 2 lbs. pork sausage; sliced
- 3 red bell peppers; chopped
- 2 sweet onions; chopped.
- 1 tbsp. brown sugar
- 1 tsp. olive oil
- Salt and black pepper to the taste
- 2 lbs. Portobello mushrooms; sliced

Instructions:
1. In a baking pan that fits your air fryer, mix sausage slices with oil, salt, pepper, bell pepper, mushrooms, onion and sugar, toss, close the air fryer basket and cook at 300 °F, for 40 minutes. Divide among plates and serve right away.

Nutrition Facts: Calories: 130; Fat: 12g; Fiber: 1g; Carbs: 13g; Protein: 18g

Short Ribs and Sauce Recipe

(Prep + Cook Time: 46 Minutes | **Servings:** 4)

Ingredients:
- 4 lbs. short ribs
- 2 green onions; chopped.
- 1 tsp. vegetable oil
- 1/2 cup soy sauce
- 1/4 cup rice wine
- 1/4 cup pear juice
- 3 garlic cloves; minced
- 3 ginger slices
- 1/2 cup water
- 2 tsp. sesame oil

Instructions:
1. Heat up a pan that fits your air fryer with the oil over medium heat, add green onions, ginger and garlic; stir and cook for 1 minute.
2. Add ribs, water, wine, soy sauce, sesame oil and pear juice; stir, close the air fryer basket and cook at 350 °F, for 35 minutes. Divide ribs and sauce on plates and serve.

Nutrition Facts: Calories: 321; Fat: 12g; Fiber: 4g; Carbs: 20g; Protein: 14g

Pork Chops and Sage Sauce Recipe
(Prep + Cook Time: 25 Minutes | **Servings:** 2)

Ingredients:
- 2 pork chops
- 1 shallot; sliced
- 1 handful sage; chopped
- Salt and black pepper to the taste
- 1 tbsp. olive oil
- 2 tbsp. butter
- 1 tsp. lemon juice

Instructions:
1. Season pork chops with salt and pepper, rub with the oil. Now place the pork chops in your air fryer and cook at 370 °F, for 10 minutes; flipping them halfway
2. Meanwhile; heat up a pan with the butter over medium heat, add shallot; stir and cook for 2 minutes.
3. Add sage and lemon juice; stir well, cook for a few more minutes and take off heat
4. Divide pork chops on plates, drizzle sage sauce all over and serve.

Nutrition Facts: Calories: 265; Fat: 6g; Fiber: 8g; Carbs: 19g; Protein: 12g

Lamb Racks and Fennel Mix Recipe
(Prep + Cook Time: 26 Minutes | **Servings:** 4)

Ingredients:
- 12 oz. lamb racks
- 2 fennel bulbs; sliced
- 2 tbsp. olive oil
- 1/8 cup apple cider vinegar
- 1 tbsp. brown sugar
- 4 figs; cut into halves
- Salt and black pepper to the taste

Instructions:
1. In a bowl; mix fennel with figs, vinegar, sugar and oil, toss to coat well, transfer to a baking pan that fits your air fryer, close the air fryer basket and cook at 350 °F, for 6 minutes.
2. Season lamb with salt and pepper, add to the baking pan with the fennel mix and air fry for 10 minutes more. Divide everything on plates and serve.

Nutrition Facts: Calories: 240; Fat: 9g; Fiber: 3g; Carbs: 15g; Protein: 12g

Balsamic Beef Recipe
(Prep + Cook Time: 1 hour 10 Minutes | **Servings:** 6)

Ingredients:
- 1 medium beef roast
- 1 tbsp. Worcestershire sauce
- 1 tbsp. honey
- 1 tbsp. soy sauce
- 1/2 cup balsamic vinegar
- 1 cup beef stock
- 4 garlic cloves; minced

Instructions:
1. In a heat proof dish that fits your air fryer, mix roast with roast with Worcestershire sauce, vinegar, stock, honey, soy sauce and garlic, toss well, close the air fryer basket and cook at 370 °F, for 1 hour
2. Slice roast, divide among plates, drizzle the sauce all over and serve

Nutrition Facts: Calories: 311; Fat: 7g; Fiber: 12g; Carbs: 20g; Protein: 16g

Beef Patties and Mushroom Sauce Recipe

(**Prep + Cook Time:** 35 Minutes | **Servings:** 6)

Ingredients:
- 2 lbs. beef; ground
- 1/2 tsp. garlic powder
- 1 tbsp. soy sauce
- 1/4 cup beef stock
- 3/4 cup flour
- 1 tbsp. parsley; chopped
- 1 tbsp. onion flakes
- Salt and black pepper to the taste

For the sauce:
- 1 cup yellow onion; chopped.
- 1/2 tsp. soy sauce
- 1/4 cup sour cream
- 1/2 cup beef stock
- 2 cups mushrooms; sliced
- 2 tbsp. bacon fat
- 2 tbsp. butter
- Salt and black pepper to the taste

Instructions:
1. In a bowl; mix beef with salt, pepper, garlic powder, 1 tbsp. soy sauce, 1/4 cup beef stock, flour, parsley and onion flakes; stir well, shape 6 patties, place them in your air fryer and cook at 350 °F, for 14 minutes.
2. Meanwhile; heat up a pan with the butter and the bacon fat over medium heat, add mushrooms; stir and cook for 4 minutes.
3. Add onions; stir and cook for 4 minutes more.
4. Add 1/2 tsp. soy sauce, sour cream and 1/2 cup stock; stir well, bring to a simmer and take off heat. Divide beef patties on plates and serve with mushroom sauce on top.

Nutrition Facts: Calories: 435; Fat: 23g; Fiber: 4g; Carbs: 6g; Protein: 32g

Side Dish Recipes

Sweet Potato Fries

(Prep + Cook Time: 30 Minutes | **Servings:** 2)

Ingredients:
- 2 sweet potatoes; peeled and cut into medium fries
- 2 tbsp. olive oil
- 1/2 tsp. curry powder
- 1/4 tsp. coriander; ground
- 2 tbsp. mayonnaise
- 1/2 tsp. cumin; ground
- 1/4 cup ketchup
- Salt and black pepper to the taste
- A pinch of ginger powder
- A pinch of cinnamon powder

Instructions:
1. In your air fryer's basket; mix sweet potato fries with salt, pepper, coriander, curry powder and oil; toss well and cook at 370 °F, for 20 minutes; flipping them once.
2. Meanwhile; in a bowl, mix ketchup with mayo, cumin, ginger and cinnamon and whisk well. Divide fries on plates; drizzle ketchup mix over them and serve as a side dish.

Nutrition Facts: Calories: 200; Fat: 5g; Fiber: 8g; Carbs: 9g; Protein: 7g

Roasted Parsnips Dish

(Prep + Cook Time: 50 Minutes | **Servings:** 6)

Ingredients:
- 2 lbs. parsnips; peeled and cut into medium chunks
- 1 tbsp. parsley flakes; dried
- 1 tbsp. olive oil
- 2 tbsp. maple syrup

Instructions:
1. Preheat your air fryer at 360 degrees F; add oil and heat it up as well.
2. Add parsnips, parsley flakes and maple syrup; toss and cook them for 40 minutes. Divide among plates and serve as a side dish.

Nutrition Facts: Calories: 124; Fat: 3g; Fiber: 3g; Carbs: 7g; Protein: 4g

Roasted Pumpkin Side Dish

(Prep + Cook Time: 22 Minutes | **Servings:** 4)

Ingredients:
- 1 ½ lb. pumpkin; deseeded, sliced and roughly chopped.
- 3 garlic cloves; minced
- 1 tbsp. olive oil
- A pinch of nutmeg; ground
- A pinch of sea salt
- A pinch of brown sugar
- A pinch of cinnamon powder

Instructions:
1. In your air fryer's basket, mix pumpkin with garlic, oil, salt, brown sugar, cinnamon and nutmeg; toss well, cover and cook at 370 °F, for 12 minutes. Divide among plates and serve as a side dish.

Nutrition Facts: Calories: 200; Fat: 5g; Fiber: 4g; Carbs: 7g; Protein: 4g

Creamy Endives

(Prep + Cook Time: 20 Minutes | **Servings:** 6)

Ingredients:
- 6 endives; trimmed and halved
- 3 tbsp. lemon juice
- 1 tsp. garlic powder
- 1/2 tsp. curry powder
- 1/2 cup Greek yogurt
- Salt and black pepper to the taste

Instructions:
1. In a bowl mix endives with garlic powder, yogurt, curry powder, salt, pepper and lemon juice; toss, leave aside for 10 minutes and transfer to your preheated air fryer at 350 degrees F. Cook endives for 10 minutes; divide them on plates and serve as a side dish.

Nutrition Facts: Calories: 100; Fat: 2g; Fiber: 2g; Carbs: 7g; Protein: 4g

Eggplant Fries Dish
(Prep + Cook Time: 15 Minutes | Servings: 4)

Ingredients:
- 1 eggplant; peeled and cut into medium fries
- 2 tbsp. milk
- 1 egg; whisked
- 2 cups panko bread crumbs
- 1/2 cup Italian cheese; shredded
- A pinch of salt and black pepper to the taste
- Cooking spray

Instructions:
1. In a bowl; mix egg with milk, salt and pepper and whisk well.
2. In another bowl; mix panko with cheese and stir.
3. Dip eggplant fries in egg mix, then coat in panko mix, place them in your air fryer greased with cooking spray and cook at 400 °F, for 5 minutes. Divide among plates and serve as a side dish.

Nutrition Facts: Calories: 162; Fat: 5g; Fiber: 5g; Carbs: 7g; Protein: 6g

Herbed Tomatoes Dish
(Prep + Cook Time: 25 Minutes | Servings: 4)

Ingredients:
- 4 big tomatoes; halved and insides scooped out
- 1 tbsp. olive oil
- 2 garlic cloves; minced
- 1/2 tsp. thyme; chopped.
- Salt and black pepper to the taste

Instructions:
1. In your air fryer, mix tomatoes with salt, pepper, oil, garlic and thyme; toss and cook at 390 °F, for 15 minutes. Divide among plates and serve them as a side dish.

Nutrition Facts: Calories: 112; Fat: 1g; Fiber: 3g; Carbs: 4g; Protein: 4g

Mushrooms and Cream
(Prep + Cook Time: 20 Minutes | Servings: 6)

Ingredients:
- 2 bacon strips; chopped.
- 1 yellow onion; chopped.
- 1 carrot; grated
- 1/2 cup sour cream
- 1 cup cheddar cheese; grated
- 1 green bell pepper; chopped.
- 24 mushrooms; stems removed
- Salt and black pepper to the taste

Instructions:
1. Heat up a pan over medium high heat; add bacon, onion, bell pepper and carrot; stir and cook for 1 minute.
2. Add salt, pepper and sour cream, stir cook for 1 minute more; take off heat and cool down.
3. Stuff mushrooms with this mix, sprinkle cheese on top and cook at 360 °F, for 8 minutes. Divide among plates and serve as a side dish.

Nutrition Facts: Calories: 211; Fat: 4g; Fiber: 7g; Carbs: 8g; Protein: 3g

Cauliflower Cakes

(Prep + Cook Time: 20 Minutes | **Servings:** 6)

Ingredients:
- 3 ½ cups cauliflower rice
- 1/2 cup parmesan; grated
- 2 eggs
- 1/4 cup white flour
- Salt and black pepper to the taste
- Cooking spray

Instructions:
1. In a bowl; mix cauliflower rice with salt and pepper, stir and squeeze excess water.
2. Transfer cauliflower to another bowl; add eggs, salt, pepper, flour and parmesan; stir really well and shape your cakes.
3. Grease your air fryer with cooking spray, heat it up at 400 degrees; add cauliflower cakes and cook them for 10 minutes flipping them halfway. Divide cakes on plates and serve as a side dish.

Nutrition Facts: Calories: 125; Fat: 2g; Fiber: 6g; Carbs: 8g; Protein: 3g

Cauliflower Rice Dish

(Prep + Cook Time: 50 Minutes | **Servings:** 8)

Ingredients:
- 3 garlic cloves; minced
- 9 oz. water chestnuts; drained
- 1 tbsp. peanut oil
- 1 tbsp. sesame oil
- 4 tbsp. soy sauce
- 3/4 cup peas
- 15 oz. mushrooms; chopped.
- 1 tbsp. ginger; grated
- Juice from 1/2 lemon
- 1 cauliflower head; riced
- 1 egg; whisked

Instructions:
1. In your air fryer; mix cauliflower rice with peanut oil, sesame oil, soy sauce, garlic, ginger and lemon juice; stir, cover and cook at 350 °F, for 20 minutes.
2. Add chestnuts, peas, mushrooms and egg; toss and cook at 360 °F, for 20 minutes more. Divide among plates and serve for breakfast.

Nutrition Facts: Calories: 142; Fat: 3g; Fiber: 2g; Carbs: 6g; Protein: 4g

Coconut Potatoes

(Prep + Cook Time: 30 Minutes | **Servings:** 4)

Ingredients:
- 2 eggs; whisked
- 2 potatoes; sliced
- 4 oz. coconut cream
- 1 tbsp. cheddar cheese; grated
- 1 tbsp. flour
- Salt and black pepper to the taste

Instructions:
1. Place potato slices in your air fryer's basket and cook at 360 °F, for 10 minutes.
2. Meanwhile; in a bowl, mix eggs with coconut cream, salt, pepper and flour.
3. Arrange potatoes in your air fryer's pan, add coconut cream mix over them, sprinkle cheese, return to air fryer's basket and cook at 400 °F, for 10 minutes more. Divide among plates and serve as a side dish.

Nutrition Facts: Calories: 170; Fat: 4g; Fiber: 1g; Carbs: 15g; Protein: 17g

Veggie Fries Dish

(Prep + Cook Time: 40 Minutes | **Servings:** 4)

Ingredients:
- 4 parsnips; cut into medium sticks
- 2 sweet potatoes cut into medium sticks
- 4 mixed carrots cut into medium sticks
- 2 tbsp. rosemary; chopped
- 2 tbsp. olive oil
- 1 tbsp. flour
- 1/2 tsp. garlic powder
- Salt and black pepper to the taste

Instructions:
1. Put veggie fries in a bowl; add oil, garlic powder, salt, pepper, flour and rosemary and toss to coat.
2. Put the sweet potatoes in your preheated air fryer; cook them for 10 minutes at 350 °F and transfer them to a platter.
3. Put the parsnip fries in your air fryer; cook for 5 minutes and transfer over potato fries.
4. Put the carrot fries in your air fryer; cook for 15 minutes at 350 °F and transfer to the platter with the other fries. Divide veggie fries on plates and serve them as a side dish.

Nutrition Facts: Calories: 100; Fat: 0g; Fiber: 4g; Carbs: 7g; Protein: 4g

Vermouth White Mushrooms

(Prep + Cook Time: 35 Minutes | **Servings:** 4)

Ingredients:
- 2 garlic cloves; minced
- 2 lbs. white mushrooms
- 1 tbsp. olive oil
- 2 tsp. herbs de Provence
- 2 tbsp. white vermouth

Instructions:
1. In your air fryer; mix oil with mushrooms, herbs de Provence and garlic; toss and cook at 350 °F, for 20 minutes.
2. Add vermouth, toss and cook for 5 minutes more. Divide among plates and serve as a side dish.

Nutrition Facts: Calories: 121; Fat: 2g; Fiber: 5g; Carbs: 7g; Protein: 4g

Delightful Cauliflower and Broccoli

(Prep + Cook Time: 17 Minutes | **Servings:** 4)

Ingredients:
- 2 cauliflower heads; florets separated and steamed
- 1 broccoli head; florets separated and steamed
- 4 anchovies
- 1 tbsp. capers; chopped.
- Zest from 1 orange; grated
- Juice from 1 orange
- A pinch of hot pepper flakes
- Salt and black pepper to the taste
- 4 tbsp. olive oil

Instructions:
1. In a bowl; mix orange zest with orange juice, pepper flakes, anchovies, capers salt, pepper and olive oil and whisk well.
2. Add broccoli and cauliflower; toss well, transfer them to your air fryer's basket and cook at 400 °F, for 7 minutes. Divide among plates and serve as a side dish with some of the orange vinaigrette drizzled on top.

Nutrition Facts: Calories: 300; Fat: 4g; Fiber: 7g; Carbs: 28g; Protein: 4g

Parmesan Button Mushrooms

(Prep + Cook Time: 25 Minutes | **Servings:** 3)

Ingredients:
- 9 button mushroom caps
- 3 cream cracker slices; crumbled
- 1 egg white
- 2 tbsp. parmesan; grated
- 1 tsp. Italian seasoning
- 1 tbsp. butter; melted
- A pinch of salt and black pepper

Instructions:
1. In a bowl; mix crackers with egg white, parmesan, Italian seasoning, butter, salt and pepper; stir well and stuff mushrooms with this mix.
2. Arrange mushrooms in your air fryer's basket and cook them at 360 °F, for 15 minutes. Divide among plates and serve as a side dish.

Nutrition Facts: Calories: 124; Fat: 4g; Fiber: 4g; Carbs: 7g; Protein: 3g

Green Beans Dish

(Prep + Cook Time: 35 Minutes | **Servings:** 4)

Ingredients:
- 1 ½ lbs. green beans; trimmed and steamed for 2 minutes
- 1/2 lb. shallots; chopped.
- 1/4 cup almonds; toasted
- 2 tbsp. olive oil
- Salt and black pepper to the taste

Instructions:
1. In your air fryer's basket, mix green beans with salt, pepper, shallots, almonds and oil; toss well and cook at 400 °F, for 25 minutes. Divide among plates and serve as a side dish.

Nutrition Facts: Calories: 152; Fat: 3g; Fiber: 6g; Carbs: 7g; Protein: 4g

Hassel-Back Potatoes

(Prep + Cook Time: 30 Minutes | **Servings:** 2)

Ingredients:
- 2 potatoes; peeled and thinly sliced almost all the way horizontally
- 2 tbsp. olive oil
- 1 tsp. garlic; minced
- 1/2 tsp. oregano; dried
- 1/2 tsp. basil; dried
- 1/2 tsp. sweet paprika
- Salt and black pepper to the taste

Instructions:
1. In a bowl; mix oil with garlic, salt, pepper, oregano, basil and paprika and whisk really well.
2. Rub potatoes with this mix; place them in your air fryer's basket and fry them at 360 °F, for 20 minutes. Divide them on plates and serve as a side dish.

Nutrition Facts: Calories: 172; Fat: 6g; Fiber: 6g; Carbs: 9g; Protein: 6g

Greek Veggie Dish

(Prep + Cook Time: 55 Minutes | **Servings:** 4)

Ingredients:
- 1 eggplant; sliced
- 1 zucchini; sliced
- 1 thyme spring; chopped.
- 2 onions; chopped
- 4 tomatoes; cut into quarters
- 2 red bell peppers; chopped.
- 2 garlic cloves; minced
- 3 tbsp. olive oil
- 1 bay leaf
- Salt and black pepper to the taste

Instructions:
1. In your air fryer's pan; mix eggplant slices with zucchini ones, bell peppers, garlic, oil, bay leaf, thyme, onions, tomatoes, salt and pepper; toss and cook them at 300 °F, for 35 minutes. Divide among plates and serve as a side dish.

Nutrition Facts: Calories: 200; Fat: 1g; Fiber: 3g; Carbs: 7g; Protein: 6g

Potato Wedges

(Prep + Cook Time: 35 Minutes | **Servings:** 4)

Ingredients:
- 2 potatoes; cut into wedges
- 1 tbsp. olive oil
- 3 tbsp. sour cream
- 2 tbsp. sweet chili sauce
- Salt and black pepper to the taste

Instructions:
1. In a bowl; mix potato wedges with oil, salt and pepper, toss well, add to air fryer's basket and cook at 360 °F, for 25 minutes; flipping them once. Divide potato wedges on plates; drizzle sour cream and chili sauce all over and serve them as a side dish.

Nutrition Facts: Calories: 171; Fat: 8g; Fiber: 9g; Carbs: 18g; Protein: 7g

Creamy Fried Potato Dish

(Prep + Cook Time: 1 hour and 30 minutes | **Servings:** 2)

Ingredients:
- 2 bacon strips; cooked and chopped.
- 1 tsp. olive oil
- 1/3 cup cheddar cheese; shredded
- 1 big potato
- 1 tbsp. green onions; chopped.
- 1 tbsp. butter
- 2 tbsp. heavy cream
- Salt and black pepper to the taste

Instructions:
1. Rub potato with oil, season with salt and pepper, place in preheated air fryer and cook at 400 °F, for 30 minutes.
2. Flip potato, cook for 30 minutes more; transfer to a cutting board, cool it down, slice in half lengthwise and scoop pulp in a bowl.
3. Add bacon, cheese, butter, heavy cream, green onions, salt and pepper; stir well and stuff potato skins with this mix.
4. Return potatoes to your air fryer and cook them at 400 °F, for 20 minutes. Divide among plates and serve as a side dish.

Nutrition Facts: Calories: 172; Fat: 5g; Fiber: 7g; Carbs: 9g; Protein: 4g

Brussels Sprouts Dish

(Prep + Cook Time: 25 Minutes | **Servings:** 4)

Ingredients:
- 1 lb. Brussels sprouts; trimmed and halved
- 6 tsp. olive oil
- 1/2 tsp. thyme; chopped.
- 1/2 cup mayonnaise
- 2 tbsp. roasted garlic; crushed
- Salt and black pepper to the taste

Instructions:
1. In your air fryer; mix Brussels sprouts with salt, pepper and oil; toss well and cook them at 390 °F, for 15 minutes.
2. Meanwhile; in a bowl, mix thyme with mayo and garlic and whisk well. Divide Brussels sprouts on plates; drizzle garlic sauce all over and serve as a side dish.

Nutrition Facts: Calories: 172; Fat: 6g; Fiber: 8g; Carbs: 12g; Protein: 6g

Potato Chips

(Prep + Cook Time: 60 Minutes | **Servings:** 4)

Ingredients:
- 4 potatoes; scrubbed, peeled into thin chips, soaked in water for 30 minutes, drained and pat dried
- 1 tbsp. olive oil
- 2 tsp. rosemary; chopped.
- Salt to taste

Instructions:
1. In a bowl; mix potato chips with salt and oil toss to coat, place them in your air fryer's basket and cook at 330 °F, for 30 minutes. Divide among plates; sprinkle rosemary all over and serve as a side dish.

Nutrition Facts: Calories: 200; Fat: 4g; Fiber: 4g; Carbs: 14g; Protein: 5g

Garlic Potatoes

(Prep + Cook Time: 30 Minutes | **Servings:** 6)

Ingredients:
- 3 lbs. red potatoes; halved
- 5 garlic cloves; minced
- 2 tbsp. parsley; chopped.
- 1/2 tsp. basil; dried
- 2 tbsp. butter
- 1/3 cup parmesan; grated
- 1/2 tsp. oregano; dried
- 1 tsp. thyme; dried
- 2 tbsp. olive oil
- Salt and black pepper to the taste

Instructions:
1. In a bowl; mix potato halves with parsley, garlic, basil, oregano, thyme, salt, pepper, oil and butter; toss really well and transfer to your air fryer's basket.
2. Cover and cook at 400 °F, for 20 minutes; flipping them once. Sprinkle parmesan on top, divide potatoes on plates and serve as a side dish.

Nutrition Facts: Calories: 162; Fat: 5g; Fiber: 5g; Carbs: 7g; Protein: 5g

Lemony Artichokes Side Dish

(Prep + Cook Time: 25 Minutes | **Servings:** 4)

Ingredients:
- 2 medium artichokes; trimmed and halved
- 2 tbsp. lemon juice
- Cooking spray
- Salt and black pepper to the taste

Instructions:
1. Grease your air fryer with cooking spray, add artichokes; drizzle lemon juice and sprinkle salt and black pepper and cook them at 380 °F, for 15 minutes. Divide them on plates and serve as a side dish.

Nutrition Facts: Calories: 121; Fat: 3g; Fiber: 6g; Carbs: 9g; Protein: 4g

Cajun Onion Wedges Dish

(Prep + Cook Time: 25 Minutes | **Servings:** 4)

Ingredients:
- 2 big white onions; cut into wedges
- 2 eggs
- 1/2 tsp. Cajun seasoning
- 1/4 cup milk
- 1/3 cup panko
- A drizzle of olive oil
- 1 ½ tsp. paprika
- 1 tsp. garlic powder
- Salt and black pepper to the taste

Instructions:
1. In a bowl; mix panko with Cajun seasoning and oil and stir.
2. In another bowl; mix egg with milk, salt and pepper and stir.
3. Sprinkle onion wedges with paprika and garlic powder, dip them in egg mix, then in bread crumbs mix; place in your air fryer's basket, cook at 360 °F, for 10 minutes; flip and cook for 5 minutes more. Divide among plates and serve as a side dish.

Nutrition Facts: Calories: 200; Fat: 2g; Fiber: 2g; Carbs: 14g; Protein: 7g

Artichokes and Tarragon Sauce Dish
(Prep + Cook Time: 28 Minutes | **Servings:** 4)

Ingredients:
- 4 artichokes; trimmed
- 2 tbsp. tarragon; chopped
- 2 tbsp. lemon juice
- 1 celery stalk; chopped.
- 1/2 cup olive oil
- 2 tbsp. chicken stock
- Lemon zest from 2 lemons; grated
- Salt to the taste

Instructions:
1. In your food processor; mix tarragon, chicken stock, lemon zest, lemon juice, celery, salt and olive oil and pulse very well.
2. In a bowl; mix artichokes with tarragon and lemon sauce; toss well, transfer them to your air fryer's basket and cook at 380 °F, for 18 minutes.
3. Divide artichokes on plates; drizzle the rest of the sauce all over and serve as a side dish.

Nutrition Facts: Calories: 215; Fat: 3g; Fiber: 8g; Carbs: 28g; Protein: 6g

Button Mushroom Dish
(Prep + Cook Time: 18 Minutes | **Servings:** 4)

Ingredients:
- 10 button mushrooms; stems removed
- 1 tbsp. Italian seasoning
- 2 tbsp. cheddar cheese; grated
- 1 tbsp. olive oil
- 2 tbsp. mozzarella; grated
- 1 tbsp. dill; chopped
- Salt and black pepper to the taste

Instructions:
1. In a bowl; mix mushrooms with Italian seasoning, salt, pepper, oil and dill and rub well.
2. Arrange mushrooms in your air fryer's basket; sprinkle mozzarella and cheddar in each and cook them at 360 °F, for 8 minutes. Divide them on plates and serve them as a side dish.

Nutrition Facts: Calories: 241; Fat: 7g; Fiber: 8g; Carbs: 14g; Protein: 6g

Fried Creamy Cabbage
(Prep + Cook Time: 30 Minutes | **Servings:** 4)

Ingredients:
- 1 green cabbage head; chopped.
- 1 yellow onion; chopped.
- 4 bacon slices; chopped.
- 1 cup whipped cream
- 2 tbsp. cornstarch
- Salt and black pepper to the taste

Instructions:
1. Put the cabbage, bacon and onion in your air fryer.
2. In a bowl; mix cornstarch with cream, salt and pepper, stir and add over cabbage. Toss, cook at 400 °F, for 20 minutes; divide among plates and serve as a side dish.

Nutrition Facts: Calories: 208; Fat: 10g; Fiber: 3g; Carbs: 16g; Protein: 5g

Rice and Mushroom Risotto
(Prep + Cook Time: 40 Minutes | **Servings:** 4)

Ingredients:
- 1 ½ cups rice
- 2 tbsp. olive oil
- 2 yellow onions; chopped.
- 2 cups beer
- 2 cups chicken stock
- 1 tbsp. butter
- 1 cup mushrooms; sliced
- 1 tsp. basil; dried
- 1 tsp. oregano; dried
- 1/2 cup parmesan; grated

Instructions:
1. In a dish that fits your air fryer, mix oil with onions, mushrooms, basil and oregano and stir.
2. Add rice, beer, butter, stock and butter; stir again, place in your air fryer's basket and cook at 350 °F, for 30 minutes. Divide among plates and serve with grated parmesan on top as a side dish.

Nutrition Facts: Calories: 142; Fat: 4g; Fiber: 4g; Carbs: 6g; Protein: 4g

Air Fried Tomatoes
(Prep + Cook Time: 15 Minutes | Servings: 4)

Ingredients:
- 1 cup buttermilk
- 1 cup panko bread crumbs
- 2 green tomatoes; sliced
- 1/2 tbsp. Creole seasoning
- 1/2 cup flour
- Cooking spray
- Salt and black pepper to the taste

Instructions:
1. Season tomato slices with salt and pepper.
2. Put the flour in a bowl; buttermilk in another and panko crumbs and Creole seasoning in a third one.
3. Dredge tomato slices in flour; then in buttermilk and panko bread crumbs, place them in your air fryer's basket greased with cooking spray and cook them at 400 °F, for 5 minutes. Divide among plates and serve as a side dish.

Nutrition Facts: Calories: 124; Fat: 5g; Fiber: 7g; Carbs: 9g; Protein: 4g

Roasted Eggplant Dish
(Prep + Cook Time: 30 Minutes | Servings: 6)

Ingredients:
- 1 ½ lbs. eggplant; cubed
- 1 tsp. onion powder
- 1 tsp. sumac
- 1 tbsp. olive oil
- 1 tsp. garlic powder
- 2 tsp. za'atar
- Juice from 1/2 lemon
- 2 bay leaves

Instructions:
1. In your air fryer; mix eggplant cubes with oil, garlic powder, onion powder, sumac, za'atar, lemon juice and bay leaves; toss and cook at 370 °F, for 20 minutes. Divide among plates and serve as a side dish.

Nutrition Facts: Calories: 172; Fat: 4g; Fiber: 7g; Carbs: 12g; Protein: 3g

Tortilla Chips
(Prep + Cook Time: 16 Minutes | Servings: 4)

Ingredients:
- 8 corn tortillas; cut into triangles
- 1 tbsp. olive oil
- A pinch of garlic powder
- A pinch of sweet paprika
- Salt and black pepper to the taste

Instructions:
1. In a bowl; mix tortilla chips with oil, add salt, pepper, garlic powder and paprika; toss well, place them in your air fryer's basket and cook them at 400 °F, for 6 minutes. Serve them as a side for a fish dish.

Nutrition Facts: Calories: 53; Fat: 1g; Fiber: 1g; Carbs: 6g; Protein: 4g

Roasted Carrots
(Prep + Cook Time: 30 Minutes | Servings: 4)

Ingredients:
- 1 lb. baby carrots
- 4 tbsp. orange juice
- 2 tsp. olive oil
- 1 tsp. herbs de Provence

Instructions:

1. In your air fryer's basket, mix carrots with herbs de Provence, oil and orange juice; toss and cook at 320 °F, for 20 minutes. Divide among plates and serve as a side dish.

Nutrition Facts: Calories: 112; Fat: 2g; Fiber: 3g; Carbs: 4g; Protein: 3g

Pumpkin Rice Dish

(**Prep + Cook Time:** 35 Minutes | **Servings:** 4)

Ingredients:
- 12 oz. white rice
- 4 cups chicken stock
- 6 oz. pumpkin puree
- 2 tbsp. olive oil
- 1 small yellow onion; chopped.
- 2 garlic cloves; minced
- 1/2 tsp. nutmeg
- 1 tsp. thyme; chopped
- 1/2 tsp. ginger; grated
- 1/2 tsp. cinnamon powder
- 1/2 tsp. allspice
- 4 oz. heavy cream

Instructions:
1. In a dish that fits your air fryer; mix oil with onion, garlic, rice, stock, pumpkin puree, nutmeg, thyme, ginger, cinnamon, allspice and cream; stir well,
2. place in your air fryer's basket and cook at 360 °F, for 30 minutes. Divide among plates and serve as a side dish.

Nutrition Facts: Calories: 261; Fat: 6g; Fiber: 7g; Carbs: 29g; Protein: 4g

Yummy Biscuits

(**Prep + Cook Time:** 30 Minutes | **Servings:** 8)

Ingredients:
- 2 ⅓ cup self-rising flour
- 1/2 cup cheddar cheese; grated
- 1 ⅓ cup buttermilk
- 1 cup flour
- 1/2 cup butter+ 1 tablespoon; melted
- 2 tbsp. sugar

Instructions:
1. In a bowl; mix self-rising flour with 1/2 cup butter, sugar, cheddar cheese and buttermilk and stir until you obtain a dough.
2. Spread 1 cup flour on a working surface, roll dough, flatten it, cut 8 circles with a cookie cutter and coat them with flour.
3. Line your air fryer's basket with tin foil, add biscuits, brush them with melted butter and cook them at 380 °F, for 20 minutes. Divide among plates and serve as a side.

Nutrition Facts: Calories: 221; Fat: 3g; Fiber: 8g; Carbs: 12g; Protein: 4g

Mushroom Cakes

(**Prep + Cook Time:** 18 Minutes | **Servings:** 8)

Ingredients:
- 4 oz. mushrooms; chopped
- 1 yellow onion; chopped.
- 1/2 tsp. nutmeg; ground
- 2 tbsp. olive oil
- 1 tbsp. butter
- 1 ½ tbsp. flour
- 1 tbsp. bread crumbs
- 14 oz. milk
- Salt and black pepper to the taste

Instructions:
1. Heat up a pan with the butter over medium high heat; add onion and mushrooms; stir, cook for 3 minutes, add flour, stir well again and take off heat.
2. Add milk gradually, salt, pepper and nutmeg; stir and leave aside to cool down completely.
3. In a bowl; mix oil with bread crumbs and whisk.
4. Take spoonfuls of the mushroom filling, add to breadcrumbs mix, coat well, shape patties out of this mix; place them in your air fryer's basket and cook at 400 °F, for 8 minutes. Divide among plates and serve as a side for a steak

Nutrition Facts: Calories: 192; Fat: 2g; Fiber: 1g; Carbs: 16g; Protein: 6g

Carrots and Rhubarb Dish

(Prep + Cook Time: 50 Minutes | **Servings:** 4)

Ingredients:
- 1 orange; peeled, cut into medium segments and zest grated
- 1 lb. baby carrots
- 2 tsp. walnut oil
- 1 lb. rhubarb; roughly chopped.
- 1/2 cup walnuts; halved
- 1/2 tsp. stevia

Instructions:
1. Add the oil in your air fryer, add carrots; toss and fry them at 380 °F, for 20 minutes.
2. Add rhubarb, orange zest, stevia and walnuts; toss and cook for 20 minutes more. Add orange segments; toss and serve as a side dish.

Nutrition Facts: Calories: 172; Fat: 2g; Fiber: 3g; Carbs: 4g; Protein: 4g

Potato Casserole Dish

(Prep + Cook Time: 55 Minutes | **Servings:** 4)

Ingredients:
- 3 lbs. sweet potatoes; scrubbed
- 1/4 cup milk
- 2 tbsp. white flour
- 1/4 tsp. allspice; ground
- 1/2 tsp. nutmeg; ground
- Salt to the taste

For the topping:
- 1/2 cup almond flour
- 1/2 cup walnuts; soaked, drained and ground
- 1/4 cup sugar
- 1 tsp. cinnamon powder
- 5 tbsp. butter
- 1/4 cup pecans; soaked, drained and ground
- 1/4 cup coconut; shredded
- 1 tbsp. chia seeds

Instructions:
1. Place potatoes in your air fryer's basket, prick them with a fork and cook at 360 °F, for 30 minutes.
2. Meanwhile; in a bowl, mix almond flour with pecans, walnuts, 1/4 cup coconut, 1/4 cup sugar, chia seeds, 1 tsp. cinnamon and the butter and stir everything.
3. Transfer potatoes to a cutting board, cool them, peel and place them in a baking pan that fits your air fryer.
4. Add milk, flour, salt, nutmeg and allspice and stir
5. Add crumble mix you've made earlier on top; place dish in your air fryer's basket and cook at 400 °F, for 8 minutes. Divide among plates and serve as a side dish.

Nutrition Facts: Calories: 162; Fat: 4g; Fiber: 8g; Carbs: 18g; Protein: 4g

Tasty Barley Risotto

(Prep + Cook Time: 40 Minutes | **Servings:** 8)

Ingredients:
- 2 lbs. sweet potato; peeled and chopped.
- 5 cups veggie stock
- 1 tsp. thyme; dried
- 1 tsp. tarragon; dried
- 3 tbsp. olive oil
- 2 yellow onions; chopped.
- 2 garlic cloves; minced
- 3/4 lb. barley
- 3 oz. mushrooms; sliced
- 2 oz. skim milk
- Salt and black pepper to the taste

Instructions:
1. Put the stock in a pot, add barley; stir, bring to a boil over medium heat and cook for 15 minutes.
2. Pre-heat your air fryer at 350 degrees F; add oil and heat it up.
3. Add barley, onions, garlic, mushrooms, milk, salt, pepper, tarragon and sweet potato; stir and cook for 15 minutes more. Divide among plates and serve as a side dish.

Nutrition Facts: Calories: 124; Fat: 4g; Fiber: 4g; Carbs: 6g; Protein: 4g

Zucchini Fries Dish
(Prep + Cook Time: 22 Minutes | Servings: 4)
Ingredients:
- 1 zucchini; cut into medium sticks
- A drizzle of olive oil
- 2 eggs; whisked
- 1 cup bread crumbs
- 1/2 cup flour
- Salt and black pepper to the taste

Instructions:
1. Put the flour in a bowl and mix with salt and pepper and stir.
2. Put the breadcrumbs in another bowl.
3. In a third bowl mix eggs with a pinch of salt and pepper.
4. Dredge zucchini fries in flour; then in eggs and in bread crumbs at the end.
5. Grease your air fryer with some olive oil, heat up at 400 degrees F; add zucchini fries and cook them for 12 minutes. Serve them as a side dish.

Nutrition Facts: Calories: 172; Fat: 3g; Fiber: 3g; Carbs: 7g; Protein: 3g

Avocado Fries Dish
(Prep + Cook Time: 20 Minutes | Servings: 4)
Ingredients:
- 1 avocado; pitted, peeled, sliced and cut into medium fries
- 1/2 cup panko bread crumbs
- 1 tbsp. lemon juice
- 1 egg; whisked
- 1 tbsp. olive oil
- Salt and black pepper to the taste

Instructions:
1. In a bowl; mix panko with salt and pepper and stir.
2. In another bowl; mix egg with a pinch of salt and whisk.
3. In a third bowl; mix avocado fries with lemon juice and oil and toss.
4. Dip fries in egg, then in panko, place them in your air fryer's basket and cook at 390 °F, for 10 minutes; shake the basket every few minutes to ensure even cooking. Divide among plates and serve as a side dish.

Nutrition Facts: Calories: 130; Fat: 11g; Fiber: 3g; Carbs: 16g; Protein: 4g

Maple Glazed Beets
(Prep + Cook Time: 50 Minutes | Servings: 8)
Ingredients:
- 3 lbs. small beets; trimmed
- 1 tbsp. duck fat
- 4 tbsp. maple syrup

Instructions:
1. Pre-heat your air fryer at 360 degrees F; add duck fat and heat it up.
2. Add beets and maple syrup; toss and cook for 40 minutes. Divide among plates and serve as a side dish.

Nutrition Facts: Calories: 121; Fat: 3g; Fiber: 2g; Carbs: 3g; Protein: 4g

Beet Wedges Dish
(Prep + Cook Time: 25 Minutes | Servings: 4)
Ingredients:
- 4 beets; washed, peeled and cut into large wedges
- 1 tbsp. olive oil
- 2 garlic cloves; minced
- 1 tsp. lemon juice
- Salt and black to the taste

Instructions:
1. In a bowl; mix beets with oil, salt, pepper, garlic and lemon juice; toss well, transfer to your air fryer's basket and cook them at 400 °F, for 15 minutes. Divide beets wedges on plates and serve as a side dish.

Nutrition Facts: Calories: 182; Fat: 6g; Fiber: 3g; Carbs: 8g; Protein: 2g

Eggplant Dish

(Prep + Cook Time: 20 Minutes | **Servings:** 4)

Ingredients:
- 8 baby eggplants; scooped in the center and pulp reserved
- 1/2 tsp. garlic powder
- 1 tbsp. olive oil
- 1 yellow onion; chopped.
- A pinch of oregano; dried
- 1 green bell pepper; chopped.
- 1 tbsp. tomato paste
- 1 bunch coriander; chopped
- 1 tomato chopped
- Salt and black pepper to the taste

Instructions:
1. Heat up a pan with the oil over medium heat, add onion; stir and cook for 1 minute.
2. Add salt, pepper, eggplant pulp, oregano, green bell pepper, tomato paste, garlic power, coriander and tomato; stir, cook for 1-2 minutes more, take off heat and cool down.
3. Stuff eggplants with this mix, place them in your air fryer's basket and cook at 360 °F, for 8 minutes. Divide eggplants on plates and serve them as a side dish.

Nutrition Facts: Calories: 200; Fat: 3g; Fiber: 7g; Carbs: 12g; Protein: 4g

Zucchini Croquettes

(Prep + Cook Time: 20 Minutes | **Servings:** 4)

Ingredients:
- 1 carrot; grated
- 1 zucchini; grated
- 2 slices of bread; crumbled
- 1 egg
- 1/2 tsp. sweet paprika
- 1 tsp. garlic; minced
- 2 tbsp. parmesan cheese; grated
- 1 tbsp. corn flour
- Salt and black pepper to the taste

Instructions:
1. Put zucchini in a bowl; add salt, leave aside for 10 minutes; squeeze excess water and transfer them to another bowl.
2. Add carrots, salt, pepper, paprika, garlic, flour, parmesan, egg and bread crumbs; stir well, shape 8 croquettes, place them in your air fryer and cook at 360 °F, for 10 minutes. Divide among plates and serve as a side dish

Nutrition Facts: Calories: 100; Fat: 3g; Fiber: 1g; Carbs: 7g; Protein: 4g

Air Fried Red Cabbage

(Prep + Cook Time: 25 Minutes | **Servings:** 4)

Ingredients:
- 1/2 cup yellow onion; chopped
- 4 garlic cloves; minced
- 1 tbsp. apple cider vinegar
- 1 cup applesauce
- 1 tbsp. olive oil
- 6 cups red cabbage; chopped
- 1 cup veggie stock
- Salt and black pepper to the taste

Instructions:
1. In a heat proof dish that fits your air fryer; mix cabbage with onion, garlic, oil, stock, vinegar, applesauce, salt and pepper; toss really well, place dish in your air fryer's basket and cook at 380 °F, for 15 minutes. Divide among plates and serve as a side dish.

Nutrition Facts: Calories: 172; Fat: 7g; Fiber: 7g; Carbs: 14g; Protein: 5g

Yellow Squash and Zucchinis Dish

(**Prep + Cook Time:** 45 Minutes | **Servings:** 4)

Ingredients:
- 1 yellow squash; halved, deseeded and cut into chunks
- 6 tsp. olive oil
- 1 lb. zucchinis; sliced
- 1/2 lb. carrots; cubed
- 1 tbsp. tarragon; chopped
- Salt and white pepper to the taste

Instructions:
1. In your air fryer's basket; mix zucchinis with carrots, squash, salt, pepper and oil; toss well and cook at 400 °F, for 25 minutes. Divide them on plates and serve as a side dish with tarragon sprinkled on top.

Nutrition Facts: Calories: 160; Fat: 2g; Fiber: 1g; Carbs: 5g; Protein: 5g

Tasty Potatoes Patties

(**Prep + Cook Time:** 18 Minutes | **Servings:** 4)

Ingredients:
- 4 potatoes; cubed, boiled and mashed
- 1 cup parmesan; grated
- 2 tbsp. white flour
- 3 tbsp. chives; chopped.
- A pinch of nutmeg
- 2 egg yolks
- Salt and black pepper to the taste

For the breading:
- 1/4 cup white flour
- 3 tbsp. vegetable oil
- 1/4 cup bread crumbs
- 2 eggs; whisked

Instructions:
1. In a bowl; mix mashed potatoes with egg yolks, salt, pepper, nutmeg, parmesan, chives and 2 tbsp. flour; stir well, shape medium cakes and place them on a plate.
2. In another bowl; mix vegetable oil with bread crumbs and stir.
3. Put whisked eggs in a third bowl and 1/4 cup flour in a forth one. Dip cakes in flour, then in eggs and in breadcrumbs at the end; place them in your air fryer's basket, cook them at 390 °F, for 8 minutes; divide among plates and serve as a side dish.

Nutrition Facts: Calories: 140; Fat: 3g; Fiber: 4g; Carbs: 17g; Protein: 4g

Colored Veggie Rice Recipe

(**Prep + Cook Time:** 35 Minutes | **Servings:** 4)

Ingredients:
- 1 cup mixed carrots; peas, corn and green beans
- 2 cups basmati rice
- 2 cups water
- 1/2 tsp. green chili; minced
- 1/2 tsp. ginger; grated
- 5 black peppercorns
- 2 whole cardamoms
- 3 garlic cloves; minced
- 2 tbsp. butter
- 1 tsp. cinnamon powder
- 1 tbsp. cumin seeds
- 2 bay leaves
- 3 whole cloves
- 1 tbsp. sugar
- Salt to the taste

Instructions:
1. Pour the water in a heat proof dish that fits your air fryer
2. Add rice, mixed veggies, green chili, grated ginger, garlic cloves, cinnamon, cloves, butter, cumin seeds, bay leaves, cardamoms, black peppercorns, salt and sugar; stir, put it in your air fryer's basket and cook at 370 °F, for 25 minutes.
3. Divide among plates and serve as a side dish.

Nutrition Facts: Calories: 283; Fat: 4g; Fiber: 8g; Carbs: 34g; Protein: 14g

Brussels Sprouts and Pomegranate Seeds Dish

(Prep + Cook Time: 15 Minutes **| Servings:** 4)

Ingredients:
- 1 lb. Brussels sprouts; trimmed and halved
- 1 cup pomegranate seeds
- 1/4 cup pine nuts; toasted
- 1 tbsp. olive oil
- 2 tbsp. veggie stock
- Salt and black pepper to the taste

Instructions:
1. In a heat proof dish that fits your air fryer; mix Brussels sprouts with salt, pepper, pomegranate seeds, pine nuts, oil and stock; stir, place in your air fryer's basket and cook at 390 °F, for 10 minutes.
2. Divide among plates and serve as a side dish.

Nutrition Facts: Calories: 152; Fat: 4g; Fiber: 7g; Carbs: 12g; Protein: 3g

Corn with Cheese and Lime

(Prep + Cook Time: 25 Minutes **| Servings:** 2)

Ingredients:
- 2 corns on the cob; husks removed
- 1/2 cup feta cheese; grated
- 2 tsp. sweet paprika
- A drizzle of olive oil
- Juice from 2 limes

Instructions:
1. Rub corn with oil and paprika, place in your air fryer and cook at 400 °F, for 15 minutes; flipping once. Divide corn on plates; sprinkle cheese on top, drizzle lime juice and serve as a side dish.

Nutrition Facts: Calories: 200; Fat: 5g; Fiber: 2g; Carbs: 6g; Protein: 6g

Fried Broccoli

(Prep + Cook Time: 30 Minutes **| Servings:** 4)

Ingredients:
- 1 broccoli head; florets separated
- 1 tbsp. duck fat
- 3 garlic cloves; minced
- Juice from 1/2 lemon
- 1 tbsp. sesame seeds

Instructions:
1. Pre-heat your air fryer at 350 degrees F; add duck fat and heat as well.
2. Add broccoli, garlic, lemon juice and sesame seeds; toss and cook for 20 minutes. Divide among plates and serve as a side dish.

Nutrition Facts: Calories: 132; Fat: 3g; Fiber: 3g; Carbs: 6g; Protein: 4g

Onion Rings Dish

(Prep + Cook Time: 20 Minutes **| Servings:** 3)

Ingredients:
- 1 onion cut into medium slices and rings separated
- 1¼ cups white flour
- 1 tsp. baking powder
- A pinch of salt
- 1 egg
- 1 cup milk
- 3/4 cup bread crumbs

Instructions:
1. In a bowl; mix flour with salt and baking powder; stir, dredge onion rings in this mix and place them on a separate plate.
2. Add milk and egg to flour mix and whisk well.
3. Dip onion rings in this mix, dredge them in breadcrumbs; put them in your air fryer's basket and cook them at 360 °F, for 10 minutes. Divide among plates and serve as a side dish for a steak.

Nutrition Facts: Calories: 140; Fat: 8g; Fiber: 20g; Carbs: 12g; Protein: 3g

Roasted Peppers Dish

(Prep + Cook Time: 20 Minutes | **Servings:** 4)

Ingredients:
- 1 red bell pepper
- 1 green bell pepper
- 1 yellow bell pepper
- 1 lettuce head; cut into strips
- 1 oz. rocket leaves
- 1 tbsp. lemon juice
- 3 tbsp. Greek yogurt
- 2 tbsp. olive oil
- Salt and black pepper to the taste

Instructions:
1. Place bell peppers in your air fryer's basket, cook at 400 °F, for 10 minutes; transfer to a bowl, leave aside for 10 minutes; peel them, discard seeds, cut them in strips, transfer to a larger bowl; add rocket leaves and lettuce strips and toss.
2. In a bowl; mix oil with lemon juice, yogurt, salt and pepper and whisk well. Add this over bell peppers mix, toss to coat, divide among plates and serve as a side salad.

Nutrition Facts: Calories: 170; Fat: 1g; Fiber: 1g; Carbs: 2g; Protein: 6g

Creamy Brussels Sprouts Side Dish

(Prep + Cook Time: 35 Minutes | **Servings:** 8)

Ingredients:
- 3 lbs. Brussels sprouts; halved
- A drizzle of olive oil
- 1 lb. bacon; chopped
- 4 tbsp. butter
- 3 shallots; chopped
- 1 cup milk
- 2 cups heavy cream
- 1/4 tsp. nutmeg; ground
- 3 tbsp. prepared horseradish
- Salt and black pepper to the taste

Instructions:
1. Preheated you air fryer at 370 degrees F; add oil, bacon, salt and pepper and Brussels sprouts and toss.
2. Add butter, shallots, heavy cream, milk, nutmeg and horseradish; toss again and cook for 25 minutes. Divide among plates and serve as a side dish.

Nutrition Facts: Calories: 214; Fat: 5g; Fiber: 8g; Carbs: 12g; Protein: 5g

Flavored Cauliflower Dish

(Prep + Cook Time: 20 Minutes | **Servings:** 4)

Ingredients:
- 12 cauliflower florets; steamed
- 1/4 tsp. turmeric powder
- 1½ tsp. red chili powder
- 1 tbsp. ginger; grated
- 2 tsp. lemon juice
- 3 tbsp. white flour
- 1/2 tsp. corn flour
- 2 tbsp. water
- Cooking spray
- Salt and black pepper to the taste

Instructions:
1. In a bowl; mix chili powder with turmeric powder, ginger paste, salt, pepper, lemon juice, white flour, corn flour and water, stir, add cauliflower, toss well and transfer them to your air fryer's basket. Coat them with cooking spray, cook them at 400 °F, for 10 minutes, divide among plates and serve as a side dish.

Nutrition Facts: Calories: 70; Fat: 1g; Fiber: 2g; Carbs: 12g; Protein: 3g

Creamy Potatoes Dish

(**Prep + Cook Time:** 30 Minutes | **Servings:** 4)

Ingredients:
- 1 ½ lbs. potatoes; peeled and cubed
- 2 tbsp. olive oil
- 1 tbsp. hot paprika
- 1 cup Greek yogurt
- Salt and black pepper to the taste

Instructions:
1. Put the potatoes in a bowl; add water to cover, leave aside for 10 minutes; drain, pat dry them, transfer to another bowl; add salt, pepper, paprika and half of the oil and toss them well.
2. Put the potatoes in your air fryer's basket and cook at 360 °F, for 20 minutes.
3. In a bowl; mix yogurt with salt, pepper and the rest of the oil and whisk. Divide potatoes on plates, drizzle yogurt dressing all over; toss them and serve as a side dish.

Nutrition Facts: Calories: 170; Fat: 3g; Fiber: 5g; Carbs: 20g; Protein: 5g

Brussels Sprouts and Potatoes

(**Prep + Cook Time:** 18 Minutes | **Servings:** 4)

Ingredients:
- 1 ½ lbs. Brussels sprouts; washed and trimmed
- 1 cup new potatoes; chopped
- 1 ½ tbsp. butter
- 1 ½ tbsp. bread crumbs
- Salt and black pepper to the taste

Instructions:
1. Put the Brussels sprouts and potatoes in your air fryer's pan, add bread crumbs, salt, pepper and butter
2. Toss well and cook at 400 °F, for 8 minutes.
3. Divide among plates and serve as a side dish.

Nutrition Facts: Calories: 152; Fat: 3g; Fiber: 7g; Carbs: 17g; Protein: 4g

Roasted Peppers Dish

(**Prep + Cook Time:** 30 Minutes | **Servings:** 4)

Ingredients:
- 4 red bell peppers; cut into medium strips
- 4 green bell peppers; cut into medium strips
- 4 yellow bell peppers; cut into medium strips
- 1 yellow onion; chopped
- 1 tbsp. sweet paprika
- 1 tbsp. olive oil
- Salt and black pepper to the taste

Instructions:
1. In your air fryer; mix red bell peppers with green and yellow ones.
2. Add paprika, oil, onion, salt and pepper; toss and cook at 350 °F, for 20 minutes. Divide among plates and serve as a side dish.

Nutrition Facts: Calories: 142; Fat: 4g; Fiber: 4g; Carbs: 7g; Protein: 4g

Wild Rice Pilaf

(**Prep + Cook Time:** 35 Minutes | **Servings:** 12)

Ingredients:
- 1 shallot; chopped.
- 1 tsp. garlic; minced
- A drizzle of olive oil
- 1 cup farro
- 1/2 cup hazelnuts; toasted and chopped
- 3/4 cup cherries; dried
- 3/4 cup wild rice
- 4 cups chicken stock
- Salt and black pepper to the taste
- 1 tbsp. parsley; chopped.
- Chopped chives for serving

Instructions:
1. In a dish that fits your air fryer; mix shallot with garlic, oil, faro, wild rice, stock, salt, pepper, parsley, hazelnuts and cherries; stir, place in your air fryer's basket and cook at 350 °F, for 25 minutes. Divide among plates and serve as a side dish.

Nutrition Facts: Calories: 142; Fat: 4g; Fiber: 4g; Carbs: 16g; Protein: 4g

Rice and Sausage Dish

(**Prep + Cook Time:** 30 Minutes | **Servings:** 4)

Ingredients:
- 2 cups white rice; already boiled
- 1 tbsp. butter
- Salt and black pepper to the taste
- 4 garlic cloves; minced
- 2 tbsp. carrot; chopped.
- 3 tbsp. cheddar cheese; grated
- 1 pork sausage; chopped
- 2 tbsp. mozzarella cheese; shredded

Instructions:
1. Pre-heat your air fryer at 350 degrees F; add butter, melt it, add garlic, stir and brown for 2 minutes.
2. Add sausage, salt, pepper, carrots and rice; stir and cook at 350 °F, for 10 minutes. Add cheddar and mozzarella; toss, divide among plates and serve as a side dish.

Nutrition Facts: Calories: 240; Fat: 12g; Fiber: 5g; Carbs: 20g; Protein: 13g

Cauliflower Bars

(**Prep + Cook Time:** 35 Minutes | **Servings:** 12)

Ingredients:
- 1 big cauliflower head; florets separated
- 1 tsp. Italian seasoning
- 1/2 cup mozzarella; shredded
- 1/4 cup egg whites
- Salt and black pepper to the taste

Instructions:
1. Put the cauliflower florets in your food processor; pulse well, spread on a lined baking pan that fits your air fryer, place them in the fryer and cook at 360 °F, for 10 minutes.
2. Transfer cauliflower to a bowl; add salt, pepper, cheese, egg whites and Italian seasoning; stir really well, spread this into a rectangle pan that fits your air fryer; press well, lock the air fryer basket and cook at 360 °F, for 15 minutes more. Cut into 12 bars, arrange them on a platter and serve as a snack

Nutrition Facts: Calories: 50; Fat: 1g; Fiber: 2g; Carbs: 3g; Protein: 3g

Vegetable Recipes

Beet, Tomato and Goat Cheese Mix Recipe
(Prep + Cook Time: 44 Minutes | **Servings:** 8)

Ingredients:
- 8 small beets; trimmed, peeled and halved
- 1 red onion; sliced
- 2 tbsp. sugar
- 1 pint mixed cherry tomatoes; halved
- 2 oz. pecans
- 2 tbsp. olive oil
- 4 oz. goat cheese; crumbled
- 1 tbsp. balsamic vinegar
- Salt and black pepper to the taste

Instructions:
1. Put the beets in your air fryer, season them with salt and pepper, cook at 350 °F, for 14 minutes and transfer to a salad bowl
2. Add onion, cherry tomatoes and pecans and toss
3. In another bowl, mix vinegar with sugar and oil, whisk well until sugar dissolves and add to salad. Also add goat cheese, toss and serve.

Nutrition Facts: Calories: 124; Fat: 7g; Fiber: 5g; Carbs: 12g; Protein: 6g

Flavored Fennel Recipe
(Prep + Cook Time: 18 Minutes | **Servings:** 4)

Ingredients:
- 2 fennel bulbs; cut into quarters
- 3 tbsp. olive oil
- Juice from 1/2 lemon
- Salt and black pepper to the taste
- 1 garlic clove; minced
- 1 red chili pepper; chopped
- 3/4 cup veggie stock
- 1/4 cup white wine
- 1/4 cup parmesan; grated

Instructions:
1. Heat up a pan that fits your air fryer with the oil over medium high heat, add garlic and chili pepper; stir and cook for 2 minutes
2. Add fennel, salt, pepper, stock, wine, lemon juice, and parmesan, toss to coat, close the air fryer basket and cook at 350 °F, for 6 minutes. Divide among plates and serve right away.

Nutrition Facts: Calories: 100; Fat: 4g; Fiber: 8g; Carbs: 4g; Protein: 4g

Broccoli Salad Recipe
(Prep + Cook Time: 18 Minutes | **Servings:** 4)

Ingredients:
- 1 broccoli head; florets separated
- 1 tbsp. Chinese rice wine vinegar
- 1 tbsp. peanut oil
- 6 garlic cloves; minced
- Salt and black pepper to the taste

Instructions:
1. In a bowl; mix broccoli with salt, pepper and half of the oil, toss, transfer to your air fryer and cook at 350 °F, for 8 minutes; shake the basket in the middle of the cooking to ensure even cooking.
2. Transfer broccoli to a salad bowl, add the rest of the peanut oil, garlic and rice vinegar, toss really well and serve.

Nutrition Facts: Calories: 121; Fat: 3g; Fiber: 4g; Carbs: 4g; Protein: 4g

Brussels Sprouts and Butter Sauce Recipe

(**Prep + Cook Time:** 14 Minutes | **Servings:** 4)

Ingredients:
- 1 lb. Brussels sprouts; trimmed
- 1/2 cup bacon; cooked and chopped.
- 2 tbsp. dill; finely chopped.
- 1 tbsp. mustard
- Salt and black pepper to the taste
- 1 tbsp. butter

Instructions:
1. Put the Brussels sprouts in your air fryer and cook them at 350 °F, for 10 minutes
2. Heat up a pan with the butter over medium high heat, add bacon, mustard and dill and whisk well. Divide Brussels sprouts on plates, drizzle butter sauce all over and serve.

Nutrition Facts: Calories: 162; Fat: 8g; Fiber: 8g; Carbs: 14g; Protein: 5g

Collard Greens and Turkey Wings Recipe

(**Prep + Cook Time:** 30 Minutes | **Servings:** 6)

Ingredients:
- 1 sweet onion; chopped
- 2 smoked turkey wings
- 2 tbsp. olive oil
- 3 garlic cloves; minced
- 2 ½ lbs. collard greens; chopped.
- 2 tbsp. apple cider vinegar
- 1 tbsp. brown sugar
- Salt and black pepper to the taste
- 1/2 tsp. crushed red pepper

Instructions:
1. Heat up a pan that fits your air fryer with the oil over medium high heat, add onions, add garlic, greens, vinegar, salt, pepper, crushed red pepper, sugar and smoked turkey, stir and cook for 2 minutes. Transfer it to the preheated air fryer and cook at 350 °F, for 15 minutes
2. Divide greens and turkey on plates and serve.

Nutrition Facts: Calories: 262; Fat: 4g; Fiber: 8g; Carbs: 12g; Protein: 4g

Swiss Chard and Sausage Recipe

(**Prep + Cook Time:** 30 Minutes | **Servings:** 8)

Ingredients:
- 8 cups Swiss chard; chopped
- 1/2 cup onion; chopped
- 1/4 cup parmesan; grated
- 1 lb. sausage; chopped
- 1 tbsp. olive oil
- 1 garlic clove; minced
- Salt and black pepper to the taste
- 3 eggs
- 2 cups ricotta cheese
- 1 cup mozzarella; shredded
- A pinch of nutmeg

Instructions:
1. Heat up a pan that fits your air fryer with the oil over medium heat, add onions, garlic, Swiss chard, salt, pepper and nutmeg; stir, cook for 2 minutes and take off heat
2. In a bowl; whisk eggs with mozzarella, parmesan and ricotta; stir, pour over Swiss chard mix, toss, close the air fryer basket and cook at 320 °F, for 17 minutes. Divide among plates and serve.

Nutrition Facts: Calories: 332; Fat: 13g; Fiber: 3g; Carbs: 14g; Protein: 23g

Collard Greens and Bacon Recipe
(Prep + Cook Time: 22 Minutes | Servings: 4)

Ingredients:
- 1 lb. collard greens
- 1 tbsp. apple cider vinegar
- 2 tbsp. chicken stock
- 3 bacon strips; chopped
- 1/4 cup cherry tomatoes; halved
- Salt and black pepper to the taste

Instructions:
1. Heat up a pan that fits your air fryer over medium heat, add bacon; stir and cook 1-2 minutes
2. Add tomatoes, collard greens, vinegar, stock, salt and pepper; stir, close the air fryer basket and cook at 320 °F, for 10 minutes. Divide among plates and serve

Nutrition Facts: Calories: 120; Fat: 3g; Fiber: 1g; Carbs: 3g; Protein: 7g

Green Beans Recipe
(Prep + Cook Time: 25 Minutes | Servings: 4)

Ingredients:
- 1 lb. red potatoes; cut into wedges
- 2 garlic cloves; minced
- 2 tbsp. olive oil
- 1 lb. green beans
- Salt and black pepper to the taste
- 1/2 tsp. oregano; dried

Instructions:
1. In a pan that fits your air fryer, combine potatoes with green beans, garlic, oil, salt, pepper and oregano, toss, close the air fryer basket and cook at 380 °F, for 15 minutes. Divide among plates and serve

Nutrition Facts: Calories: 211; Fat: 6g; Fiber: 7g; Carbs: 8g; Protein: 5g

Cheesy Brussels Sprouts Recipe
(Prep + Cook Time: 18 Minutes | Servings: 4)

Ingredients:
- 1 lb. Brussels sprouts; washed
- Juice of 1 lemon
- 2 tbsp. butter
- 3 tbsp. parmesan; grated
- Salt and black pepper to the taste

Instructions:
1. Put the Brussels sprouts in your air fryer, cook them at 350 °F, for 8 minutes and transfer them to a bowl
2. Heat up a pan with the butter over medium heat, add lemon juice, salt and pepper, whisk well and add to Brussels sprouts. Add parmesan, toss until parmesan melts and serve.

Nutrition Facts: Calories: 152; Fat: 6g; Fiber: 6g; Carbs: 8g; Protein: 12g

Okra and Corn Salad Recipe
(Prep + Cook Time: 22 Minutes | Servings: 6)

Ingredients:
- 1 lb. okra; trimmed
- 6 scallions; chopped
- 28 oz. canned tomatoes; chopped.
- 3 green bell peppers; chopped
- Salt and black pepper to the taste
- 2 tbsp. olive oil
- 1 tsp. sugar
- 1 cup con

Instructions:
1. Heat up a pan that fits your air fryer with the oil over medium high heat, add scallions and bell peppers; stir and cook for 5 minutes
2. Add okra, salt, pepper, sugar, tomatoes and corn; stir, close the air fryer basket and cook at 360 °F, for 7 minutes. Divide okra mix on plates and serve warm.

Nutrition Facts: Calories: 152; Fat: 4g; Fiber: 3g; Carbs: 18g; Protein: 4g

Artichokes and Sauce Recipe
(Prep + Cook Time: 16 Minutes | Servings: 2)

Ingredients:
- 2 artichokes; trimmed
- 2 garlic cloves; minced

For the sauce:
- 3 anchovy fillets
- 1/4 cup coconut oil
- A drizzle of olive oil
- 1 tbsp. lemon juice
- 1/4 cup extra virgin olive oil
- 3 garlic cloves

Instructions:
1. In a bowl; mix artichokes with oil, 2 garlic cloves and lemon juice, toss well, transfer to your air fryer, cook at 350 °F, for 6 minutes and divide among plates
2. In your food processor, mix coconut oil with anchovy, 3 garlic cloves and olive oil, blend very well, drizzle over artichokes and serve.

Nutrition Facts: Calories: 261; Fat: 4g; Fiber: 7g; Carbs: 20g; Protein: 12g

Eggplant Hash Recipe
(Prep + Cook Time: 30 Minutes | Servings: 4)

Ingredients:
- 1 eggplant; roughly chopped.
- 1/2 lb. cherry tomatoes; halved
- 1/2 cup olive oil
- 1 tsp. Tabasco sauce
- 1/4 cup mint; chopped
- 1/4 cup basil; chopped
- Salt and black pepper to the taste

Instructions:
1. Heat up a pan that fits your air fryer with half of the oil over medium high heat, add eggplant pieces, cook for 3 minutes; flip, cook them for 3 minutes more and transfer to a bowl
2. Heat up the same pan with the rest of the oil over medium high heat, add tomatoes; stir and cook for 1-2 minutes.
3. Return eggplant pieces to the pan, add salt, black pepper, basil, mint and Tabasco sauce, close the air fryer basket and cook at 320 °F, for 6 minutes. Divide among plates and serve

Nutrition Facts: Calories: 120; Fat: 1g; Fiber: 4g; Carbs: 8g; Protein: 15g

Brussels Sprouts and Tomatoes Mix Recipe
(Prep + Cook Time: 15 Minutes | Servings: 4)

Ingredients:
- 1 lb. Brussels sprouts; trimmed
- 6 cherry tomatoes; halved
- 1/4 cup green onions; chopped.
- 1 tbsp. olive oil
- Salt and black pepper to the taste

Instructions:
1. Season Brussels sprouts with salt and pepper, put them in your air fryer and cook at 350 °F, for 10 minutes
2. Transfer them to a bowl, add salt, pepper, cherry tomatoes, green onions and olive oil, toss well and serve.

Nutrition Facts: Calories: 121; Fat: 4g; Fiber: 4g; Carbs: 11g; Protein: 4g

Potatoes and Tomatoes Mix Recipe
(Prep + Cook Time: 26 Minutes | **Servings:** 4)

Ingredients:
- 1 ½ lbs. red potatoes; quartered
- 2 tbsp. olive oil
- 1 tsp. sweet paprika
- 1 tbsp. rosemary; chopped
- 1-pint cherry tomatoes
- Salt and black pepper to the taste
- 3 garlic cloves; minced

Instructions:
1. In a bowl; mix potatoes with tomatoes, oil, paprika, rosemary, garlic, salt and pepper, toss, transfer to your air fryer and cook at 380 °F, for 16 minutes. Divide among plates and serve

Nutrition Facts: Calories: 192; Fat: 4g; Fiber: 4g; Carbs: 20g; Protein: 25g

Spinach Pie Recipe
(Prep + Cook Time: 25 Minutes | **Servings:** 4)

Ingredients:
- 7 oz. flour
- 2 tbsp. butter
- 7 oz. spinach
- 1 tbsp. olive oil
- 1 yellow onion; chopped
- 2 eggs
- 2 tbsp. milk
- 3 oz. cottage cheese
- Salt and black pepper to the taste

Instructions:
1. In your food processor, mix flour with butter, 1 egg, milk, salt and pepper, blend well, transfer to a bowl, knead, cover and leave for 10 minutes
2. Heat up a pan with the oil over medium high heat, add onion and spinach; stir and cook for 2 minutes.
3. Add salt, pepper, the remaining egg and cottage cheese; stir well and take off heat
4. Divide dough in 4 pieces, roll each piece, place on the bottom of a ramekin, add spinach filling over dough, place ramekins in your air fryer's basket and cook at 360 °F, for 15 minutes.

Nutrition Facts: Calories: 250; Fat: 12g; Fiber: 2g; Carbs: 23g; Protein: 12g

Cherry Tomatoes Skewers Recipe
(Prep + Cook Time: 36 Minutes | **Servings:** 4)

Ingredients:
- 24 cherry tomatoes
- 3 tbsp. balsamic vinegar
- 3 garlic cloves; minced
- 1 tbsp. thyme; chopped
- 2 tbsp. olive oil
- Salt and black pepper to the taste

For the dressing:
- 2 tbsp. balsamic vinegar
- Salt and black pepper to the taste
- 4 tbsp. olive oil

Instructions:
1. In a bowl; mix 2 tbsp. oil with 3 tbsp. vinegar, 3 garlic cloves, thyme, salt and black pepper and whisk well.
2. Add tomatoes, toss to coat and leave aside for 30 minutes
3. Arrange 6 tomatoes on one skewer and repeat with the rest of the tomatoes.
4. Place them in your air fryer and cook at 360 °F, for 6 minutes
5. In another bowl, mix 2 tbsp. vinegar with salt, pepper and 4 tbsp. oil and whisk well. Arrange tomato skewers on plates and serve with the dressing drizzled on top.

Nutrition Facts: Calories: 140; Fat: 1g; Fiber: 1g; Carbs: 2g; Protein: 7g

Stuffed Baby Peppers Recipe

(Prep + Cook Time: 16 Minutes | **Servings:** 4)

Ingredients:
- 12 baby bell peppers; cut into halves lengthwise
- 1 lb. shrimp; cooked, peeled and deveined
- 1/4 tsp. red pepper flakes; crushed
- 6 tbsp. jarred basil pesto
- 1 tbsp. lemon juice
- 1 tbsp. olive oil
- Salt and black pepper to the taste
- A handful parsley; chopped

Instructions:
1. In a bowl; mix shrimp with pepper flakes, pesto, salt, black pepper, lemon juice, oil and parsley, whisk very well and stuff bell pepper halves with this mix
2. Place them in your air fryer and cook at 320 °F, for 6 minutes; Arrange peppers on plates and serve.

Nutrition Facts: Calories: 130; Fat: 2g; Fiber: 1g; Carbs: 3g; Protein: 15g

Beet Salad and Parsley Dressing Recipe

(Prep + Cook Time: 24 Minutes | **Servings:** 4)

Ingredients:
- 4 beets
- 2 tbsp. balsamic vinegar
- A bunch of parsley; chopped
- 1 tbsp. extra virgin olive oil
- 1 garlic clove; chopped
- 2 tbsp. capers
- Salt and black pepper to the taste

Instructions:
1. Put the beets in your air fryer and cook them at 360 °F, for 14 minutes.
2. Meanwhile; in a bowl, mix parsley with garlic, salt, pepper, olive oil and capers and stir very well
3. Transfer beets to a cutting board, leave them to cool down, peel them, slice put them in a salad bowl
4. Add vinegar, drizzle the parsley dressing all over and serve.

Nutrition Facts: Calories: 70; Fat: 2g; Fiber: 1g; Carbs: 6g; Protein: 4g

Herbed Eggplant and Zucchini Mix Recipe

(Prep + Cook Time: 18 Minutes | **Servings:** 4)

Ingredients:
- 1 eggplant; roughly cubed
- 3 zucchinis; roughly cubed
- 2 tbsp. lemon juice
- 1 tsp. thyme; dried
- Salt and black pepper to the taste
- 1 tsp. oregano; dried
- 3 tbsp. olive oil

Instructions:
1. Put the eggplant in a dish that fits your air fryer, add zucchinis, lemon juice, salt, pepper, thyme, oregano and olive oil, toss, close the air fryer basket and cook at 360 °F, for 8 minutes
2. Divide among plates and serve right away.

Nutrition Facts: Calories: 152; Fat: 5g; Fiber: 7g; Carbs: 19g; Protein: 5g

Peppers Stuffed with Beef Recipe
(Prep + Cook Time: 65 Minutes | **Servings:** 4)

Ingredients:
- 1-pound beef; ground
- 1 tsp. coriander; ground
- 1 onion; chopped
- 3 garlic cloves; minced
- 1/2 tsp. turmeric powder
- 1 tbsp. hot curry powder
- 2 tbsp. olive oil
- 1 tbsp. ginger; grated
- 1/2 tsp. cumin; ground
- Salt and black pepper to the taste
- 1 egg
- 4 bell peppers; cut into halves and seeds removed
- 1/3 cup raisins
- 1/3 cup walnuts; chopped

Instructions:
1. Heat up a pan with the oil over medium high heat, add onion; stir and cook for 4 minutes.
2. Add garlic and beef; stir and cook for 10 minutes
3. Add coriander, ginger, cumin, curry powder, salt, pepper, turmeric, walnuts and raisins; stir take off heat and mix with the egg.
4. Stuff pepper halves with this mix and palace them in your air fryer and cook at 320 °F, for 20 minutes. Divide among plates and serve

Nutrition Facts: Calories: 170; Fat: 4g; Fiber: 3g; Carbs: 7g; Protein: 12g

Beets and Blue Cheese Salad Recipe
(Prep + Cook Time: 24 Minutes | **Servings:** 6)

Ingredients:
- 6 beets; peeled and quartered
- 1/4 cup blue cheese; crumbled
- 1 tbsp. olive oil
- Salt and black pepper to the taste

Instructions:
1. Put the beets in your air fryer, cook them at 350 °F, for 14 minutes and transfer them to a bowl.
2. Add blue cheese, salt, pepper and oil, toss and serve

Nutrition Facts: Calories: 100; Fat: 4g; Fiber: 4g; Carbs: 10g; Protein: 5g

Radish Hash Recipe
(Prep + Cook Time: 17 Minutes | **Servings:** 4)

Ingredients:
- 4 eggs
- 1 lb. radishes; sliced
- 1/2 tsp. garlic powder
- 1/2 tsp. onion powder
- 1/3 cup parmesan; grated
- Salt and black pepper to the taste

Instructions:
1. In a bowl; mix radishes with salt, pepper, onion and garlic powder, eggs and parmesan and stir well
2. Transfer radishes to a pan that fits your air fryer and cook at 350 °F, for 7 minutes
3. Divide hash on plates and serve.

Nutrition Facts: Calories: 80; Fat: 5g; Fiber: 2g; Carbs: 5g; Protein: 7g

Flavored Fried Tomatoes Recipe
(**Prep + Cook Time:** 25 Minutes | **Servings:** 8)

Ingredients:
- 1 jalapeno pepper; chopped
- 4 garlic cloves; minced
- 1/2 tsp. oregano; dried
- 1/4 cup basil; chopped.
- 2 lbs. cherry tomatoes; halved
- Salt and black pepper to the taste
- 1/4 cup olive oil
- 1/2 cup parmesan; grated

Instructions:
1. In a bowl; mix tomatoes with garlic, jalapeno, season with salt, pepper and oregano and drizzle the oil, toss to coat, close the air fryer basket and cook at 380 °F, for 15 minutes
2. Transfer tomatoes to a bowl, add basil and parmesan, toss and serve.

Nutrition Facts: Calories: 140; Fat: 2g; Fiber: 2g; Carbs: 6g; Protein: 8g

Mexican Peppers Recipe
(**Prep + Cook Time:** 35 Minutes | **Servings:** 4)

Ingredients:
- 4 bell peppers; tops cut off and seeds removed
- 1/2 cup tomato juice
- 1/4 cup yellow onion; chopped
- 1/4 cup green peppers; chopped.
- 2 cups tomato sauce
- 2 tbsp. jarred jalapenos; chopped.
- 4 chicken breasts
- 1 cup tomatoes; chopped
- Salt and black pepper to the taste
- 2 tsp. onion powder
- 1/2 tsp. red pepper; crushed
- 1 tsp. chili powder
- 1/2 tsp. garlic powder
- 1 tsp. cumin; ground

Instructions:
1. In a pan that fits your air fryer, mix chicken breasts with tomato juice, jalapenos, tomatoes, onion, green peppers, salt, pepper, onion powder, red pepper, chili powder, garlic powder, oregano and cumin; stir well, close the air fryer basket and cook at 350 °F, for 15 minutes
2. Shred meat using 2 forks; stir, stuff bell peppers with this mix, place them in your air fryer and cook at 320 °F, for 10 minutes more. Divide stuffed peppers on plates and serve

Nutrition Facts: Calories: 180; Fat: 4g; Fiber: 3g; Carbs: 7g; Protein: 14g

Balsamic Artichokes Recipe
(**Prep + Cook Time:** 17 Minutes | **Servings:** 4)

Ingredients:
- 4 big artichokes; trimmed
- 2 tbsp. lemon juice
- 2 tsp. balsamic vinegar
- 1 tsp. oregano; dried
- 1/4 cup extra virgin olive oil
- 2 garlic cloves; minced
- Salt and black pepper to the taste

Instructions:
1. Season artichokes with salt and pepper, rub them with half of the oil and half of the lemon juice, put them in your air fryer and cook at 360 °F, for 7 minutes
2. Meanwhile; in a bowl, mix the rest of the lemon juice with vinegar, the remaining oil, salt, pepper, garlic and oregano and stir very well
3. Arrange artichokes on a platter, drizzle the balsamic vinaigrette over them and serve.

Nutrition Facts: Calories: 200; Fat: 3g; Fiber: 6g; Carbs: 12g; Protein: 4g

Beets and Arugula Salad Time Recipe
(Prep + Cook Time: 20 Minutes | Servings: 4)

Ingredients:
- 1 ½ lbs. beets; peeled and quartered
- 2 tbsp. brown sugar
- 2 scallions; chopped
- 2 tsp. mustard
- A drizzle of olive oil
- 2 tsp. orange zest; grated
- 2 tbsp. cider vinegar
- 1/2 cup orange juice
- 2 cups arugula

Instructions:
1. Rub beets with the oil and orange juice, place them in your air fryer and cook at 350 °F, for 10 minutes
2. Transfer beet quarters to a bowl, add scallions, arugula and orange zest and toss
3. In a separate bowl, mix sugar with mustard and vinegar, whisk well, add to salad, toss and serve.

Nutrition Facts: Calories: 121; Fat: 2g; Fiber: 3g; Carbs: 11g; Protein: 4g

Sesame Mustard Greens Recipe
(Prep + Cook Time: 21 Minutes | Servings: 4)

Ingredients:
- 2 garlic cloves; minced
- 3 tbsp. veggie stock
- 1/4 tsp. dark sesame oil
- 1 lb. mustard greens; torn
- 1 tbsp. olive oil
- 1/2 cup yellow onion; sliced
- Salt and black pepper to the taste

Instructions:
1. Heat up a pan that fits your air fryer with the oil over medium heat, add onions; stir and brown them for 5 minutes.
2. Add garlic, stock, greens, salt and pepper; stir, close the air fryer basket and cook at 350 °F, for 6 minutes. Add sesame oil, toss to coat, divide among plates and serve

Nutrition Facts: Calories: 120; Fat: 3g; Fiber: 1g; Carbs: 3g; Protein: 7g

Garlic Tomatoes Recipe
(Prep + Cook Time: 25 Minutes | Servings: 4)

Ingredients:
- 4 garlic cloves; crushed
- 1 lb. mixed cherry tomatoes
- 3 thyme springs; chopped.
- 1/4 cup olive oil
- Salt and black pepper to the taste

Instructions:
1. In a bowl; mix tomatoes with salt, black pepper, garlic, olive oil and thyme, toss to coat, close the air fryer basket and cook at 360 °F, for 15 minutes. Divide tomatoes mix on plates and serve

Nutrition Facts: Calories: 100; Fat: 0g; Fiber: 1g; Carbs: 1g; Protein: 6g

Broccoli and Tomatoes Fried Stew Recipe
(Prep + Cook Time: 30 Minutes | Servings: 4)

Ingredients:
- 28 oz. canned tomatoes; pureed
- 1 broccoli head; florets separated
- 2 tsp. coriander seeds
- 1 tbsp. olive oil
- 1 yellow onion; chopped
- A pinch of red pepper; crushed
- 1 small ginger piece; chopped
- 1 garlic clove; minced
- Salt and black pepper to the taste

Instructions:
1. Heat up a pan that fits your air fryer with the oil over medium heat, add onions, salt, pepper and red pepper; stir and cook for 7 minutes

2. Add ginger, garlic, coriander seeds, tomatoes and broccoli; stir, close the air fryer basket and cook at 360 °F, for 12 minutes. Divide into bowls and serve.

Nutrition Facts: Calories: 150; Fat: 4g; Fiber: 2g; Carbs: 7g; Protein: 12g

Cheesy Artichokes Recipe

(Prep + Cook Time: 16 Minutes | **Servings:** 6)

Ingredients:
- 14 oz. canned artichoke hearts
- 8 oz. cream cheese
- 8 oz. mozzarella; shredded
- 1/2 cup sour cream
- 3 garlic cloves; minced
- 16 oz. parmesan cheese; grated
- 10 oz. spinach
- 1/2 cup chicken stock
- 1/2 cup mayonnaise
- 1 tsp. onion powder

Instructions:
1. In a pan that fits your air fryer, mix artichokes with stock, garlic, spinach, cream cheese, sour cream, onion powder and mayo, toss, close the air fryer basket and cook at 350 °F, for 6 minutes
2. Add mozzarella and parmesan; stir well and serve.

Nutrition Facts: Calories: 261; Fat: 12g; Fiber: 2g; Carbs: 12g; Protein: 15g

Stuffed Eggplants Recipe

(Prep + Cook Time: 40 Minutes | **Servings:** 4)

Ingredients:
- 4 small eggplants; halved lengthwise
- 1/2 cup cauliflower; chopped.
- 1 tsp. oregano; chopped
- 1/2 cup parsley; chopped
- Salt and black pepper to the taste
- 10 tbsp. olive oil
- 2 ½ lbs. tomatoes; cut into halves and grated
- 1 green bell pepper; chopped.
- 1 yellow onion; chopped
- 1 tbsp. garlic; minced
- 3 oz. feta cheese; crumbled

Instructions:
1. Season eggplants with salt, pepper and 4 tbsp. oil, toss, put them in your air fryer and cook at 350 °F, for 16 minutes.
2. Meanwhile; heat up a pan with 3 tbsp. oil over medium high heat, add onion; stir and cook for 5 minutes.
3. Add bell pepper, garlic and cauliflower; stir, cook for 5 minutes; take off heat, add parsley, tomato, salt, pepper, oregano and cheese and whisk everything
4. Stuff eggplants with the veggie mix, drizzle the rest of the oil over them, put them in your air fryer and cook at 350 °F, for 6 minutes more. Divide among plates and serve right away

Nutrition Facts: Calories: 240; Fat: 4, fiber, 2g; Carbs: 19g; Protein: 2g

Fried Asparagus Recipe

(Prep + Cook Time: 25 Minutes | **Servings:** 4)

Ingredients:
- 2 lbs. fresh asparagus; trimmed
- 1/2 tsp. oregano; dried
- 1/4 tsp. red pepper flakes
- 1/4 cup olive oil
- Salt and black pepper to the taste
- 1 tsp. lemon zest
- 4 oz. feta cheese; crumbled
- 4 garlic cloves; minced
- 2 tbsp. parsley; finely chopped.
- Juice from 1 lemon

Instructions:
1. In a bowl; mix oil with lemon zest, garlic, pepper flakes and oregano and whisk.
2. Add asparagus, cheese, salt and pepper, toss, transfer to your air fryer's basket and cook at 350 °F, for 8 minutes.
3. Divide asparagus on plates, drizzle lemon juice and sprinkle parsley on top and serve

Nutrition Facts: Calories: 162; Fat: 13g; Fiber: 5g; Carbs: 12g; Protein: 8g

Collard Greens Mix Recipe

(Prep + Cook Time: 20 Minutes | **Servings:** 4)

Ingredients:
- 1 bunch collard greens; trimmed
- 2 tbsp. olive oil
- 2 tbsp. tomato puree
- 1 tbsp. balsamic vinegar
- 1 tsp. sugar
- 1 yellow onion; chopped
- 3 garlic cloves; minced
- Salt and black pepper to the taste

Instructions:
1. In a dish that fits your air fryer, mix oil, garlic, vinegar, onion and tomato puree and whisk
2. Add collard greens, salt, pepper and sugar, toss, close the air fryer basket and cook at 320 °F, for 10 minutes. Divide collard greens mix on plates and serve

Nutrition Facts: Calories: 121; Fat: 3g; Fiber: 3g; Carbs: 7g; Protein: 3g

Spanish Greens Recipe

(Prep + Cook Time: 18 Minutes | **Servings:** 4)

Ingredients:
- 1 apple; cored and chopped.
- 1 yellow onion; sliced
- 1/4 cup pine nuts; toasted
- 1/4 cup balsamic vinegar
- 3 tbsp. olive oil
- 1/4 cup raisins
- 6 garlic cloves; chopped
- 5 cups mixed spinach and chard
- Salt and black pepper to the taste
- A pinch of nutmeg

Instructions:
1. Heat up a pan that fits your air fryer with the oil over medium high heat, add onion; stir and cook for 3 minutes
2. Add apple, garlic, raisins, vinegar, mixed spinach and chard, nutmeg, salt and pepper; stir and transfer this to the preheated air fryer and cook at 350 °F, for 5 minutes
3. Divide among plates, sprinkle pine nuts on top and serve.

Nutrition Facts: Calories: 120; Fat: 1g; Fiber: 2g; Carbs: 3g; Protein: 6g

Stuffed Tomatoes Recipe

(Prep + Cook Time: 25 Minutes | **Servings:** 4)

Ingredients:
- 4 tomatoes; tops cut off and pulp scooped and chopped.
- 1 yellow onion; chopped.
- 1 tbsp. butter
- 2 tbsp. celery; chopped
- 1/2 cup mushrooms; chopped.
- 1 tbsp. bread crumbs
- 1 cup cottage cheese
- Salt and black pepper to the taste
- 1/4 tsp. caraway seeds
- 1 tbsp. parsley; chopped

Instructions:
1. Heat up a pan with the butter over medium heat, melt it, add onion and celery; stir and cook for 3 minutes.
2. Add tomato pulp and mushrooms; stir and cook for 1 minute more
3. Add salt, pepper, crumbled bread, cheese, caraway seeds and parsley; stir, cook for 4 minutes more and take off heat.
4. Stuff tomatoes with this mix, place them in your air fryer and cook at 350 °F, for 8 minutes. Divide stuffed tomatoes on plates and serve

Nutrition Facts: Calories: 143; Fat: 4g; Fiber: 6g; Carbs: 4g; Protein: 4g

Zucchini Mix Recipe

(Prep + Cook Time: 24 Minutes | **Servings:** 6)

Ingredients:
- 6 zucchinis; halved and then sliced
- 3 garlic cloves; minced
- 2 oz. parmesan; grated
- 3/4 cup heavy cream
- Salt and black pepper to the taste
- 1 tbsp. butter
- 1 tsp. oregano; dried
- 1/2 cup yellow onion; chopped

Instructions:
1. Heat up a pan that fits your air fryer with the butter over medium high heat, add onion; stir and cook for 4 minutes
2. Add garlic, zucchinis, oregano, salt, pepper and heavy cream, toss, close the air fryer basket and cook at 350 °F, for 10 minutes. Add parmesan; stir, divide among plates and serve.

Nutrition Facts: Calories: 160; Fat: 4g; Fiber: 2g; Carbs: 8g; Protein: 8g

Broccoli Hash Recipe

(Prep + Cook Time: 38 Minutes | **Servings:** 2)

Ingredients:
- 10 oz. mushrooms; halved
- 1 broccoli head; florets separated
- 1 garlic clove; minced
- 1 tbsp. balsamic vinegar
- 1 avocado; peeled and pitted
- A pinch of red pepper flakes
- 1 yellow onion; chopped.
- 1 tbsp. olive oil
- Salt and black pepper
- 1 tsp. basil; dried

Instructions:
1. In a bowl; mix mushrooms with broccoli, onion, garlic and avocado.
2. In another bowl, mix vinegar, oil, salt, pepper and basil and whisk well
3. Pour this over veggies, toss to coat, leave aside for 30 minutes; transfer to your air fryer's basket and cook at 350 °F, for 8 minutes; Divide among plates and serve with pepper flakes on top

Nutrition Facts: Calories: 182; Fat: 3g; Fiber: 3g; Carbs: 5g; Protein: 8g

Crispy Potatoes and Parsley Recipe

(Prep + Cook Time: 20 Minutes | **Servings:** 4)

Ingredients:
- 1 lb. gold potatoes; cut into wedges
- 2 tbsp. olive
- Juice from 1/2 lemon
- Salt and black pepper to the taste
- 1/4 cup parsley leaves; chopped.

Instructions:
1. Rub potatoes with salt, pepper, lemon juice and olive oil, put them in your air fryer and cook at 350 °F, for 10 minutes
2. Divide among plates, sprinkle parsley on top and serve.

Nutrition Facts: Calories: 152; Fat: 3g; Fiber: 7g; Carbs: 17g; Protein: 4g

Sweet Baby Carrots Dish Recipe

(Prep + Cook Time: 20 Minutes | **Servings:** 4)

Ingredients:
- 2 cups baby carrots
- A pinch of salt and black pepper
- 1 tbsp. brown sugar
- 1/2 tbsp. butter; melted

Instructions:
1. In a dish that fits your air fryer, mix baby carrots with butter, salt, pepper and sugar, toss, close the air fryer basket and cook at 350 °F, for 10 minutes. Divide among plates and serve

Nutrition Facts: Calories: 100; Fat: 2g; Fiber: 3g; Carbs: 7g; Protein: 4g

Zucchini Noodles Recipe

(Prep + Cook Time: 30 Minutes | **Servings:** 6)

Ingredients:
- 3 zucchinis; cut with a spiralizer
- 16 oz. mushrooms; sliced
- 2 cups tomatoes sauce
- 2 tbsp. olive oil
- 2 cups spinach; torn
- 1/4 cup sun dried tomatoes; chopped
- 1 tsp. garlic; minced
- 1/2 cup cherry tomatoes; halved
- Salt and black pepper to the taste
- A handful basil; chopped.

Instructions:
1. Put zucchini noodles in a bowl, season salt and black pepper and leave them aside for 10 minutes.
2. Heat up a pan that fits your air fryer with the oil over medium high heat, add garlic; stir and cook for 1 minute
3. Add mushrooms, sun dried tomatoes, cherry tomatoes, spinach, cayenne, sauce and zucchini noodles; stir, close the air fryer basket and cook at 320 °F, for 10 minutes
4. Divide among plates and serve with basil sprinkled on top.

Nutrition Facts: Calories: 120; Fat: 1g; Fiber: 1g; Carbs: 2g; Protein: 9g

Creamy Green Beans Recipe

(Prep + Cook Time: 25 Minutes | **Servings:** 4)

Ingredients:
- 1/2 cup heavy cream
- 2 lbs. green beans
- 2 tsp. lemon zest; grated
- 1 cup mozzarella; shredded
- 2/3 cup parmesan; grated
- Salt and black pepper to the taste
- A pinch of red pepper flakes

Instructions:
1. Put the beans in a dish that fits your air fryer, add heavy cream, salt, pepper, lemon zest, pepper flakes, mozzarella and parmesan, toss, close the air fryer basket and cook at 350 °F, for 15 minutes
2. Divide among plates and serve right away.

Nutrition Facts: Calories: 231; Fat: 6g; Fiber: 7g; Carbs: 8g; Protein: 5g

Greek Potato Mix Recipe

(Prep + Cook Time: 30 Minutes | **Servings:** 2)

Ingredients:
- 2 medium potatoes; cut into wedges
- 1 yellow onion; chopped.
- 1 bay leaf
- 1/2 cup chicken stock
- 2 tbsp. Greek yogurt
- 2 tbsp. butter
- 1 small carrot; roughly chopped.
- 1 ½ tbsp. flour
- Salt and black pepper to the taste

Instructions:
1. Heat up a pan that fits your air fryer with the butter over medium high heat, add onion and carrot; stir and cook for 3-4 minutes
2. Add potatoes, flour, chicken stock, salt, pepper and bay leaf; stir, close the air fryer basket and cook at 320 °F, for 16 minutes. Add Greek yogurt, toss, divide among plates and serve

Nutrition Facts: Calories: 198; Fat: 3g; Fiber: 2g; Carbs: 6g; Protein: 8g

Portobello Mushrooms Recipe
(**Prep + Cook Time:** 22 Minutes | **Servings:** 4)

Ingredients:
- 4 Portobello mushrooms; stems removed and chopped.
- 10 basil leaves
- 1 cup baby spinach
- 3 garlic cloves; chopped
- 1 cup almonds; roughly chopped.
- 1 tbsp. parsley
- 1/4 cup olive oil
- 8 cherry tomatoes; halved
- Salt and black pepper to the taste

Instructions:
1. In your food processor, mix basil with spinach, garlic, almonds, parsley, oil, salt, black pepper to the taste and mushroom stems and blend well
2. Stuff each mushroom with this mix, place them in your air fryer and cook at 350 °F, for 12 minutes. Divide mushrooms on plates and serve.

Nutrition Facts: Calories: 145; Fat: 3g; Fiber: 2g; Carbs: 6g; Protein: 17g

Green Beans and Parmesan Recipe
(**Prep + Cook Time:** 18 Minutes | **Servings:** 4)

Ingredients:
- 12 oz. green beans
- 2 tsp. garlic; minced
- 1 egg; whisked
- 1/3 cup parmesan; grated
- 2 tbsp. olive oil
- Salt and black pepper to the taste

Instructions:
1. In a bowl; mix oil with salt, pepper, garlic and egg and whisk well.
2. Add green beans to this mix, toss well and sprinkle parmesan all over
3. Transfer green beans to your air fryer and cook them at 390 °F, for 8 minutes. Divide green beans on plates and serve them right away.

Nutrition Facts: Calories: 120; Fat: 8g; Fiber: 2g; Carbs: 7g; Protein: 4g

Asian Turnips Salad Recipe
(**Prep + Cook Time:** 22 Minutes | **Servings:** 4)

Ingredients:
- 20 oz. turnips; peeled and chopped.
- 1 tsp. garlic; minced
- 1 tsp. ginger; grated
- 1/2 tsp. turmeric powder
- 2 tbsp. butter
- 2 yellow onions; chopped
- 2 tomatoes; chopped
- 1 tsp. cumin; ground
- 1 tsp. coriander; ground
- 2 green chilies; chopped
- Salt and black pepper to the taste
- A handful coriander leaves; chopped

Instructions:
1. Heat up a pan that fits your air fryer with the butter, melt it, add green chilies, garlic and ginger; stir and cook for 1 minute
2. Add onions, salt, pepper, tomatoes, turmeric, cumin, ground coriander and turnips; stir, close the air fryer basket and cook at 350 °F, for 10 minutes
3. Divide among plates, sprinkle fresh coriander on top and serve.

Nutrition Facts: Calories: 100; Fat: 3g; Fiber: 6g; Carbs: 12g; Protein: 4g

Green Beans and Potatoes Recipe

(**Prep + Cook Time:** 25 Minutes | **Servings:** 5)

Ingredients:
- 2 lbs. green beans
- 6 new potatoes; halved
- Salt and black pepper to the taste
- 6 bacon slices; cooked and chopped.
- A drizzle of olive oil

Instructions:
1. In a bowl; mix green beans with potatoes, salt, pepper and oil, toss, transfer to your air fryer and cook at 390 °F, for 15 minutes. Divide among plates and serve with bacon sprinkled on top

Nutrition Facts: Calories: 374; Fat: 15g; Fiber: 12g; Carbs: 28g; Protein: 12g

Swiss Chard Salad Recipe

(**Prep + Cook Time:** 23 Minutes | **Servings:** 4)

Ingredients:
- 1 bunch Swiss chard; torn
- 1/4 cup pine nuts; toasted
- 1/4 cup raisins
- 2 tbsp. olive oil
- 1 small yellow onion; chopped
- A pinch of red pepper flakes
- 1 tbsp. balsamic vinegar
- Salt and black pepper to the taste

Instructions:
1. Heat up a pan that fits your air fryer with the oil over medium heat, add chard and onions; stir and cook for 5 minutes
2. Add salt, pepper, pepper flakes, raisins, pine nuts and vinegar; stir, close the air fryer basket and cook at 350 °F, for 8 minutes. Divide among plates and serve.

Nutrition Facts: Calories: 120; Fat: 2g; Fiber: 1g; Carbs: 8g; Protein: 8g

Green Beans and Tomatoes Recipe

(**Prep + Cook Time:** 25 Minutes | **Servings:** 4)

Ingredients:
- 1-pint cherry tomatoes
- 2 tbsp. olive oil
- 1 lb. green beans
- Salt and black pepper to the taste

Instructions:
1. In a bowl; mix cherry tomatoes with green beans, olive oil, salt and pepper, toss, transfer to your air fryer and cook at 400 °F, for 15 minutes. Divide among plates and serve right away

Nutrition Facts: Calories: 162; Fat: 6g; Fiber: 5g; Carbs: 8g; Protein: 9g

Rutabaga and Cherry Tomatoes Mix Recipe

(**Prep + Cook Time:** 25 Minutes | **Servings:** 4)

Ingredients:
- 1 garlic clove; minced
- 3/4 cup cashews; soaked for a couple of hours and drained
- 1 tbsp. shallot; chopped
- 2 tbsp. nutritional yeast
- 1/2 cup veggie stock
- 2 tsp. lemon juice
- Salt and black pepper to the taste

For the pasta:
- 1 cup cherry tomatoes; halved
- 2 rutabagas; peeled and cut into thick noodles
- 5 tsp. olive oil
- 1/4 tsp. garlic powder

Instructions:
1. Place tomatoes and rutabaga noodles in a pan that fits your air fryer, drizzle the oil over them, season with salt, black pepper and garlic powder, toss to coat and cook in your air fryer at 350 °F, for 15 minutes

2. Meanwhile; in a food processor, mix garlic with shallots, cashews, veggie stock, nutritional yeast, lemon juice, a pinch of sea salt and black pepper to the taste and blend well
3. Divide rutabaga pasta on plates, top with tomatoes, drizzle the sauce over them and serve.

Nutrition Facts: Calories: 160; Fat: 2g; Fiber: 5g; Carbs: 10g; Protein: 8g

Stuffed Poblano Peppers Recipe

(**Prep + Cook Time:** 25 Minutes | **Servings:** 4)

Ingredients:
- 10 poblano peppers; tops cut off and deseeded
- 2 tsp. garlic; minced
- 1 white onion; chopped
- 1 tbsp. olive oil
- 8 oz. mushrooms; chopped.
- 1/2 cup cilantro; chopped
- Salt and black pepper to the taste

Instructions:
1. Heat up a pan with the oil over medium high heat, add onion and mushrooms; stir and cook for 5 minutes.
2. Add garlic, cilantro, salt and black pepper; stir and cook for 2 minutes
3. Divide this mix into poblanos and place them into the air fryer basket cook at 350 °F, for 15 minutes. Divide among plates and serve

Nutrition Facts: Calories: 150; Fat: 3g; Fiber: 2g; Carbs: 7g; Protein: 10g

Balsamic Potatoes Recipe

(**Prep + Cook Time:** 30 Minutes | **Servings:** 4)

Ingredients:
- 1 ½ lbs. baby potatoes; halved
- 2 garlic cloves; chopped.
- 2 red onions; chopped
- 1 ½ tbsp. balsamic vinegar
- 2 thyme springs; chopped
- 9 oz. cherry tomatoes
- 3 tbsp. olive oil
- Salt and black pepper to the taste

Instructions:
1. In your food processor, mix garlic with onions, oil, vinegar, thyme, salt and pepper and pulse really well.
2. In a bowl; mix potatoes with tomatoes and balsamic marinade, toss well, transfer to your air fryer and cook at 380 °F, for 20 minutes. Divide among plates and serve

Nutrition Facts: Calories: 301; Fat: 6g; Fiber: 8g; Carbs: 18g; Protein: 6g

Sweet Potatoes Mix Recipe

(**Prep + Cook Time:** 25 Minutes | **Servings:** 4)

Ingredients:
- 3 sweet potatoes; cubed
- 4 tbsp. olive oil
- 4 garlic cloves; minced
- 1/2 lb. bacon; chopped
- 2 tbsp. balsamic vinegar
- A handful dill; chopped.
- 2 green onions; chopped.
- Juice from 1 lime
- Salt and black pepper to the taste
- A pinch of cinnamon powder
- A pinch of red pepper flakes

Instructions:
1. Arrange bacon and sweet potatoes in your air fryer's basket, add garlic and half of the oil, toss well and cook at 350 °F and bake for 15 minutes
2. Meanwhile; in a bowl, mix vinegar with lime juice, olive oil, green onions, pepper flakes, dill, salt, pepper and cinnamon and whisk. Transfer bacon and sweet potatoes to a salad bowl, add salad dressing, toss well and serve right away

Nutrition Facts: Calories: 170; Fat: 3g; Fiber: 2g; Carbs: 5g; Protein: 12g

Asian Potatoes Recipe

(**Prep + Cook Time:** 22 Minutes | **Servings:** 4)

Ingredients:
- 1 tbsp. coriander seeds
- 1 tbsp. cumin seeds
- 2 tsp. fenugreek; dried
- 5 potatoes; boiled, peeled and cubed
- Salt and black pepper to the taste
- 1/2 tsp. turmeric powder
- 1/2 tsp. red chili powder
- 1 tsp. pomegranate powder
- 1 tbsp. pickled mango; chopped
- 2 tbsp. olive oil

Instructions:
1. Heat up a pan that fits your air fryer with the oil over medium heat, add coriander and cumin seeds; stir and cook for 2 minutes
2. Add salt, pepper, turmeric, chili powder, pomegranate powder, mango, fenugreek and potatoes, toss, close the air fryer basket and cook at 360 °F, for 10 minutes.
3. Divide among plates and serve hot.

Nutrition Facts: Calories: 251; Fat: 7g; Fiber: 4g; Carbs: 12g; Protein: 7g

Tomato and Basil Tart Recipe

(**Prep + Cook Time:** 24 Minutes | **Servings:** 2)

Ingredients:
- 1 bunch basil; chopped
- 4 eggs
- 1 garlic clove; minced
- 1/4 cup cheddar cheese; grated
- 1/2 cup cherry tomatoes; halved
- Salt and black pepper to the taste

Instructions:
1. In a bowl; mix eggs with salt, black pepper, cheese and basil and whisk well.
2. Pour this into a baking pan that fits your air fryer, arrange tomatoes on top, place the baking pan in the air fryer basket then lock it and cook at 320 °F, for 14 minutes
3. Slice and serve right away.

Nutrition Facts: Calories: 140; Fat: 1g; Fiber: 1g; Carbs: 2g; Protein: 10g

Tomatoes and Bell Pepper Sauce Recipe

(**Prep + Cook Time:** 25 Minutes | **Servings:** 4)

Ingredients:
- 2 red bell peppers; chopped
- 2 garlic cloves; minced
- 2 tbsp. olive oil
- 1 tbsp. balsamic vinegar
- 1 lb. cherry tomatoes; halved
- 1 tsp. rosemary; dried
- 3 bay leaves
- Salt and black pepper to the taste

Instructions:
1. In a bowl mix tomatoes with garlic, salt, black pepper, rosemary, bay leaves, half of the oil and half of the vinegar, toss to coat, transfer this to air fryer and roast them at 320 °F, for 15 minutes
2. Meanwhile; in your food processor, mix bell peppers with a pinch of sea salt, black pepper, the rest of the oil and the rest of the vinegar and blend very well.
3. Divide roasted tomatoes on plates, drizzle the bell peppers sauce over them and serve

Nutrition Facts: Calories: 123; Fat: 1g; Fiber: 1g; Carbs: 8g; Protein: 10g

Spicy Cabbage Recipe

(Prep + Cook Time: 18 Minutes | **Servings:** 4)

Ingredients:
- 1/4 cups apple juice
- 1/2 tsp. cayenne pepper
- 1 cabbage; cut into 8 wedges
- 1 tbsp. sesame seed oil
- 1 carrot; grated
- 1/4 cup apple cider vinegar
- 1 tsp. red pepper flakes; crushed

Instructions:
1. In a pan that fits your air fryer, combine cabbage with oil, carrot, vinegar, apple juice, cayenne and pepper flakes, toss, Put it in the preheated air fryer and cook at 350 °F, for 8 minutes
2. Divide cabbage mix on plates and serve.

Nutrition Facts: Calories: 100; Fat: 4g; Fiber: 2g; Carbs: 11g; Protein: 7g

Potatoes and Tomato Sauce Recipe

(Prep + Cook Time: 26 Minutes | **Servings:** 4)

Ingredients:
- 2 lbs. potatoes; cubed
- 4 garlic cloves; minced
- 1 yellow onion; chopped.
- 1 cup tomato sauce
- 1/2 tsp. oregano; dried
- 1/2 tsp. parsley; dried
- 2 tbsp. basil; chopped
- 2 tbsp. olive oil

Instructions:
1. Heat up a pan that fits your air fryer with the oil over medium heat, add onion; stir and cook for 1-2 minutes.
2. Add garlic, potatoes, parsley, tomato sauce and oregano; stir, close the air fryer basket and cook at 370 °F and cook for 16 minutes. Add basil, toss everything, divide among plates and serve

Nutrition Facts: Calories: 211; Fat: 6g; Fiber: 8g; Carbs: 14g; Protein: 6g

Italian Eggplant Stew Recipe

(Prep + Cook Time: 25 Minutes | **Servings:** 4)

Ingredients:
- 1 red onion; chopped
- 2 garlic cloves; chopped
- 1 bunch parsley; chopped.
- 2 tbsp. capers; chopped
- 1 handful green olives; pitted and sliced
- Salt and black pepper to the taste
- 1 tsp. oregano; dried
- 2 eggplants; cut into medium chunks
- 2 tbsp. olive oil
- 5 tomatoes; chopped
- 3 tbsp. herb vinegar

Instructions:
1. Heat up a pan that fits your air fryer with the oil over medium heat, add eggplant, oregano, salt and pepper; stir and cook for 5 minutes
2. Add garlic, onion, parsley, capers, olives, vinegar and tomatoes; stir, close the air fryer basket and cook at 360 °F, for 15 minutes. Divide into bowls and serve.

Nutrition Facts: Calories: 170; Fat: 13g; Fiber: 3g; Carbs: 5g; Protein: 7g

Snack and Appetizer Recipes

Spicy Fish Nuggets

(Prep + Cook Time: 22 Minutes | **Servings:** 4)

Ingredients:
- 28 oz. fish fillets; skinless and cut into medium pieces
- 5 tbsp. flour
- 1 egg; whisked
- 5 tbsp. water
- 3 oz. panko bread crumbs
- 1 tbsp. garlic powder
- 1 tbsp. smoked paprika
- 4 tbsp. homemade mayonnaise
- Lemon juice from 1/2 lemon
- Salt and black pepper to the taste
- 1 tsp. dill; dried
- Cooking spray

Instructions:
1. In a bowl; mix flour with water and stir well.
2. Add egg, salt and pepper and whisk well.
3. In a second bowl; mix panko with garlic powder and paprika and stir well.
4. Dip fish pieces in flour and egg mix and then in panko mix, place them in your air fryer's basket, spray them with cooking oil and cook at 400 °F, for 12 minutes.
5. Meanwhile; in a bowl mix mayo with dill and lemon juice and whisk well. Arrange fish nuggets on a platter and serve with dill mayo on the side.

Nutrition Facts: Calories: 332; Fat: 12g; Fiber: 6g; Carbs: 17g; Protein: 15g

Cauliflower Snack

(Prep + Cook Time: 25 Minutes | **Servings:** 4)

Ingredients:
- 4 cups cauliflower florets
- 1 cup panko bread crumbs
- 1/4 cup buffalo sauce
- 1/4 cup butter; melted
- Mayonnaise for serving

Instructions:
1. In a bowl; mix buffalo sauce with butter and whisk well.
2. Dip cauliflower florets in this mix and coat them in panko bread crumbs.
3. Place them in your air fryer's basket and cook at 350 °F, for 15 minutes. Arrange them on a platter and serve with mayo on the side.

Nutrition Facts: Calories: 241; Fat: 4g; Fiber: 7g; Carbs: 8g; Protein: 4g

Tasty Banana Snack

(Prep + Cook Time: 15 Minutes | **Servings:** 8)

Ingredients:
- 1 banana; peeled and sliced into 16 pieces
- 16 baking cups crust
- 1/4 cup peanut butter
- 3/4 cup chocolate chips
- 1 tbsp. vegetable oil

Instructions:
1. Put the chocolate chips in a small pot, heat up over low heat; stir until it melts and take off heat.
2. In a bowl; mix peanut butter with coconut oil and whisk well.
3. Spoon 1 tsp. chocolate mix in a cup, add 1 banana slice and top with 1 tsp. butter mix. Repeat with the rest of the cups, place them all into a dish that fits your air fryer, cook at 320 °F, for 5 minutes; transfer to a freezer and keep there until you serve them as a snack.

Nutrition Facts: Calories: 70; Fat: 4g; Fiber: 1g; Carbs: 10g; Protein: 1g

Chestnut and Shrimp Rolls
(Prep + Cook Time: 25 Minutes | **Servings:** 4)

Ingredients:
- 1/2 lb. already cooked shrimp; chopped.
- 8 oz. water chestnuts; chopped.
- 1/2 lb. shiitake mushrooms; chopped.
- 2 cups cabbage; chopped.
- 2 tbsp. olive oil
- 1 garlic clove; minced
- 1 tsp. ginger; grated
- 3 scallions; chopped
- 1 tbsp. water
- 1 egg yolk
- 6 spring roll wrappers
- Salt and black pepper to the taste

Instructions:
1. Heat up a pan with the oil over medium high heat, add cabbage, shrimp, chestnuts, mushrooms, garlic, ginger, scallions, salt and pepper; stir and cook for 2 minutes.
2. In a bowl; mix egg with water and stir well. Arrange roll wrappers on a working surface, divide shrimp and veggie mix on them, seal edges with egg wash, place them all in your air fryer's basket, cook at 360 °F, for 15 minutes; transfer to a platter and serve as an appetizer.

Nutrition Facts: Calories: 140; Fat: 3g; Fiber: 1g; Carbs: 12g; Protein: 3g

Chicken Breast Sticks
(Prep + Cook Time: 26 Minutes | **Servings:** 4)

Ingredients:
- 1 lb. chicken breast; skinless, boneless and cut into medium sticks
- 1 tsp. sweet paprika
- 1 cup panko bread crumbs
- 1 egg; whisked
- Salt and black pepper to the taste
- 3/4 cup white flour
- 1/2 tbsp. olive oil
- Zest from 1 lemon; grated

Instructions:
1. In a bowl; mix paprika with flour, salt, pepper and lemon zest and stir.
2. Put whisked egg in another bowl and the panko breadcrumbs in a third one.
3. Dredge chicken pieces in flour, egg and panko and place them in your lined air fryer's basket; drizzle the oil over them, cook at 400 °F, for 8 minutes; flip and cook for 8 more minutes. Arrange them on a platter and serve as a snack.

Nutrition Facts: Calories: 254; Fat: 4g; Fiber: 7g; Carbs: 20g; Protein: 22g

Honey Chicken Wings
(Prep + Cook Time: 1 hour and 22 minutes | **Servings:** 8)

Ingredients:
- 16 chicken wings; halved
- 2 tbsp. soy sauce
- 2 tbsp. honey
- 2 tbsp. lime juice
- Salt and black pepper to the taste

Instructions:
1. In a bowl; mix chicken wings with soy sauce, honey, salt, pepper and lime juice; toss well and keep in the fridge for 1 hour.
2. Transfer chicken wings to your air fryer and cook them at 360 °F, for 12 minutes; flipping them halfway. Arrange them on a platter and serve as an appetizer.

Nutrition Facts: Calories: 211; Fat: 4g; Fiber: 7g; Carbs: 14g; Protein: 3g

Pesto Crackers

(**Prep + Cook Time:** 27 Minutes | **Servings:** 6)

Ingredients:
- 1¼ cups flour
- 2 tbsp. basil pesto
- 1/2 tsp. baking powder
- 1/4 tsp. basil; dried
- 1 garlic clove; minced
- 3 tbsp. butter
- Salt and black pepper to the taste

Instructions:
1. In a bowl; mix salt, pepper, baking powder, flour, garlic, cayenne, basil, pesto and butter and stir until you obtain a dough.
2. Spread this dough on a lined baking pan that fits your air fryer; put it in the air fryer and bake at 325 °F and for 17 minutes. Leave aside to cool down, cut crackers and serve them as a snack.

Nutrition Facts: Calories: 200; Fat: 20g; Fiber: 1g; Carbs: 4g; Protein: 7g

Salmon Meatballs Snack

(**Prep + Cook Time:** 22 Minutes | **Servings:** 4)

Ingredients:
- 1 lb. salmon; skinless and chopped.
- 3 tbsp. cilantro; minced
- 2 garlic cloves; minced
- 1/2 tsp. paprika
- 1/4 cup panko
- 1/2 tsp. oregano; ground
- 1 small yellow onion; chopped
- 1 egg white
- Salt and black pepper to the taste
- Cooking spray

Instructions:
1. In your food processor, mix salmon with onion, cilantro, egg white, garlic cloves, salt, pepper, paprika and oregano and stir well.
2. Add panko, blend again and shape meatballs from this mix using your palms.
3. Place them in your air fryer's basket; spray them with cooking spray and cook at 320 °F, for 12 minutes. shake the basket in the middle of the cooking to ensure even cooking. Arrange meatballs on a platter and serve them as an appetizer.

Nutrition Facts: Calories: 289; Fat: 12g; Fiber: 3g; Carbs: 22g; Protein: 23g

Sweet Popcorn Snack

(**Prep + Cook Time:** 15 Minutes | **Servings:** 4)

Ingredients:
- 2 tbsp. corn kernels
- 2 ½ tbsp. butter
- 2 oz. brown sugar

Instructions:
1. Put the corn kernels in your air fryer's pan, cook at 400 °F, for 6 minutes; transfer them to a tray, spread and leave aside for now.
2. Heat up a pan over low heat, add butter, melt it, add sugar and stir until it dissolves.
3. Add popcorn, toss to coat, take off heat and spread on the tray again. Cool down, divide into bowls and serve as a snack.

Nutrition Facts: Calories: 70; Fat: 0.2g; Fiber: 0g; Carbs: 1g; Protein: 1g

Cabbage Spring Rolls

(Prep + Cook Time: 35 Minutes | **Servings:** 8)

Ingredients:
- 2 cups green cabbage; shredded
- 2 yellow onions; chopped.
- 1 carrot; grated
- 10 spring roll sheets
- 2 tbsp. corn flour
- 2 tbsp. water
- 1/2 chili pepper; minced
- 1 tbsp. ginger; grated
- 3 garlic cloves; minced
- 1 tsp. sugar
- 1 tsp. soy sauce
- 2 tbsp. olive oil
- Salt and black pepper to the taste

Instructions:
1. Heat up a pan with the oil over medium heat, add cabbage, onions, carrots, chili pepper, ginger, garlic, sugar, salt, pepper and soy sauce; stir well, cook for 2-3 minutes; take off heat and cool down.
2. Cut spring roll sheets in squares, divide cabbage mix on each and roll them.
3. In a bowl; mix corn flour with water; stir well and seal spring rolls with this mix.
4. Place spring rolls in your air fryer's basket and cook them at 360 °F, for 10 minutes.
5. Flip roll and cook them for 10 minutes more. Arrange on a platter and serve them as an appetizer.

Nutrition Facts: Calories: 214; Fat: 4g; Fiber: 4g; Carbs: 12g; Protein: 4g

Salmon Patties

(Prep + Cook Time: 30 Minutes | **Servings:** 4)

Ingredients:
- 3 big potatoes; boiled, drained and mashed
- 1 egg
- 1 big salmon fillet; skinless, boneless
- 2 tbsp. bread crumbs
- 2 tbsp. parsley; chopped
- 2 tbsp. dill; chopped
- Salt and black pepper to the taste
- Cooking spray

Instructions:
1. Place salmon in your air fryer's basket and cook for 10 minutes at 360 degrees F.
2. Transfer salmon to a cutting board, cool it down; flake it and put it in a bowl.
3. Add mashed potatoes, salt, pepper, dill, parsley, egg and bread crumbs; stir well and shape 8 patties out of this mix. Place salmon patties in your air fryer's basket, spry them with cooking oil, cook at 360 °F, for 12 minutes; flipping them halfway, transfer them to a platter and serve as an appetizer.

Nutrition Facts: Calories: 231; Fat: 3g; Fiber: 7g; Carbs: 14g; Protein: 4g

Tasty Crab Sticks

(Prep + Cook Time: 30 Minutes | **Servings:** 4)

Ingredients:
- 10 crabsticks; halved
- 2 tsp. Cajun seasoning
- 2 tsp. sesame oil

Instructions:
1. Put the crab sticks in a bowl; add sesame oil and Cajun seasoning; toss, transfer them to your air fryer's basket and cook at 350 °F, for 12 minutes. Arrange on a platter and serve as an appetizer.

Nutrition Facts: Calories: 110; Fat: 0g; Fiber: 1g; Carbs: 4g; Protein: 2g 5

Zucchini Chips

(**Prep + Cook Time:** 1 hour 10 Minutes | **Servings:** 6)

Ingredients:
- 3 zucchinis; thinly sliced
- 2 tbsp. olive oil
- 2 tbsp. balsamic vinegar
- Salt and black pepper to the taste

Instructions:
1. In a bowl; mix oil with vinegar, salt and pepper and whisk well.
2. Add zucchini slices, toss to coat well; close the air fryer basket and cook at 200 °F, for 1 hour. Serve zucchini chips cold as a snack.

Nutrition Facts: Calories: 40; Fat: 3g; Fiber: 7g; Carbs: 3g; Protein: 7g

Coco Chicken Bites

(**Prep + Cook Time:** 23 Minutes | **Servings:** 4)

Ingredients:
- 8 chicken tenders
- 2 tsp. garlic powder
- 2 eggs
- 3/4 cup coconut; shredded
- 3/4 cup panko bread crumbs
- Salt and black pepper to the taste
- Cooking spray

Instructions:
1. In a bowl; mix eggs with salt, pepper and garlic powder and whisk well.
2. In another bowl; mix coconut with panko and stir well.
3. Dip chicken tenders in eggs mix and then coat in coconut one well.
4. Spray chicken bites with cooking spray, place them in your air fryer's basket and cook them at 350 °F, for 10 minutes. Arrange them on a platter and serve as an appetizer.

Nutrition Facts: Calories: 252; Fat: 4g; Fiber: 2g; Carbs: 14g; Protein: 24g

Beef Rolls

(**Prep + Cook Time:** 24 Minutes | **Servings:** 4)

Ingredients:
- 2 lbs. beef steak; opened and flattened with a meat tenderizer
- 3 oz. red bell pepper; roasted and chopped.
- 6 slices provolone cheese
- Salt and black pepper to the taste
- 1 cup baby spinach
- 3 tbsp. pesto

Instructions:
1. Arrange flattened beef steak on a cutting board, spread pesto all over, add cheese in a single layer, add bell peppers, spinach, salt and pepper to the taste.
2. Roll your steak, secure with toothpicks, season again with salt and pepper; place roll in your air fryer's basket and cook at 400 °F, for 14 minutes; rotating roll halfway. Leave aside to cool down, cut into 2 inch smaller rolls, arrange on a platter and serve them as an appetizer.

Nutrition Facts: Calories: 230; Fat: 1g; Fiber: 3g; Carbs: 12g; Protein: 10g

Jerky Beef Snack

(**Prep + Cook Time:** 3 hour and 30 minutes | **Servings:** 6)

Ingredients:
- 2 lbs. beef round; sliced
- 2 tbsp. black peppercorns
- 2 cups soy sauce
- 2 tbsp. black pepper
- 1/2 cup Worcestershire sauce

Instructions:
1. In a bowl; mix soy sauce with black peppercorns, black pepper and Worcestershire sauce and whisk well.
2. Add beef slices; toss to coat and leave aside in the fridge for 6 hours.

3. Place the beef rounds in your air fryer and cook them at 370 °F, for 1 hour and 30 minutes. Transfer to a bowl and serve cold.

Nutrition Facts: Calories: 300; Fat: 12g; Fiber: 4g; Carbs: 3g; Protein: 8g

Delightful Chickpeas Snack
(**Prep + Cook Time:** 20 Minutes | **Servings:** 4)

Ingredients:
- 15 oz. canned chickpeas; drained
- 1 tsp. smoked paprika
- 1/2 tsp. cumin; ground
- 1 tbsp. olive oil
- Salt and black pepper to the taste

Instructions:
1. In a bowl; mix chickpeas with oil, cumin, paprika, salt and pepper; toss to coat, place them in your fryer's basket and cook at 390 °F, for 10 minutes. Divide into bowls and serve as a snack.

Nutrition Facts: Calories: 140; Fat: 1g; Fiber: 6g; Carbs: 20g; Protein: 6g

Tasty Apple Chips
(**Prep + Cook Time:** 20 Minutes | **Servings:** 2)

Ingredients:
- 1 apple; cored and sliced
- 1/2 tsp. cinnamon powder
- 1 tbsp. white sugar
- A pinch of salt

Instructions:
1. In a bowl; mix apple slices with salt, sugar and cinnamon; toss, transfer to your air fryer's basket, cook for 10 minutes at 390 °F, flipping once. Divide apple chips in bowls and serve as a snack.

Nutrition Facts: Calories: 70; Fat: 0g; Fiber: 4g; Carbs: 3g; Protein: 1g

Zucchini Cakes
(**Prep + Cook Time:** 22 Minutes | **Servings:** 12)

Ingredients:
- 3 zucchinis; grated
- 1/2 cup whole wheat flour
- 1 yellow onion; chopped.
- 1/2 cup dill; chopped
- 1 egg
- 2 garlic cloves; minced
- Cooking spray
- Salt and black pepper to the taste

Instructions:
1. In a bowl; mix zucchinis with garlic, onion, flour, salt, pepper, egg and dill; stir well, shape small patties out of this mix, spray them with cooking spray; place them in your air fryer's basket and cook at 370 °F, for 6 minutes on each side. Serve them as a snack right away.

Nutrition Facts: Calories: 60; Fat: 1g; Fiber: 2g; Carbs: 6g; Protein: 2g

Fried Dill Pickles
(**Prep + Cook Time:** 15 Minutes | **Servings:** 4)

Ingredients:
- 16 oz. jarred dill pickles; cut into wedges and pat dried
- 1/2 cup white flour
- 1 egg
- 1/4 cup ranch sauce
- 1/4 cup milk
- 1/2 tsp. garlic powder
- 1/2 tsp. sweet paprika
- Cooking spray

Instructions:
1. In a bowl; combine milk with egg and whisk well.
2. In a second bowl; mix flour with salt, garlic powder and paprika and stir as well

3. Dip pickles in flour, then in egg mix and again in flour and place them in your air fryer. Grease them with cooking spray, cook pickle wedges at 400 °F, for 5 minutes; transfer to a bowl and serve with ranch sauce on the side.

Nutrition Facts: Calories: 109; Fat: 2g; Fiber: 2g; Carbs: 10g; Protein: 4g

Succulent Chicken Dip

(**Prep + Cook Time:** 35 Minutes | **Servings:** 10)

Ingredients:
- 2 cups chicken meat; cooked and shredded
- 2 tsp. curry powder
- 4 scallions; chopped.
- 3 tbsp. butter; melted
- 1 cup yogurt
- 12 oz. cream cheese
- 6 oz. Monterey jack cheese; grated
- 1/3 cup raisins
- 1/4 cup cilantro; chopped.
- 1/2 cup almonds; sliced
- 1/2 cup chutney
- Salt and black pepper to the taste

Instructions:
1. In a bowl mix cream cheese with yogurt and whisk using your mixer.
2. Add curry powder, scallions, chicken meat, raisins, cheese, cilantro, salt and pepper and stir everything. Spread this into a baking pan that fist your air fryer; sprinkle almonds on top, place in your air fryer, bake at 300 degrees for 25 minutes; divide into bowls, top with chutney and serve as an appetizer.

Nutrition Facts: Calories: 240; Fat: 10g; Fiber: 2g; Carbs: 24g; Protein: 12g

Olives Balls

(**Prep + Cook Time:** 14 Minutes | **Servings:** 6)

Ingredients:
- 8 black olives; pitted and minced
- 2 tbsp. sun dried tomato pesto
- 14 pepperoni slices; chopped.
- 4 oz. cream cheese
- 1 tbsp. basil; chopped.
- Salt and black pepper to the taste

Instructions:
1. In a bowl; mix cream cheese with salt, pepper, basil, pepperoni, pesto and black olives; stir well and shape small balls out of this mix. Place them in your air fryer's basket, cook at 350 °F, for 4 minutes; arrange on a platter and serve as a snack.

Nutrition Facts: Calories: 100; Fat: 1g; Fiber: 0g; Carbs: 8g; Protein: 3g

Cheering Chicken Breast Rolls

(**Prep + Cook Time:** 32 Minutes | **Servings:** 4)

Ingredients:
- 4 chicken breasts; boneless and skinless
- 1 cup sun dried tomatoes; chopped.
- 2 cups baby spinach
- 1 ½ tbsp. Italian seasoning
- 4 mozzarella slices
- A drizzle of olive oil
- Salt and black pepper to the taste

Instructions:
1. Flatten chicken breasts using a meat tenderizer, divide tomatoes, mozzarella and spinach, season with salt, pepper and Italian seasoning, roll and seal them.
2. Place them in your air fryer's basket; drizzle some oil over them and cook at 375 °F, for 17 minutes; flipping once. Arrange chicken rolls on a platter and serve them as an appetizer.

Nutrition Facts: Calories: 300; Fat: 1g; Fiber: 4g; Carbs: 7g; Protein: 10g

Sweet Potato Spread

(Prep + Cook Time: 20 Minutes | **Servings:** 10)

Ingredients:
- 1 cup sweet potatoes; peeled and chopped.
- 19 oz. canned garbanzo beans; drained.
- 5 garlic cloves; minced
- 1/2 tsp. cumin; ground
- 2 tbsp. water
- 1/4 cup tahini
- 2 tbsp. lemon juice
- 1 tbsp. olive oil
- A pinch of salt and white pepper

Instructions:
1. Put the potatoes in your air fryer's basket, cook them at 360 °F, for 15 minutes; cool them down, peel, put them in your food processor and pulse well. basket,
2. Add sesame paste, garlic, beans, lemon juice, cumin, water and oil and pulse really well. Add salt and pepper, pulse again; divide into bowls and serve.

Nutrition Facts: Calories: 200; Fat: 3g; Fiber: 10g; Carbs: 20g; Protein: 11g

Cheese Sticks

(Prep + Cook Time: 1 hour and 18 minutes | **Servings:** 4)

Ingredients:
- 8 mozzarella cheese strings; cut into halves
- 2 eggs; whisked
- Salt and black pepper to the taste
- 1 garlic clove; minced
- 1 cup parmesan; grated
- 1 tbsp. Italian seasoning
- Cooking spray

Instructions:
1. In a bowl; mix parmesan with salt, pepper, Italian seasoning and garlic and stir well.
2. Put whisked eggs in another bowl.
3. Dip mozzarella sticks in egg mixture; then in cheese mix.
4. Dip them again in egg and in parmesan mix and keep them in the freezer for 1 hour.
5. Spray cheese sticks with cooking oil; place them in your air fryer's basket and cook at 390 °F, for 8 minutes flipping them halfway. Arrange them on a platter and serve as an appetizer.

Nutrition Facts: Calories: 140; Fat: 5g; Fiber: 1g; Carbs: 3g; Protein: 4g

Banana Chips

(Prep + Cook Time: 25 Minutes | **Servings:** 4)

Ingredients:
- 4 bananas; peeled and sliced
- 1/2 tsp. turmeric powder
- 1/2 tsp. chaat masala
- 1 tsp. olive oil
- A pinch of salt

Instructions:
1. In a bowl; mix banana slices with salt, turmeric, chaat masala and oil; toss and leave aside for 10 minutes.
2. Transfer banana slices to your preheated air fryer at 360 °F and cook them for 15 minutes flipping them once. Serve as a snack.

Nutrition Facts: Calories: 121; Fat: 1g; Fiber: 2g; Carbs: 3g; Protein: 3g

Mexican Style Apple Snack

(Prep + Cook Time: 15 Minutes | **Servings:** 4)

Ingredients:
- 3 big apples; cored, peeled and cubed
- 2 tsp. lemon juice
- 1/2 cup clean caramel sauce
- 1/4 cup pecans; chopped.
- 1/2 cup dark chocolate chips

Instructions:
1. In a bowl; mix apples with lemon juice; stir and transfer to a pan that fits your air fryer.
2. Add chocolate chips, pecans, drizzle the caramel sauce, toss; close the air fryer basket and cook at 320 °F, for 5 minutes. Toss gently, divide into small bowls and serve right away as a snack.

Nutrition Facts: Calories: 200; Fat: 4g; Fiber: 3g; Carbs: 20g; Protein: 3g

Greek Style Lamb Meatballs

(Prep + Cook Time: 18 Minutes | **Servings:** 10)

Ingredients:
- 4 oz. lamb meat; minced
- 1 slice of bread; toasted and crumbled
- 2 tbsp. feta cheese; crumbled
- 1/2 tbsp. lemon peel; grated
- 1 tbsp. oregano; chopped
- Salt and black pepper to the taste

Instructions:
1. In a bowl; combine meat with bread crumbs, salt, pepper, feta, oregano and lemon peel; stir well, shape 10 meatballs and place them in you air fryer. Cook at 400 °F, for 8 minutes; arrange them on a platter and serve as an appetizer.

Nutrition Facts: Calories: 234; Fat: 12g; Fiber: 2g; Carbs: 20g; Protein: 22g

Bacon Jalapeno Balls

(Prep + Cook Time: 14 Minutes | **Servings:** 3)

Ingredients:
- 3 bacon slices; cooked and crumbled
- 1 jalapeno pepper; chopped.
- 3 oz. cream cheese
- 1/4 tsp. onion powder
- 1/2 tsp. parsley; dried
- 1/4 tsp. garlic powder
- Salt and black pepper to the taste

Instructions:
1. In a bowl; mix cream cheese with jalapeno pepper, onion and garlic powder, parsley, bacon salt and pepper and stir well. Shape small balls out of this mix, place them in your air fryer's basket, cook at 350 °F, for 4 minutes; arrange on a platter and serve as an appetizer.

Nutrition Facts: Calories: 172; Fat: 4g; Fiber: 1g; Carbs: 12g; Protein: 5g

Chicken Wings

(Prep + Cook Time: 1 hours 10 Minutes | **Servings:** 2)

Ingredients:
- 16 pieces' chicken wings
- 1/4 cup honey
- 1/4 cup butter
- 3/4 cup potato starch
- 4 tbsp. garlic; minced
- Salt and black pepper to the taste

Instructions:
1. In a bowl; mix chicken wings with salt, pepper and potato starch; toss well, transfer to your air fryer's basket, cook them at 380 °F, for 25 minutes and at 400 °F, for 5 minutes more.
2. Meanwhile; heat up a pan with the butter over medium high heat, melt it, add garlic; stir, cook for 5 minutes and then mix with salt, pepper and honey.
3. Whisk well, cook over medium heat for 20 minutes and take off heat. Arrange chicken wings on a platter; drizzle honey sauce all over and serve as an appetizer.

Nutrition Facts: Calories: 244; Fat: 7g; Fiber: 3g; Carbs: 19g; Protein: 8g

Broccoli Patties
(Prep + Cook Time: 20 Minutes | **Servings:** 12)

Ingredients:
- 4 cups broccoli florets
- 1 ½ cup almond flour
- 1 tsp. paprika
- 2 eggs
- 1/4 cup olive oil
- 2 cups cheddar cheese; grated
- 1 tsp. garlic powder
- 1/2 tsp. apple cider vinegar
- 1/2 tsp. baking soda
- Salt and black pepper to the taste

Instructions:
1. Put the broccoli florets in your food processor; add salt and pepper, blend well and transfer to a bowl.
2. Add almond flour, salt, pepper, paprika, garlic powder, baking soda, cheese, oil, eggs and vinegar; stir well and shape 12 patties out of this mix.
3. Place them in your preheated air fryer's basket and cook at 350 °F, for 10 minutes. Arrange patties on a platter and serve as an appetizer.

Nutrition Facts: Calories: 203; Fat: 12g; Fiber: 2g; Carbs: 14g; Protein: 2g

Seafood Appetizer
(Prep + Cook Time: 35 Minutes | **Servings:** 4)

Ingredients:
- 1 cup baby shrimp; peeled and deveined
- 1/2 cup yellow onion; chopped.
- 1 cup green bell pepper; chopped.
- 1 cup crabmeat; flaked
- 1 cup homemade mayonnaise
- 1 tsp. Worcestershire sauce
- 1 cup celery; chopped.
- 2 tbsp. bread crumbs
- 1 tbsp. butter
- 1 tsp. sweet paprika
- Salt and black pepper to the taste

Instructions:
1. In a bowl; mix shrimp with crab meat, bell pepper, onion, mayo, celery, salt and pepper and stir.
2. Add Worcestershire sauce; stir again and pour everything into a baking pan that fits your air fryer.
3. Sprinkle bread crumbs and add butter, close the air fryer basket and cook at 320 °F, for 25 minutes; shake the basket every few minutes to ensure even cooking. Divide into bowl and serve with paprika sprinkled on top as an appetizer.

Nutrition Facts: Calories: 200; Fat: 1g; Fiber: 2g; Carbs: 5g; Protein: 1g

White Mushrooms Appetizer
(Prep + Cook Time: 20 Minutes | **Servings:** 4)

Ingredients:
- 24 oz. white mushroom caps
- 1/2 cup Mexican cheese; shredded
- 4 oz. cream cheese; soft
- 1/4 cup sour cream
- 1 cup shrimp; cooked, peeled, deveined and chopped.
- 1/4 cup mayonnaise
- 1 tsp. garlic powder
- 1 small yellow onion; chopped.
- Salt and black pepper to the taste
- 1 tsp. curry powder

Instructions:
1. In a bowl; mix mayo with garlic powder, onion, curry powder, cream cheese, sour cream, Mexican cheese, shrimp, salt and pepper to the taste and whisk well.
2. Stuff mushrooms with this mix; place them in your air fryer's basket and cook at 300 °F, for 10 minutes. Arrange on a platter and serve as an appetizer.

Nutrition Facts: Calories: 200; Fat: 20g; Fiber: 3g; Carbs: 16g; Protein: 14g

Shrimp Muffins

(**Prep + Cook Time:** 36 Minutes | **Servings:** 6)

Ingredients:
- 1 spaghetti squash; peeled and halved
- 2 tbsp. mayonnaise
- 1 ½ cups panko
- 1 tsp. parsley flakes
- 1 cup mozzarella; shredded
- 8 oz. shrimp; peeled, cooked and chopped
- 1 garlic clove; minced
- Salt and black pepper to the taste
- Cooking spray

Instructions:
1. Put the squash halves in your air fryer; cook at 350 °F, for 16 minutes; leave aside to cool down and scrape flesh into a bowl.
2. Add salt, pepper, parsley flakes, panko, shrimp, mayo and mozzarella and stir well.
3. Spray a muffin tray that fits your air fryer with cooking spray and divide squash and shrimp mix in each cup.
4. Place the caps in the fryer and cook at 360 °F, for 10 minutes. Arrange muffins on a platter and serve as a snack.

Nutrition Facts: Calories: 60; Fat: 2g; Fiber: 0.4g; Carbs: 4g; Protein: 4g

Stuffed Peppers

(**Prep + Cook Time:** 18 Minutes | **Servings:** 8)

Ingredients:
- 8 small bell peppers; tops cut off and seeds removed
- 3.5 oz. goat cheese; cut into 8 pieces
- 1 tbsp. olive oil
- Salt and black pepper to the taste

Instructions:
1. In a bowl; mix cheese with oil with salt and pepper and toss to coat. Stuff each pepper with goat cheese, place them in your air fryer's basket, cook at 400 °F, for 8 minutes; arrange on a platter and serve as an appetizer.

Nutrition Facts: Calories: 120; Fat: 1g; Fiber: 1g; Carbs: 12g; Protein: 8g

Herbed Tomatoes

(**Prep + Cook Time:** 30 Minutes | **Servings:** 2)

Ingredients:
- 2 tomatoes; halved
- 1 tsp. parsley; dried
- 1 tsp. basil; dried
- 1 tsp. oregano; dried
- 1 tsp. rosemary; dried
- Cooking spray
- Salt and black pepper to the taste

Instructions:
1. Spray tomato halves with cooking oil, season with salt, pepper, parsley, basil, oregano and rosemary over them.
2. Place them in your air fryer's basket and cook at 320 °F, for 20 minutes. Arrange them on a platter and serve as an appetizer.

Nutrition Facts: Calories: 100; Fat: 1g; Fiber: 1g; Carbs: 4g; Protein: 1g

Spicy Stuffed Peppers

(Prep + Cook Time: 30 Minutes | **Servings:** 6)

Ingredients:
- 1 lb. mini bell peppers; halved
- 1 lb. beef meat; ground
- 1½ cups cheddar cheese; shredded
- Salt and black pepper to the taste
- 1 tsp. garlic powder
- 1 tsp. sweet paprika
- 1/2 tsp. oregano; dried
- 1/4 tsp. red pepper flakes
- 1 tbsp. chili powder
- 1 tsp. cumin; ground
- Sour cream for serving

Instructions:
1. In a bowl; mix chili powder with paprika, salt, pepper, cumin, oregano, pepper flakes and garlic powder and stir.
2. Heat up a pan over medium heat, add beef; stir and brown for 10 minutes.
3. Add chili powder mix; stir, take off heat and stuff pepper halves with this mix.
4. Sprinkle cheese all over, place peppers in your air fryer's basket and cook them at 350 °F, for 6 minutes. Arrange peppers on a platter and serve them with sour cream on the side.

Nutrition Facts: Calories: 170; Fat: 22g; Fiber: 3g; Carbs: 6g; Protein: 27g

Fish Sticks

(Prep + Cook Time: 22 Minutes | **Servings:** 2)

Ingredients:
- 4 white fish filets; boneless, skinless and cut into medium sticks
- 4 oz. bread crumbs
- 4 tbsp. olive oil
- 1 egg; whisked
- Salt and black pepper to the taste

Instructions:
1. In a bowl; mix bread crumbs with oil and stir well.
2. Put the egg in a second bowl; add salt and pepper and whisk well.
3. Dip fish stick in egg and them in bread crumb mix, place them in your air fryer's basket and cook at 360 °F, for 12 minutes. Arrange fish sticks on a platter and serve as an appetizer.

Nutrition Facts: Calories: 160; Fat: 3g; Fiber: 5g; Carbs: 12g; Protein: 3g

Traditional Sweet Bacon Snack

(Prep + Cook Time: 40 Minutes | **Servings:** 16)

Ingredients:
- 16 bacon slices
- 1/2 tsp. cinnamon powder
- 1 tbsp. avocado oil
- 3 oz. dark chocolate
- 1 tsp. maple extract

Instructions:
1. Arrange bacon slices in your air fryer's basket; sprinkle cinnamon mix over them and cook them at 300 °F, for 30 minutes.
2. Heat up a pan with the oil over medium heat, add chocolate and stir until it melts.
3. Add maple extract; stir, take off heat and leave aside to cool down a bit.
4. Take bacon strips out of the oven; leave them to cool down, dip each in chocolate mix; place them on a parchment paper and leave them to cool down completely. Serve cold as a snack.

Nutrition Facts: Calories: 200; Fat: 4g; Fiber: 5g; Carbs: 12g; Protein: 3g

Special Empanadas
(Prep + Cook Time: 35 Minutes | **Servings:** 4)

Ingredients:
- 1 package empanada shells
- 1 tbsp. olive oil
- 1/2 tsp. cumin; ground
- 1/4 cup tomato salsa
- 1 egg yolk whisked with 1 tbsp. water
- 1 lb. beef meat; ground
- 1 yellow onion; chopped
- Salt and black pepper to the taste
- 2 garlic cloves; minced
- 1 green bell pepper; chopped

Instructions:
1. Heat up a pan with the oil over medium high heat; add beef and brown on all sides.
2. Add onion, garlic, salt, pepper, bell pepper and tomato salsa; stir and cook for 15 minutes.
3. Divide cooked meat in empanada shells, brush them with egg wash and seal.
4. Place them in your air fryer's steamer basket and cook at 350 °F, for 10 minutes. Arrange on a platter and serve as an appetizer.

Nutrition Facts: Calories: 274; Fat: 17g; Fiber: 14g; Carbs: 20g; Protein: 7g

Appetizing Cajun Shrimp
(Prep + Cook Time: 15 Minutes | **Servings:** 2)

Ingredients:
- 20 tiger shrimp; peeled and deveined
- 1/2 tsp. old bay seasoning
- 1 tbsp. olive oil
- 1/4 tsp. smoked paprika
- Salt and black pepper to the taste

Instructions:
1. In a bowl; mix shrimp with oil, salt, pepper, old bay seasoning and paprika and toss to coat.
2. Place shrimp in your air fryer's basket and cook at 390 °F, for 5 minutes. Arrange them on a platter and serve as an appetizer.

Nutrition Facts: Calories: 162; Fat: 6g; Fiber: 4g; Carbs: 8g; Protein: 14g

Bread Sticks Snack
(Prep + Cook Time: 20 Minutes | **Servings:** 2)

Ingredients:
- 4 bread slices; each cut into 4 sticks
- 1 tbsp. honey
- 1/4 cup brown sugar
- 2 eggs
- 1/4 cup milk
- 1 tsp. cinnamon powder
- A pinch of nutmeg

Instructions:
1. In a bowl; mix eggs with milk, brown sugar, cinnamon, nutmeg and honey and whisk well.
2. Dip bread sticks in this mix; place them in your air fryer's basket and cook at 360 °F, for 10 minutes. Divide bread sticks into bowls and serve as a snack.

Nutrition Facts: Calories: 140; Fat: 1g; Fiber: 4g; Carbs: 8g; Protein: 4g

Roasted Pepper Rolls
(Prep + Cook Time: 20 Minutes | **Servings:** 8)

Ingredients:
- 1 yellow bell pepper; halved
- 4 oz. feta cheese; crumbled
- 1 green onion; chopped
- 2 tbsp. oregano; chopped.
- 1 orange bell pepper; halved
- Salt and black pepper to the taste

Instructions:
1. In a bowl; mix cheese with onion, oregano, salt and pepper and whisk well.
2. Place bell pepper halves in your air fryer's basket, cook at 400 °F, for 10 minutes; transfer to a cutting board, cool down and peel. Divide cheese mix on each bell pepper half, roll, secure with toothpicks, arrange on a platter and serve as an appetizer.

Nutrition Facts: Calories: 170; Fat: 1g; Fiber: 2g; Carbs: 8g; Protein: 5g

Crispy Shrimp Snack
(Prep + Cook Time: 15 Minutes | **Servings:** 4)

Ingredients:
- 12 big shrimp; deveined and peeled
- 1 cup panko bread crumbs
- 1 cup white flour
- 2 egg whites
- 1 cup coconut; shredded
- Salt and black pepper to the taste

Instructions:
1. In a bowl; mix panko with coconut and stir.
2. Put the flour, salt and pepper in a second bowl and whisk egg whites in a third one.
3. Dip shrimp in flour, egg whites mix and coconut, place them all in your air fryer's basket; cook at 350 °F, for 10 minutes flipping halfway. Arrange on a platter and serve as an appetizer.

Nutrition Facts: Calories: 140; Fat: 4g; Fiber: 0g; Carbs: 3g; Protein: 4g

Radish Chips
(Prep + Cook Time: 20 Minutes | **Servings:** 4)

Ingredients:
- 15 radishes; sliced
- 1 tbsp. chives; chopped.
- Cooking spray
- Salt and black pepper to the taste

Instructions:
1. Arrange radish slices in your air fryer's basket, spray them with cooking oil, season with salt and black pepper to the taste, cook them at 350 °F, for 10 minutes;
2. Flipping them halfway, transfer to bowls and serve with chives sprinkled on top.

Nutrition Facts: Calories: 80; Fat: 1g; Fiber: 1g; Carbs: 1g; Protein: 1g

Healthy Spinach Balls
(Prep + Cook Time: 17 Minutes | **Servings:** 30)

Ingredients:
- 16 oz. spinach
- 1/3 cup parmesan; grated
- 4 tbsp. butter; melted
- 2 eggs
- 1 cup flour
- 1/4 tsp. nutmeg; ground
- 1/3 cup feta cheese; crumbled
- 1 tbsp. onion powder
- 3 tbsp. whipping cream
- 1 tsp. garlic powder
- Salt and black pepper to the taste

Instructions:
1. In your blender, mix spinach with butter, eggs, flour, feta cheese, parmesan, nutmeg, whipping cream, salt, pepper, onion and garlic pepper, blend very well and keep in the freezer for 10 minutes.
2. Shape 30 spinach balls; place them in your air fryer's basket and cook at 300 °F, for 7 minutes. Serve as a party appetizer.

Nutrition Facts: Calories: 60; Fat: 5g; Fiber: 1g; Carbs: 1g; Protein: 2g

Shrimp and Calamari Snack

(Prep + Cook Time: 30 Minutes | **Servings:** 1)

Ingredients:
- 8 oz. calamari; cut into medium rings
- 1/2 tsp. turmeric powder
- 2 tbsp. avocado; chopped
- 7 oz. shrimp; peeled and deveined
- 1 eggs
- 3 tbsp. white flour
- 1 tbsp. olive oil
- 1 tsp. tomato paste
- 1 tbsp. mayonnaise
- 1 tsp. lemon juice
- A splash of Worcestershire sauce
- Salt and black pepper to the taste

Instructions:
1. In a bowl; whisk egg with oil, add calamari rings and shrimp and toss to coat.
2. In another bowl; mix flour with salt, pepper and turmeric and stir.
3. Dredge calamari and shrimp in this mix, place them in your air fryer's basket and cook at 350 °F, for 9 minutes; flipping them once.
4. Meanwhile; in a bowl, mix avocado with mayo and tomato paste and mash using a fork.
5. Add Worcestershire sauce, lemon juice, salt and pepper and stir well. Arrange calamari and shrimp on a platter and serve with the sauce on the side.

Nutrition Facts: Calories: 288; Fat: 23g; Fiber: 3g; Carbs: 10g; Protein: 15g

Holyday Beef Patties

(Prep + Cook Time: 18 Minutes | **Servings:** 4)

Ingredients:
- 14 oz. beef; minced
- 1/2 tsp. nutmeg; ground
- 2 tbsp. ham; cut into strips
- 1 leek; chopped
- 3 tbsp. bread crumbs
- Salt and black pepper to the taste

Instructions:
1. In a bowl; mix beef with leek, salt, pepper, ham, breadcrumbs and nutmeg; stir well and shape small patties out of this mix. Place them in your air fryer's basket, cook at 400 °F, for 8 minutes; arrange on a platter and serve as an appetizer.

Nutrition Facts: Calories: 260; Fat: 12g; Fiber: 3g; Carbs: 12g; Protein: 21g

Sausage Balls Snack

(Prep + Cook Time: 25 Minutes | **Servings:** 9)

Ingredients:
- 4 oz. sausage meat; ground
- 1 tsp. sage
- 1/2 tsp. garlic; minced
- 1 small onion; chopped.
- 3 tbsp. breadcrumbs
- Salt and black pepper to the taste

Instructions:
1. In a bowl; mix sausage with salt, pepper, sage, garlic, onion and breadcrumbs; stir well and shape small balls out of this mix. Put them in your air fryer's basket, cook at 360 °F, for 15 minutes; divide into bowls and serve as a snack.

Nutrition Facts: Calories: 130; Fat: 7g; Fiber: 1g; Carbs: 13g; Protein: 4g

Party Beef Rolls

(Prep + Cook Time: 25 Minutes | **Servings:** 4)

Ingredients:
- 14 oz. beef stock
- 8 sage leaves
- 4 ham slices
- 1 tbsp. butter; melted
- 7 oz. white wine
- 4 beef cutlets
- Salt and black pepper to the taste

Instructions:
1. Heat up a pan with the stock over medium high heat, add wine, cook until it reduces, take off heat and divide into small bowls
2. Season cutlets with salt and pepper; cover with sage and roll each in ham slices.
3. Brush rolls with butter, place them in your air fryer's basket and cook at 400 °F, for 15 minutes. Arrange rolls on a platter and serve them with the gravy on the side.

Nutrition Facts: Calories: 260; Fat: 12g; Fiber: 1g; Carbs: 22g; Protein: 21g

Cheesy Chicken Wings

(Prep + Cook Time: 22 Minutes | **Servings:** 6)

Ingredients:
- 6 lb. chicken wings; halved
- 1/2 tsp. Italian seasoning
- 1 tsp. garlic powder
- 1 egg
- 2 tbsp. butter
- 1/2 cup parmesan cheese; grated
- A pinch of red pepper flakes; crushed
- Salt and black pepper to the taste

Instructions:
1. Arrange chicken wings in your air fryer's basket and cook at 390 °F and cook for 9 minutes.
2. Meanwhile; in your blender, mix butter with cheese, egg, salt, pepper, pepper flakes, garlic powder and Italian seasoning and blend very well.
3. Take chicken wings out; pour cheese sauce over them, toss to coat well and cook in your air fryer's basket at 390 °F, for 3 minutes. Serve them as an appetizer.

Nutrition Facts: Calories: 204; Fat: 8g; Fiber: 1g; Carbs: 18g; Protein: 14g

Tuna Cakes

(Prep + Cook Time: 20 Minutes | **Servings:** 12)

Ingredients:
- 15 oz. canned tuna; drain and flaked
- 1 tsp. parsley; dried
- 1/2 cup red onion; chopped.
- 1 tsp. garlic powder
- 3 eggs
- 1/2 tsp. dill; dried
- Salt and black pepper to the taste
- Cooking spray

Instructions:
1. In a bowl; mix tuna with salt, pepper, dill, parsley, onion, garlic powder and eggs; stir well and shape medium cakes out of this mix.
2. Place tuna cakes in your air fryer's basket, spray them with cooking oil and cook at 350 °F, for 10 minutes; flipping them halfway. Arrange them on a platter and serve as an appetizer.

Nutrition Facts: Calories: 140; Fat: 2g; Fiber: 1g; Carbs: 8g; Protein: 6g

Cheesy Zucchini Snack

(Prep + Cook Time: 18 Minutes | **Servings:** 4)

Ingredients:
- 1 cup mozzarella; shredded
- 1/4 cup tomato sauce
- 1 zucchini; sliced
- Salt and black pepper to the taste
- A pinch of cumin
- Cooking spray

Instructions:
1. Arrange zucchini slices in your air fryer's basket; spray them with cooking oil, spread tomato sauce all over, them, season with salt, pepper, cumin, sprinkle mozzarella at the end and cook them at 320 °F, for 8 minutes. Arrange them on a platter and serve as a snack.

Nutrition Facts: Calories: 150; Fat: 4g; Fiber: 2g; Carbs: 12g; Protein: 4g

Pure Pumpkin Muffins

(Prep + Cook Time: 25 Minutes | **Servings:** 18)

Ingredients:
- 3/4 cup pumpkin puree
- 1/4 cup butter
- 1/2 tsp. nutmeg; ground
- 1 tsp. cinnamon powder
- 1/2 tsp. baking soda
- 2 tbsp. flaxseed meal
- 1/4 cup flour
- 1/2 cup sugar
- 1 egg
- 1/2 tsp. baking powder

Instructions:
1. In a bowl; mix butter with pumpkin puree and egg and blend well.
2. Add flaxseed meal, flour, sugar, baking soda, baking powder, nutmeg and cinnamon and stir well.
3. Spoon this into a muffin pan that fits your fryer and bake at 350 °F and for 15 minutes. Serve muffins cold as a snack.

Nutrition Facts: Calories: 50; Fat: 3g; Fiber: 1g; Carbs: 2g; Protein: 2g

Kale and Celery Crackers

(Prep + Cook Time: 30 Minutes | **Servings:** 6)

Ingredients:
- 2 cups flax seed; ground
- 1 bunch basil; chopped
- 1/2 bunch celery; chopped.
- 2 cups flax seed; soaked overnight and drained
- 4 bunches kale; chopped
- 4 garlic cloves; minced
- 1/3 cup olive oil

Instructions:
1. In your food processor mix ground flaxseed with celery, kale, basil and garlic and blend well.
2. Add oil and soaked flaxseed and blend again, spread in your air fryer's pan; cut into medium crackers and cook them at 380 °F, for 20 minutes. Divide into bowls and serve as an appetizer.

Nutrition Facts: Calories: 143; Fat: 1g; Fiber: 2g; Carbs: 8g; Protein: 4g

Cheesy Chicken Rolls

(Prep + Cook Time: 30 Minutes | **Servings:** 12)

Ingredients:
- 4 oz. blue cheese; crumbled
- 2 celery stalks; finely chopped.
- 1/2 cup tomato sauce
- 12 egg roll wrappers
- 2 cups chicken; cooked and chopped.
- 2 green onions; chopped
- Salt and black pepper to the taste
- Cooking spray

Instructions:
1. In a bowl; mix chicken meat with blue cheese, salt, pepper, green onions, celery and tomato sauce; stir well and keep in the fridge for 2 hours.

2. Place egg wrappers on a working surface, divide chicken mix on them, roll and seal edges. Place rolls in your air fryer's basket, spray them with cooking oil and cook at 350 °F, for 10 minutes; flipping them halfway.

Nutrition Facts: Calories: 220; Fat: 7g; Fiber: 2g; Carbs: 14g; Protein: 10g

Egg White Chips Snack

(Prep + Cook Time: 13 Minutes | **Servings:** 2)

Ingredients:
- 4 eggs whites
- 1/2 tbsp. water
- 2 tbsp. parmesan; shredded
- Salt and black pepper to the taste

Instructions:
1. In a bowl; mix egg whites with salt, pepper and water and whisk well.
2. Spoon this into a muffin pan that fits your air fryer, sprinkle cheese on top; close the air fryer basket and cook at 350 °F, for 8 minutes. Arrange egg white chips on a platter and serve as a snack.

Nutrition Facts: Calories: 180; Fat: 2g; Fiber: 1g; Carbs: 12g; Protein: 7g

Party Pork Rolls

(Prep + Cook Time: 50 Minutes | **Servings:** 4)

Ingredients:
- 1 (15 oz.) pork fillet
- 1/2 tsp. chili powder
- 1 tsp. cinnamon powder
- 1 red onion; chopped
- 3 tbsp. parsley; chopped
- 1 garlic clove; minced
- 2 tbsp. olive oil
- 1 ½ tsp. cumin; ground
- Salt and black pepper to the taste

Instructions:
1. In a bowl; mix cinnamon with garlic, salt, pepper, chili powder, oil, onion, parsley and cumin and stir well
2. Put the pork fillet on a cutting board, flatten it using a meat tenderizer. And use a meat tenderizer to flatten it.
3. Spread onion mix on pork, roll tight, cut into medium rolls, place them in your preheated air fryer at 360 °F and cook them for 35 minutes. Arrange them on a platter and serve as an appetizer

Nutrition Facts: Calories: 304; Fat: 12g; Fiber: 1g; Carbs: 15g; Protein: 23g

Wrapped Shrimp

(Prep + Cook Time: 18 Minutes | **Servings:** 16)

Ingredients:
- 10 oz. already cooked shrimp; peeled and deveined
- 2 tbsp. olive oil
- 1/3 cup blackberries; ground
- 11 prosciutto sliced
- 1/3 cup red wine
- 1 tbsp. mint; chopped.

Instructions:
1. Wrap each shrimp in a prosciutto slices, drizzle the oil over them, rub well, place in your preheated air fryer at 390 °F and fry them for 8 minutes.
2. Meanwhile; heat up a pan with ground blackberries over medium heat, add mint and wine; stir, cook for 3 minutes and take off heat. Arrange shrimp on a platter, drizzle blackberries sauce over them and serve as an appetizer.

Nutrition Facts: Calories: 224; Fat: 12g; Fiber: 2g; Carbs: 12g; Protein: 14g

Dessert Recipes

Mini Lava Cakes Recipe

(Prep + Cook Time: 30 Minutes | **Servings:** 3)

Ingredients:
- 1 egg
- 1/2 tsp. baking powder
- 4 tbsp. sugar
- 2 tbsp. olive oil
- 1 tbsp. cocoa powder
- 4 tbsp. milk
- 4 tbsp. flour
- 1/2 tsp. orange zest

Instructions:
1. In a bowl; mix egg with sugar, oil, milk, flour, salt, cocoa powder, baking powder and orange zest; stir very well and pour this into greased ramekins
2. Add ramekins to your air fryer and cook at 320 °F, for 20 minutes. Serve lava cakes warm.

Nutrition Facts: Calories: 201; Fat: 7g; Fiber: 8g; Carbs: 23g; Protein: 4g

Tomato Cake Recipe

(Prep + Cook Time: 40 Minutes | **Servings:** 4)

Ingredients:
- 1 ½ cups flour
- 1 tsp. cinnamon powder
- 1 cup tomatoes chopped
- 1/2 cup olive oil
- 1 tsp. baking powder
- 1 tsp. baking soda
- 3/4 cup maple syrup
- 2 tbsp. apple cider vinegar

Instructions:
1. In a bowl; mix flour with baking powder, baking soda, cinnamon and maple syrup and stir well.
2. In another bowl, mix tomatoes with olive oil and vinegar and stir well
3. Combine the 2 mixtures; stir well, pour into a greased round pan that fits your air fryer, and cook at 360 °F, for 30 minutes. Leave cake to cool down, slice and serve.

Nutrition Facts: Calories: 153; Fat: 2g; Fiber: 1g; Carbs: 25g; Protein: 4g

Lentils and Dates Brownies Recipe

(Prep + Cook Time: 25 Minutes | **Servings:** 8)

Ingredients:
- 28 oz. canned lentils; rinsed and drained
- 1/2 tsp. baking soda
- 4 tbsp. almond butter
- 12 dates
- 1 tbsp. honey
- 1 banana; peeled and chopped.
- 2 tbsp. cocoa powder

Instructions:
1. In your food processor, mix lentils with butter, banana, cocoa, baking soda and honey and blend really well.
2. Add dates, pulse a few more times, pour this into a greased pan that fits your air fryer, spread evenly, and bake at 360 °F for 15 minutes.
3. Take brownies mix out of the oven, cut, arrange on a platter and serve

Nutrition Facts: Calories: 162; Fat: 4g; Fiber: 2g; Carbs: 3g; Protein: 4g

Plum Cake Recipe

(Prep + Cook Time: 1 hour and 20 Minutes | **Servings:** 8)

Ingredients:
- 1 ¾ lbs. plums; pitted and cut into quarters
- 1 package dried yeast
- 7 oz. flour
- 5 tbsp. sugar
- 3 oz. warm milk
- 1 oz. butter; soft
- 1 egg; whisked
- Zest from 1 lemon; grated
- 1 oz. almond flakes

Instructions:
1. In a bowl; mix yeast with butter, flour and 3 tbsp. sugar and stir well
2. Add milk and egg and whisk for 4 minutes until you obtain a dough
3. Arrange the dough in a spring form pan that fits your air fryer and which you've greased with some butter, cover and leave aside for 1 hour. Arrange plumps on top of the butter, sprinkle the rest of the sugar.
4. Place the pan in your air fryer and bake at 350 degrees F, for 36 minutes; cool down, sprinkle almond flakes and lemon zest on top, slice and serve.

Nutrition Facts: Calories: 192; Fat: 4g; Fiber: 2g; Carbs: 6g; Protein: 7g

Strawberry Cobbler Recipe

(Prep + Cook Time: 35 Minutes | **Servings:** 6)

Ingredients:
- 3/4 cup sugar
- 6 cups strawberries; halved
- 1/8 tsp. baking powder
- 1 tbsp. lemon juice
- 1/2 cup flour
- 1/2 cup water
- 3 ½ tbsp. olive oil
- A pinch of baking soda
- Cooking spray

Instructions:
1. In a bowl; mix strawberries with half of sugar, sprinkle some flour, add lemon juice, whisk and pour into the baking pan that fits your air fryer and greased with cooking spray
2. In another bowl, mix flour with the rest of the sugar, baking powder and soda and stir well.
3. Add the olive oil and mix until the whole thing with your hands
4. Add 1/2 cup water and spread over strawberries.
5. Place the dish and lock the air fryer basket. bake at 355 °F for 25 minutes. Leave cobbler aside to cool down, slice and serve.

Nutrition Facts: Calories: 221; Fat: 3g; Fiber: 3g; Carbs: 6g; Protein: 9g

Carrot Cake Recipe

(Prep + Cook Time: 55 Minutes | **Servings:** 6)

Ingredients:
- 5 oz. flour
- 3/4 tsp. baking powder
- 1/4 tsp. nutmeg; ground
- 1/2 tsp. baking soda
- 1/2 tsp. cinnamon powder
- 1/2 cup sugar
- 1/3 cup carrots; grated
- 1/3 cup pecans; toasted and chopped.
- 1/4 cup pineapple juice
- 1/2 tsp. allspice
- 1 egg
- 3 tbsp. yogurt
- 4 tbsp. sunflower oil
- 1/3 cup coconut flakes; shredded
- Cooking spray

Instructions:
1. In a bowl; mix flour with baking soda and powder, salt, allspice, cinnamon and nutmeg and stir.
2. In another bowl, mix egg with yogurt, sugar, pineapple juice, oil, carrots, pecans and coconut flakes and stir well

3. Combine the two mixtures and stir well, pour this into a spring form pan that fits your air fryer which you've greased with some cooking spray, transfer to your air fryer and cook on 320 °F, for 45 minutes.
4. Leave cake to cool down, then cut and serve it.

Nutrition Facts: Calories: 200; Fat: 6g; Fiber: 20g; Carbs: 22g; Protein: 4g

Banana Bread Recipe

(Prep + Cook Time: 50 Minutes | **Servings:** 6)

Ingredients:
- 3/4 cup sugar
- 1/3 cup butter
- 1/3 cup milk
- 1 tsp. vanilla extract
- 1 egg
- 2 bananas; mashed
- 1 tsp. baking powder
- 1 ½ cups flour
- 1/2 tsp. baking soda
- 1 ½ tsp. cream of tartar
- Cooking spray

Instructions:
1. In a bowl; mix milk with cream of tartar, sugar, butter, egg, vanilla and bananas and stir everything.
2. In another bowl, mix flour with baking powder and baking soda
3. Combine the 2 mixtures; stir well, pour this into a cake pan greased with some cooking spray, close the air fryer basket and cook at 320 °F, for 40 minutes. Take bread out, leave aside to cool down, slice and serve it.

Nutrition Facts: Calories: 292; Fat: 7g; Fiber: 8g; Carbs: 28g; Protein: 4g

Banana Cake Recipe

(Prep + Cook Time: 40 Minutes | **Servings:** 4)

Ingredients:
- 1 banana; peeled and mashed
- 1 tbsp. butter; soft
- 1 egg
- 1/3 cup brown sugar
- 1 tsp. baking powder
- 1/2 tsp. cinnamon powder
- 2 tbsp. honey
- 1 cup white flour
- Cooking spray

Instructions:
1. Spray a cake pan with some cooking spray and leave aside.
2. In a bowl; mix butter with sugar, banana, honey, egg, cinnamon, baking powder and flour and whisk
3. Pour this into a cake pan greased with cooking spray, close the air fryer basket and cook at 350 °F, for 30 minutes. Leave cake to cool down, slice and serve

Nutrition Facts: Calories: 232; Fat: 4g; Fiber: 1g; Carbs: 34g; Protein: 4g

Blueberry Scones Recipe

(Prep + Cook Time: 20 Minutes | **Servings:** 10)

Ingredients:
- 1 cup white flour
- 1 cup blueberries
- 5 tbsp. sugar
- 2 tsp. vanilla extract
- 2 eggs
- 1/2 cup heavy cream
- 1/2 cup butter
- 2 tsp. baking powder

Instructions:
1. In a bowl; mix flour, salt, baking powder and blueberries and stir
2. In another bowl, mix heavy cream with butter, vanilla extract, sugar and eggs and stir well
3. Combine the 2 mixtures, knead until you obtain your dough, shape 10 triangles from this mix, place them on a lined baking pan that fits your air fryer and cook them at 320 °F, for 10 minutes. Serve them cold.

Nutrition Facts: Calories: 130; Fat: 2g; Fiber: 2g; Carbs: 4g; Protein: 3g

Strawberry Donuts Recipe
(Prep + Cook Time: 25 Minutes | Servings: 4)

Ingredients:
- 8 oz. flour
- 1 tbsp. brown sugar
- 4 oz. whole milk
- 1 tsp. baking powder
- 1 tbsp. white sugar
- 1 egg
- 2 ½ tbsp. butter

For the strawberry icing:
- 1/2 tsp. pink coloring
- 1/4 cup strawberries; chopped.
- 2 tbsp. butter
- 3.5 oz. icing sugar
- 1 tbsp. whipped cream

Instructions:
1. In a bowl; mix butter, 1 tbsp. brown sugar, 1 tbsp. white sugar and flour and stir
2. In a second bowl, mix egg with 1 ½ tbsp. butter and milk and stir well.
3. Combine the 2 mixtures; stir, shape donuts from this mix, place them in your air fryer's basket and cook at 360 °F, for 15 minutes
4. Put 1 tbsp. butter, icing sugar, food coloring, whipped cream and strawberry puree and whisk well. Arrange donuts on a platter and serve with strawberry icing on top

Nutrition Facts: Calories: 250; Fat: 12g; Fiber: 1g; Carbs: 32g; Protein: 4g

Chocolate Cookies Recipe
(Prep + Cook Time: 35 Minutes | Servings: 12)

Ingredients:
- 1 tsp. vanilla extract
- 2 cups flour
- 1/2 cup butter
- 1 egg
- 4 tbsp. sugar
- 1/2 cup unsweetened chocolate chips

Instructions:
1. Heat up a pan with the butter over medium heat; stir and cook for 1 minute
2. In a bowl; mix egg with vanilla extract and sugar and stir well
3. Add melted butter, flour and half of the chocolate chips and stir everything.
4. Transfer this to a pan that fits your air fryer, spread the rest of the chocolate chips on top, close the air fryer basket and bake at 330 °F for 25 minutes. Slice when it's cold and serve

Nutrition Facts: Calories: 230; Fat: 12g; Fiber: 2g; Carbs: 4g; Protein: 5g

Bread Dough and Amaretto Dessert Recipe
(Prep + Cook Time: 22 Minutes | Servings: 12)

Ingredients:
- 1 lb. bread dough
- 1 cup heavy cream
- 12 oz. chocolate chips
- 1 cup sugar
- 1/2 cup butter; melted
- 2 tbsp. amaretto liqueur

Instructions:
1. Roll dough, cut into 20 slices and then cut each slice in halves.
2. Brush dough pieces with butter, sprinkle sugar, place them in your air fryer's basket after you've brushed it some butter, cook them at 350 °F, for 5 minutes; flip them, cook for 3 minutes more and transfer to a platter
3. Heat up a pan with the heavy cream over medium heat, add chocolate chips and stir until they melt. Add liqueur; stir again, transfer to a bowl and serve bread dippers with this sauce

Nutrition Facts: Calories: 200; Fat: 1g; Fiber: 0g; Carbs: 6g; Protein: 6g

Plum and Currant Tart Recipe

(**Prep + Cook Time:** 65 Minutes | **Servings:** 6)

Ingredients:
For the crumble:
- 1/4 cup almond flour
- 1/4 cup millet flour
- 1 cup brown rice flour
- 1/2 cup cane sugar
- 10 tbsp. butter; soft
- 3 tbsp. milk

For the filling:
- 1 lb. small plums; pitted and halved
- 1 cup white currants
- 2 tbsp. cornstarch
- 3 tbsp. sugar
- 1/2 tsp. vanilla extract
- 1/2 tsp. cinnamon powder
- 1/4 tsp. ginger powder
- 1 tsp. lime juice

Instructions:
1. In a bowl; mix brown rice flour with 1/2 cup sugar, millet flour, almond flour, butter and milk and stir until you obtain a sand like dough
2. Reserve 1/4 of the dough, press the rest of the dough into a tart pan that fits your air fryer and keep in the fridge for 30 minutes.
3. Meanwhile; in a bowl, mix plums with currants, 3 tbsp. sugar, cornstarch, vanilla extract, cinnamon, ginger and lime juice and stir well
4. Pour this over tart crust, crumble reserved dough on top, close the air fryer basket and cook at 350 °F, for 35 minutes. Leave tart to cool down, slice and serve.

Nutrition Facts: Calories: 200; Fat: 5g; Fiber: 4g; Carbs: 8g; Protein: 6g

Strawberry Pie Recipe

(**Prep + Cook Time:** 30 Minutes | **Servings:** 12)

Ingredients:
For the crust: y
- 1 cup coconut; shredded
- 1/4 cup butter
- 1 cup sunflower seeds

For the filling:
- 1/2 cup heavy cream
- 8 oz. strawberries; chopped for serving
- 1 tsp. gelatin
- 8 oz. cream cheese
- 1/2 tbsp. lemon juice
- 1/4 tsp. stevia
- 4 oz. strawberries
- 2 tbsp. water

Instructions:
1. In your food processor, mix sunflower seeds with coconut, a pinch of salt and butter, pulse and press this on the bottom of a cake pan that fits your air fryer
2. Heat up a pan with the water over medium heat, add gelatin; stir until it dissolves, leave aside to cool down, add this to your food processor, mix with 4 oz. strawberries, cream cheese, lemon juice and stevia and blend well
3. Add heavy cream; stir well and spread this over crust.
4. Top with 8 oz. strawberries, close the air fryer basket and cook at 330 °F, for 15 minutes. Keep in the fridge until you serve it.

Nutrition Facts: Calories: 234; Fat: 23g; Fiber: 2g; Carbs: 6g; Protein: 7g

Pears and Espresso Cream Recipe

(Prep + Cook Time: 40 Minutes | **Servings:** 4)

Ingredients:
- 4 pears; halved and cored
- 2 tbsp. water
- 2 tbsp. lemon juice
- 1 tbsp. sugar
- 2 tbsp. butter

For the cream:
- 1 cup whipping cream
- 2 tbsp. espresso; cold
- 1 cup mascarpone
- 1/3 cup sugar

Instructions:
1. In a bowl; mix pears halves with lemon juice, 1 tbsp. sugar, butter and water, toss well, transfer them to your air fryer and cook at 360 °F, for 30 minutes
2. Meanwhile; in a bowl, mix whipping cream with mascarpone, ⅓ cup sugar and espresso, whisk really well and keep in the fridge until pears are done.
3. Divide pears on plates, top with espresso cream and serve them

Nutrition Facts: Calories: 211; Fat: 5g; Fiber: 7g; Carbs: 8g; Protein: 7g

Pumpkin Cookies Recipe

(Prep + Cook Time: 25 Minutes | **Servings:** 24)

Ingredients:
- 2 ½ cups flour
- 1/2 tsp. baking soda
- 2 tbsp. butter
- 1 tsp. vanilla extract
- 1 tbsp. flax seed; ground
- 3 tbsp. water
- 1/2 cup pumpkin flesh; mashed
- 1/4 cup honey
- 1/2 cup dark chocolate chips

Instructions:
1. In a bowl; mix flax seed with water; stir and leave aside for a few minutes.
2. In another bowl, mix flour with salt and baking soda
3. In a third bowl, mix honey with pumpkin puree, butter, vanilla extract and flaxseed.
4. Combine flour with honey mix and chocolate chips and stir
5. Scoop 1 tbsp. of cookie dough on a lined baking pan that fits your air fryer, repeat with the rest of the dough, transfer them in your air fryer and cook at 350 °F, for 15 minutes.
6. Leave cookies to cool down and serve.

Nutrition Facts: Calories: 140; Fat: 2g; Fiber: 2g; Carbs: 7g; Protein: 10g

Coffee Cheesecakes Recipe

(Prep + Cook Time: 30 Minutes | **Servings:** 6)

Ingredients:
For the cheesecakes:
- 1/3 cup sugar
- 8 oz. cream cheese
- 2 tbsp. butter
- 3 eggs
- 3 tbsp. coffee
- 1 tbsp. caramel syrup

For the frosting:
- 3 tbsp. caramel syrup
- 8 oz. mascarpone cheese; soft
- 3 tbsp. butter
- 2 tbsp. sugar

Instructions:
1. In your blender, mix cream cheese with eggs, 2 tbsp. butter, coffee, 1 tbsp. caramel syrup and ⅓ cup sugar and pulse very well, spoon into a cupcakes pan that fits your air fryer, place the cupcake pan in the fryer and cook at 320 °F and bake for 20 minutes

2. Leave aside to cool down and then keep in the freezer for 3 hours. Meanwhile; in a bowl, mix 3 tbsp. butter with 3 tbsp. caramel syrup, 2 tbsp. sugar and mascarpone, blend well, spoon this over cheesecakes and serve them.

Nutrition Facts: Calories: 254; Fat: 23g; Fiber: 0g; Carbs: 21g; Protein: 5g

Cheesecake Recipe

(**Prep + Cook Time:** 25 Minutes | **Servings:** 15)

Ingredients:
- 1 lb. cream cheese
- 1/2 tsp. vanilla extract
- 1 cup graham crackers; crumbled
- 2 tbsp. butter
- 2 eggs
- 4 tbsp. sugar

Instructions:
1. In a bowl; mix crackers with butter.
2. Press crackers mix on the bottom of a lined cake pan, close the air fryer basket and cook at 350 °F, for 4 minutes
3. Meanwhile; in a bowl, mix sugar with cream cheese, eggs and vanilla and whisk well.
4. Spread filling over crackers crust and cook your cheesecake in your air fryer at 310 °F, for 15 minutes. Leave cake in the fridge for 3 hours, slice and serve

Nutrition Facts: Calories: 245; Fat: 12g; Fiber: 1g; Carbs: 20g; Protein: 3g

Cinnamon Rolls and Cream Cheese Dip Recipe

(**Prep + Cook Time:** 2 hours 15 Minutes | **Servings:** 8)

Ingredients:
- 1 lb. bread dough
- 3/4 cup brown sugar
- 1/4 cup butter; melted
- 1 ½ tbsp. cinnamon; ground

For the cream cheese dip:
- 2 tbsp. butter
- 1 ¼ cups sugar
- 1/2 tsp. vanilla
- 4 oz. cream cheese

Instructions:
1. Roll dough on a floured working surface; shape a rectangle and brush with 1/4 cup butter.
2. In a bowl; mix cinnamon with sugar; stir, sprinkle this over dough, roll dough into a log, seal well and cut into 8 pieces
3. Leave rolls to rise for 2 hours, place them in your air fryer's basket, cook at 350 °F, for 5 minutes; flip them, cook for 4 minutes more and transfer to a platter
4. In a bowl; mix cream cheese with butter, sugar and vanilla and whisk really well. Serve your cinnamon rolls with this cream cheese dip.

Nutrition Facts: Calories: 200; Fat: 1g; Fiber: 0g; Carbs: 5g; Protein: 6g

Granola Recipe

(**Prep + Cook Time:** 45 Minutes | **Servings:** 4)

Ingredients:
- 1 cup coconut; shredded
- 1/2 cup almonds
- 1/2 cup pecans; chopped.
- 2 tbsp. sugar
- 1/2 cup pumpkin seeds
- 1/2 cup sunflower seeds
- 2 tbsp. sunflower oil
- 1 tsp. nutmeg; ground
- 1 tsp. apple pie spice mix

Instructions:
1. In a bowl; mix almonds and pecans with pumpkin seeds, sunflower seeds, coconut, nutmeg and apple pie spice mix and stir well
2. Heat up a pan with the oil over medium heat, add sugar and stir well.
3. Pour this over nuts and coconut mix and stir well

4. Spread this on a lined baking pan that fits your air fryer, close the air fryer basket and cook at 300 °F and bake for 25 minutes. Leave your granola to cool down, cut and serve.

Nutrition Facts: Calories: 322; Fat: 7g; Fiber: 8g; Carbs: 12g; Protein: 7g

Chocolate Cake Recipe

(**Prep + Cook Time:** 40 Minutes | **Servings:** 12)

Ingredients:
- 3/4 cup white flour
- 3/4 cup whole wheat flour
- 1 tsp. baking soda
- 3/4 tsp. pumpkin pie spice
- 3/4 cup sugar
- 1/2 tsp. vanilla extract
- 2/3 cup chocolate chips
- 1 banana; mashed
- 1/2 tsp. baking powder
- 2 tbsp. canola oil
- 1/2 cup Greek yogurt
- 8 oz. canned pumpkin puree
- 1 egg
- Cooking spray

Instructions:
1. In a bowl; mix white flour with whole wheat flour, salt, baking soda and powder and pumpkin spice and stir
2. In another bowl, mix sugar with oil, banana, yogurt, pumpkin puree, vanilla and egg and stir using a mixer
3. Combine the 2 mixtures, add chocolate chips; stir, pour this into a greased Bundt pan that fits your air fryer.
4. Close the air fryer basket and cook at 330 °F, for 30 minutes
5. Leave the cake to cool down, before cutting and serving it.

Nutrition Facts: Calories: 232; Fat: 7g; Fiber: 7g; Carbs: 29g; Protein: 4g

Lemon Bars Recipe

(**Prep + Cook Time:** 35 Minutes | **Servings:** 6)

Ingredients:
- 4 eggs
- 1 cup butter; soft
- 2 ¼ cups flour
- Juice from 2 lemons
- 2 cups sugar

Instructions:
1. In a bowl; mix butter with 1/2 cup sugar and 2 cups flour; stir well, press on the bottom of a pan that fits your air fryer, Place the pan in the fryer and cook at 350 °F, for 10 minutes
2. In another bowl, mix the rest of the sugar with the rest of the flour, eggs and lemon juice, whisk well and spread over crust. And air fry at 350 °F, for 15 minutes more, leave aside to cool down, cut bars and serve them.

Nutrition Facts: Calories: 125; Fat: 4g; Fiber: 4g; Carbs: 16g; Protein: 2g

Orange Cake Recipe

(**Prep + Cook Time:** 42 Minutes | **Servings:** 12)

Ingredients:
- 1 orange, peeled and cut into quarters
- 1 tsp. vanilla extract
- 6 eggs
- 2 tbsp. orange zest
- 4 oz. cream cheese
- 1 tsp. baking powder
- 9 oz. flour
- 2 oz. sugar+ 2 tbsp.
- 4 oz. yogurt

Instructions:
1. In your food processor, pulse orange very well
2. Add flour, 2 tbsp. sugar, eggs, baking powder, vanilla extract and pulse well again.
3. Transfer this into 2 spring form pans, Put one by one in your fryer and cook at 330 °F, for 16 minutes

4. Meanwhile; in a bowl, mix cream cheese with orange zest, yogurt and the rest of the sugar and stir well.
5. Place one cake layer on a plate, add half of the cream cheese mix, add the other cake layer and top with the rest of the cream cheese mix. Spread it well, slice and serve.

Nutrition Facts: Calories: 200; Fat: 13g; Fiber: 2g; Carbs: 9g; Protein: 8g

Peach Pie Recipe

(Prep + Cook Time: 45 Minutes | **Servings:** 4)

Ingredients:
- 1 pie dough
- 2 ¼ lbs. peaches; pitted and chopped.
- 2 tbsp. cornstarch
- 1 tbsp. dark rum
- 1 tbsp. lemon juice
- 1/2 cup sugar
- 2 tbsp. flour
- A pinch of nutmeg; ground
- 2 tbsp. butter; melted

Instructions:
1. Roll pie dough into a pie pan that fits your air fryer and press well.
2. In a bowl; mix peaches with cornstarch, sugar, flour, nutmeg, rum, lemon juice and butter and stir well.
3. Pour and spread this into pie pan, close the air fryer basket and cook at 350 °F, for 35 minutes. Serve warm or cold

Nutrition Facts: Calories: 231; Fat: 6g; Fiber: 7g; Carbs: 9g; Protein: 5g

Cocoa Cake Recipe

(Prep + Cook Time: 27 Minutes | **Servings:** 6)

Ingredients:
- 3.5 oz. butter; melted
- 3 oz. flour
- 3 eggs
- 3 oz. sugar
- 1 tsp. cocoa powder
- 1/2 tsp. lemon juice

Instructions:
1. In a bowl; mix 1 tbsp. butter with cocoa powder and whisk
2. In another bowl, mix the rest of the butter with sugar, eggs, flour and lemon juice, whisk well and pour half into a cake pan that fits your air fryer
3. Add half of the cocoa mix, spread, add the rest of the butter layer and top with the rest of cocoa.
4. Close the air fryer basket and cook at 360 °F, for 17 minutes. Cool cake down before slicing and serving.

Nutrition Facts: Calories: 340; Fat: 11g; Fiber: 3g; Carbs: 25g; Protein: 5g

Apple Bread Recipe

(Prep + Cook Time: 50 Minutes | **Servings:** 6)

Ingredients:
- 3 cups apples; cored and cubed
- 1 cup sugar
- 1 tbsp. baking powder
- 1 stick butter
- 1 tbsp. vanilla
- 2 eggs
- 1 tbsp. apple pie spice
- 2 cups white flour
- 1 cup water

Instructions:
1. In a bowl mix egg with 1 butter stick, apple pie spice and sugar and stir using your mixer.
2. Add apples and stir again well
3. In another bowl, mix baking powder with flour and stir.
4. Combine the 2 mixtures; stir and pour into a spring form pan
5. Put the spring form pan in your air fryer and cook at 320 °F, for 40 minutes Slice and serve.

Nutrition Facts: Calories: 192; Fat: 6g; Fiber: 7g; Carbs: 14g; Protein: 7g

Bread Pudding Recipe
(**Prep + Cook Time:** 1 hour 10 Minutes | **Servings:** 4)

Ingredients:
- 6 glazed doughnuts; crumbled
- 1 cup cherries
- 4 egg yolks
- 1/4 cup sugar
- 1/2 cup chocolate chips.
- 1 ½ cups whipping cream
- 1/2 cup raisins

Instructions:
1. In a bowl; mix cherries with egg yolks and whipping cream and stir well.
2. In another bowl, mix raisins with sugar, chocolate chips and doughnuts and stir
3. Combine the 2 mixtures, transfer everything to a greased pan that fits your air fryer and cook at 310 °F, for 1 hour. Chill pudding before cutting and serving it

Nutrition Facts: Calories: 302; Fat: 8g; Fiber: 2g; Carbs: 23g; Protein: 10g

Fried Bananas Recipe
(**Prep + Cook Time:** 25 Minutes | **Servings:** 4)

Ingredients:
- 8 bananas; peeled and halved
- 1/2 cup corn flour
- 3 tbsp. butter
- 3 tbsp. cinnamon sugar
- 1 cup panko
- 2 eggs

Instructions:
1. Heat up a pan with the butter over medium high heat, add panko; stir and cook for 4 minutes and then transfer to a bowl
2. Roll each in flour, eggs and panko mix, arrange them in your air fryer's basket, dust with cinnamon sugar and cook at 280 °F, for 10 minutes. Serve right away.

Nutrition Facts: Calories: 164; Fat: 1g; Fiber: 4g; Carbs: 32g; Protein: 4g

Macaroons Recipe
(**Prep + Cook Time:** 18 Minutes | **Servings:** 20)

Ingredients:
- 2 cup coconut; shredded
- 4 egg whites
- 2 tbsp. sugar
- 1 tsp. vanilla extract

Instructions:
1. In a bowl; mix egg whites with stevia and beat using your mixer.
2. Add coconut and vanilla extract, whisk again, shape small balls out of this mix, place them in your air fryer and cook at 340 °F, for 8 minutes. Serve cold.

Nutrition Facts: Calories: 55; Fat: 6g; Fiber: 1g; Carbs: 2g; Protein: 1g

Walnuts Brownies
(**Prep + Cook Time:** 27 Minutes | **Servings:** 4)

Ingredients:
- 1 egg
- 1/3 cup cocoa powder
- 1/3 cup sugar
- 1/4 cup walnuts; chopped.
- 7 tbsp. butter
- 1/2 tsp. baking powder
- 1/2 tsp. vanilla extract
- 1/4 cup white flour
- 1 tbsp. peanut butter

Instructions:
1. Heat up a pan with 6 tbsp. butter and the sugar over medium heat; stir, cook for 5 minutes; transfer this to a bowl, add salt, vanilla extract, cocoa powder, egg, baking powder, walnuts and flour; stir the whole thing really well and pour into a pan that fits your air fryer

2. In a bowl; mix 1 tbsp. butter with peanut butter, heat up in your microwave for a few seconds; stir well and drizzle this over brownies mix
3. Place the pan into your air fryer and bake at 320 °F and bake for 17 minutes. Leave brownies to cool down, cut and serve.

Nutrition Facts: Calories: 223; Fat: 32g; Fiber: 1g; Carbs: 3g; Protein: 6g

Rhubarb Pie Recipe

(Prep + Cook Time: 1 hour 15 Minutes | **Servings:** 6)

Ingredients:
- 1 ¼ cups almond flour
- 5 tbsp. cold water

For the filling:
- 3 cups rhubarb; chopped.
- 1/2 tsp. nutmeg; ground
- 1 tbsp. butter
- 3 tbsp. flour

- 8 tbsp. butter
- 1 tsp. sugar

- 1 ½ cups sugar
- 2 eggs
- 2 tbsp. low fat milk

Instructions:
1. In a bowl; mix 1 ¼ cups flour with 1 tsp. sugar, 8 tbsp. butter and cold water; stir and knead until you obtain a dough
2. Transfer dough to a floured working surface, shape a disk, flatten, wrap in plastic, keep in the fridge for about 30 minutes; roll and press on the bottom of a pie pan that fits your air fryer
3. In a bowl; mix rhubarb with 1 ½ cups sugar, nutmeg, 3 tbsp. flour and whisk.
4. In another bowl, whisk eggs with milk, add to rhubarb mix, pour the whole mix into the pie crust, close the air fryer basket and cook at 390 °F, for 45 minutes. Cut and serve it cold

Nutrition Facts: Calories: 200; Fat: 2g; Fiber: 1g; Carbs: 6g; Protein: 3g

Crispy Apples Recipe

(Prep + Cook Time: 20 Minutes | **Servings:** 4)

Ingredients:
- 5 apples; cored and cut into chunks
- 1/4 cup flour
- 3/4 cup old fashioned rolled oats
- 2 tsp. cinnamon powder
- 4 tbsp. butter

- 1/2 tsp. nutmeg powder
- 1 tbsp. maple syrup
- 1/2 cup water
- 1/4 cup brown sugar

Instructions:
1. Put the apples in a pan that fits your air fryer, add cinnamon, nutmeg, maple syrup and water
2. In a bowl; mix butter with oats, sugar, salt and flour; stir, drop spoonfuls of this mix on top of apples, close the air fryer basket and cook at 350 °F, for 10 minutes. Serve warm.

Nutrition Facts: Calories: 200; Fat: 6g; Fiber: 8g; Carbs: 29g; Protein: 12g

Pumpkin Pie Recipe

(Prep + Cook Time: 25 Minutes | **Servings:** 9)

Ingredients:
- 1 tbsp. sugar
- 1 tbsp. butter

For the pumpkin pie filling:
- 3.5 oz. pumpkin flesh; chopped.
- 3 oz. water
- 1 egg; whisked

- 2 tbsp. water
- 2 tbsp. flour

- 1 tsp. mixed spice
- 1 tsp. nutmeg
- 1 tbsp. sugar

Instructions:
1. Pour 3 oz. water in a pot, bring to a boil over medium high heat, add pumpkin, egg, 1 tbsp. sugar, spice and nutmeg; stir, boil for 20 minutes; take off heat and blend using an immersion blender
2. In a bowl; mix flour with butter, 1 tbsp. sugar and 2 tbsp. water and knead your dough well.
3. Grease a pie pan that fits your air fryer with butter, press dough into the pan, fill with pumpkin pie filling, place in your air fryer's basket and cook at 360 °F, for 15 minutes. Slice and serve warm

Nutrition Facts: Calories: 200; Fat: 5g; Fiber: 2g; Carbs: 5g; Protein: 6g

Black Tea Cake Recipe

(**Prep + Cook Time:** 45 Minutes | **Servings:** 12)

Ingredients:
- 3 ½ cups flour
- 6 tbsp. black tea powder
- 1/2 cup olive oil
- 1 tsp. baking soda
- 2 cups milk
- 1/2 cup butter
- 2 cups sugar
- 4 eggs
- 2 tsp. vanilla extract
- 3 tsp. baking powder

For the cream:
- 6 tbsp. honey
- 1 cup butter; soft
- 4 cups sugar

Instructions:
1. Put the milk in a pot, heat up over medium heat, add tea; stir well, take off heat and leave aside to cool down.
2. In a bowl; mix 1/2 cup butter with 2 cups sugar, eggs, vegetable oil, vanilla extract, baking powder, baking soda and 3 ½ cups flour and stir everything really well
3. Pour this into 2 greased round pans, Place each one by one in the fryer at 330 °F and bake for 25 minutes.
4. In a bowl; mix 1 cup butter with honey and 4 cups sugar and stir really well
5. Arrange one cake on a platter, spread the cream all over, top with the other cake and keep in the fridge until you serve it.

Nutrition Facts: Calories: 200; Fat: 4g; Fiber: 4g; Carbs: 6g; Protein: 2g

Cocoa Cookies Recipe

(**Prep + Cook Time:** 24 Minutes | **Servings:** 12)

Ingredients:
- 6 oz. coconut oil; melted
- 6 eggs
- 1/2 tsp. baking powder
- 4 oz. cream cheese
- 3 oz. cocoa powder
- 2 tsp. vanilla
- 5 tbsp. sugar

Instructions:
1. In a blender, mix eggs with coconut oil, cocoa powder, baking powder, vanilla, cream cheese and swerve and stir using a mixer
2. Pour this into a lined baking pan that fits your air fryer, Place the baking pan in the fryer and bake at 320 °F and for 14 minutes. Slice cookie sheet into rectangles and serve.

Nutrition Facts: Calories: 178; Fat: 14g; Fiber: 2g; Carbs: 3g; Protein: 5g

Mandarin Pudding Recipe
(Prep + Cook Time: 60 Minutes | **Servings:** 8)

Ingredients:
- 1 mandarin; peeled and sliced
- Juice from 2 mandarins
- 2 tbsp. brown sugar
- 3/4 cup white flour
- 3/4 cup almonds; ground
- 4 oz. butter; soft
- 2 eggs; whisked
- 3/4 cup sugar
- Honey for serving

Instructions:
1. Grease a loaf pan with some butter, sprinkle brown sugar on the bottom and arrange mandarin slices.
2. In a bowl; mix butter with sugar, eggs, almonds, flour and mandarin juice; stir, spoon this over mandarin slices, place pan in your air fryer and cook at 360 °F, for 40 minutes
3. Transfer pudding to a plate and serve with honey on top

Nutrition Facts: Calories: 162; Fat: 3g; Fiber: 2g; Carbs: 3g; Protein: 6g

Figs and Coconut Butter Mix Recipe
(Prep + Cook Time: 10 Minutes | **Servings:** 3)

Ingredients:
- 12 figs; halved
- 2 tbsp. coconut butter
- 1/4 cup sugar
- 1 cup almonds; toasted and chopped

Instructions:
1. Put the butter in a pan that fits your air fryer and melt over medium high heat
2. Add figs, sugar and almonds, toss, close the air fryer basket and cook at 300 °F, for 4 minutes.
3. Divide into bowls and serve cold.

Nutrition Facts: Calories: 170; Fat: 4g; Fiber: 5g; Carbs: 7g; Protein: 9g

Strawberry Shortcakes Recipe
(Prep + Cook Time: 65 Minutes | **Servings:** 6)

Ingredients:
- 1/4 cup sugar+ 4 tbsp.
- 1 ½ cup flour
- 1 tsp. baking powder
- 1 tbsp. mint; chopped
- 1 tsp. lime zest; grated
- 1/4 tsp. baking soda
- 1/3 cup butter
- 1 cup buttermilk
- 1 egg; whisked
- 2 cups strawberries; sliced
- Cooking spray
- 1 tbsp. rum
- 1/2 cup whipping cream

Instructions:
1. In a bowl; mix flour with 1/4 cup sugar, baking powder and baking soda and stir
2. In another bowl, mix buttermilk with egg; stir, add to flour mix and whisk.
3. Spoon this dough into 6 jars greased with cooking spray, cover with tin foil, arrange them in your air fryer cook at 360 °F, for 45 minutes
4. Meanwhile; in a bowl, mix strawberries with 3 tbsp. sugar, rum, mint and lime zest; stir and leave aside in a cold place
5. In another bowl, mix whipping cream with 1 tbsp. sugar and stir. Take jars out, divide strawberry mix and whipped cream on top and serve.

Nutrition Facts: Calories: 164; Fat: 2g; Fiber: 3g; Carbs: 5g; Protein: 2g

Lemon Tart Recipe
(Prep + Cook Time: 1 hour 35 Minutes | **Servings:** 6)

Ingredients:
For the crust:
- 2 cups white flour
- 12 tbsp. cold butter
- 3 tbsp. ice water
- 2 tbsp. sugar
- A pinch of salt

For the filling:
- 2 eggs; whisked
- 1 ¼ cup sugar
- Zest from 2 lemons; grated
- 10 tbsp. melted and chilled butter
- Juice from 2 lemons

Instructions:
1. In a bowl; mix 2 cups flour with a pinch of salt and 2 tbsp. sugar and whisk.
2. Add 12 tbsp. butter and the water, knead until you obtain a dough, shape a ball, wrap in foil and keep in the fridge for 1 hour
3. Transfer dough to a floured surface, flatten it, arrange on the bottom of a tart pan, prick with a fork, keep in the fridge for 20 minutes; Put the pan in your air fryer and bake at 360 °F for 15 minutes.
4. In a bowl; mix 1 ¼ cup sugar with eggs, 10 tbsp. butter, lemon juice and lemon zest and whisk very well. Pour this into pie crust, spread evenly, lock the air fryer basket and cook at 360 °F, for 20 minutes. Cut and serve it

Nutrition Facts: Calories: 182; Fat: 4g; Fiber: 1g; Carbs: 2g; Protein: 3g

Chocolate and Pomegranate Bars Recipe
(Prep + Cook Time: 2 hours 10 Minutes | **Servings:** 6)

Ingredients:
- 1/2 cup milk
- 1/2 cup almonds; chopped
- 1 tsp. vanilla extract
- 1 ½ cups dark chocolate; chopped
- 1/2 cup pomegranate seeds

Instructions:
1. Heat up a pan with the milk over medium low heat, add chocolate; stir for 5 minutes; take off heat add vanilla extract, half of the pomegranate seeds and half of the nuts and stir
2. Pour this into a lined baking pan, spread, sprinkle a pinch of salt, the rest of the pomegranate arils and nuts, close the air fryer basket and cook at 300 °F, for 4 minutes. Keep in the fridge for 2 hours before serving.

Nutrition Facts: Calories: 68; Fat: 1g; Fiber: 4g; Carbs: 6g; Protein: 1g

Sweet Squares Recipe
(Prep + Cook Time: 40 Minutes | **Servings:** 6)

Ingredients:
- 1 cup flour
- 1/2 cup butter; soft
- 2 tbsp. lemon juice
- 2 eggs; whisked
- 1 cup sugar
- 1/4 cup powdered sugar
- 2 tsp. lemon peel; grated
- 1/2 tsp. baking powder

Instructions:
1. In a bowl; mix flour with powdered sugar and butter; stir well, press on the bottom of a pan that fits your air fryer, place the pan in your fryer and bake at 350 °F, for 14 minutes
2. In another bowl, mix sugar with lemon juice, lemon peel, eggs and baking powder; stir using your mixer and spread over baked crust. Bake for 15 minutes more, leave aside to cool down, cut into medium squares and serve cold

Nutrition Facts: Calories: 100; Fat: 4g; Fiber: 1g; Carbs: 12g; Protein: 1g

Wrapped Pears Recipe

(Prep + Cook Time: 25 Minutes | **Servings:** 4)

Ingredients:
- 4 puff pastry sheets
- 1 egg; whisked
- 1/2 tsp. cinnamon powder
- 14 oz. vanilla custard
- 2 pears; halved
- 2 tbsp. sugar

Instructions:
1. Place puff pastry slices on a working surface, add spoonfuls of vanilla custard in the center of each, top with pear halves and wrap
2. Brush pears with egg, sprinkle sugar and cinnamon, place them in your air fryer's basket and cook at 320 °F, for 15 minutes. Divide parcels on plates and serve.

Nutrition Facts: Calories: 200; Fat: 2g; Fiber: 1g; Carbs: 14g; Protein: 3g

Tangerine Cake Recipe

(Prep + Cook Time: 30 Minutes | **Servings:** 8)

Ingredients:
- 3/4 cup sugar
- 2 cups flour
- 1/2 tsp. vanilla extract
- 1/4 cup olive oil
- 1/2 cup milk
- 1 tsp. cider vinegar
- Juice and zest from 2 lemons
- Juice and zest from 1 tangerine
- Tangerine segments; for serving

Instructions:
1. In a bowl; mix flour with sugar and stir
2. In another bowl, mix oil with milk, vinegar, vanilla extract, lemon juice and zest and tangerine zest and whisk very well. Add flour; stir well, pour this into a cake pan that fits your air fryer.
3. Now place the cake pan into your air fryer and cook at 360 °F, for 20 minutes. Serve right away with tangerine segments on top.

Nutrition Facts: Calories: 190; Fat: 1g; Fiber: 1g; Carbs: 4g; Protein: 4g

Lentils Cookies Recipe

(Prep + Cook Time: 35 Minutes | **Servings:** 36)

Ingredients:
- 1 cup white flour
- 1/2 cup brown sugar
- 1/2 cup white sugar
- 1/2 tsp. nutmeg; ground
- 1 cup canned lentils; drained and mashed
- 1 cup butter; soft
- 1 egg
- 1 cup water
- 1 tsp. cinnamon powder
- 1 cup whole wheat flour
- 1 tsp. baking powder
- 2 tsp. almond extract
- 1 cup raisins
- 1 cup rolled oats
- 1 cup coconut; unsweetened and shredded

Instructions:
1. In a bowl; mix white and whole wheat flour with salt, cinnamon, baking powder and nutmeg and stir.
2. In a bowl; mix butter with white and brown sugar and stir using your kitchen mixer for 2 minutes
3. Add egg, almond extract, lentils mix, flour mix, oats, raisins and coconut and stir everything well.
4. Scoop tbsp. of dough on a lined baking pan that fits your air fryer, Place the baking pan in your air fryer and cook at 350 °F, for 15 minutes. Arrange cookies on a serving platter and serve

Nutrition Facts: Calories: 154; Fat: 2g; Fiber: 2g; Carbs: 4g; Protein: 7g

Plum Bars Recipe

(**Prep + Cook Time:** 26 Minutes | **Servings:** 8)

Ingredients:
- 2 cups dried plums
- 6 tbsp. water
- 2 tbsp. butter; melted
- 1 egg; whisked
- 2 cup rolled oats
- 1 cup brown sugar
- 1/2 tsp. baking soda
- 1 tsp. cinnamon powder
- Cooking spray

Instructions:
1. In your food processor, mix plums with water and blend until you obtain a sticky spread.
2. In a bowl; mix oats with cinnamon, baking soda, sugar, egg and butter and whisk really well.
3. Press half of the oats mix in a baking pan that fits your air fryer sprayed with cooking oil, spread plums mix and top with the other half of the oats mix
4. Close the air fryer basket and cook at 350 °F, for 16 minutes. Leave mix aside to cool down, cut into medium bars and serve

Nutrition Facts: Calories: 111; Fat: 5g; Fiber: 6g; Carbs: 12g; Protein: 6g

Sweet Potato Cheese Cake Recipe

(**Prep + Cook Time:** 15 Minutes | **Servings:** 4)

Ingredients:
- 3/4 cup milk
- 1 tsp. vanilla extract
- 4 tbsp. butter; melted
- 6 oz. mascarpone; soft
- 8 oz. cream cheese; soft
- ⅔ cup graham crackers; crumbled
- ⅔ cup sweet potato puree
- 1/4 tsp. cinnamon powder

Instructions:
1. In a bowl; mix butter with crumbled crackers; stir well, press on the bottom of a cake pan that fits your air fryer and keep in the fridge for now.
2. In another bowl, mix cream cheese with mascarpone, sweet potato puree, milk, cinnamon and vanilla and whisk really well. Spread this over crust.
3. Place the Pan in your air fryer and cook at 300 °F, for 4 minutes and keep in the fridge for a few hours before serving.

Nutrition Facts: Calories: 172; Fat: 4g; Fiber: 6g; Carbs: 8g; Protein: 3g

Berries Mix Recipe

(**Prep + Cook Time:** 11 Minutes | **Servings:** 4)

Ingredients:
- 1 lb. strawberries; halved
- 2 tbsp. lemon juice
- 1 ½ cups blueberries
- 1 ½ tbsp. maple syrup
- 1 ½ tbsp. champagne vinegar
- 1 tbsp. olive oil
- 1/4 cup basil leaves; torn

Instructions:
1. In a pan that fits your air fryer, mix lemon juice with maple syrup and vinegar, bring to a boil over medium high heat, add oil, blueberries and strawberries; stir,
2. Close the air fryer basket and cook at 310 °F, for 6 minutes
3. Sprinkle basil on top and serve!

Nutrition Facts: Calories: 163; Fat: 4g; Fiber: 4g; Carbs: 10g; Protein: 2g.1

Ginger Cheesecake Recipe

(**Prep + Cook Time:** 2 hours and 30 Minutes | **Servings:** 6)

Ingredients:
- 1/2 cup ginger cookies; crumbled
- 16 oz. cream cheese; soft
- 2 tsp. butter; melted
- 1/2 tsp. vanilla extract
- 1/2 tsp. nutmeg; ground
- 2 eggs
- 1/2 cup sugar
- 1 tsp. rum

Instructions:
1. Grease a pan with the butter and spread cookie crumbs on the bottom
2. In a bowl; beat cream cheese with nutmeg, vanilla, rum and eggs, whisk well and spread over the cookie crumbs.
3. Close the air fryer basket and cook at 340 °F, for 20 minutes. Leave cheesecake to cool down and keep in the fridge for 2 hours before slicing and serving it

Nutrition Facts: Calories: 412; Fat: 12g; Fiber: 6g; Carbs: 20g; Protein: 6g

Cocoa and Almond Bars Recipe

(**Prep + Cook Time:** 34 Minutes | **Servings:** 6)

Ingredients:
- 1/4 cup cocoa nibs
- 1 cup almonds; soaked and drained
- 1/4 cup coconut; shredded
- 8 dates; pitted and soaked
- 2 tbsp. cocoa powder
- 1/4 cup hemp seeds
- 1/4 cup goji berries

Instructions:
1. Put almonds in your food processor, blend, add hemp seeds, cocoa nibs, cocoa powder, goji, coconut and blend very well
2. Add dates, blend well again, spread on a lined baking pan that fits your air fryer and cook at 320 °F, for 4 minutes. Cut into equal parts and keep in the fridge for 30 minutes before serving.

Nutrition Facts: Calories: 140; Fat: 6g; Fiber: 3g; Carbs: 7g; Protein: 19g

Fried Apples Recipe

(**Prep + Cook Time:** 27 Minutes | **Servings:** 4)

Ingredients:
- 4 big apples; cored
- 1 tbsp. cinnamon; ground
- A handful raisins
- Raw honey to the taste

Instructions:
1. Fill each apple with raisins, sprinkle cinnamon, drizzle honey, put them in your air fryer and cook at 367 °F, for 17 minutes. Leave them to cool down and serve

Nutrition Facts: Calories: 220; Fat: 3g; Fiber: 4g; Carbs: 6g; Protein: 10g

Cashew Bars Recipe

(**Prep + Cook Time:** 25 Minutes | **Servings:** 6)

Ingredients:
- 1/4 cup almond meal
- 1 tbsp. almond butter
- 1 ½ cups cashews; chopped
- 4 dates; chopped
- 3/4 cup coconut; shredded
- 1/3 cup honey
- 1 tbsp. chia seeds

Instructions:
1. In a bowl; mix honey with almond meal and almond butter and stir well.
2. Add cashews, coconut, dates and chia seeds and stir well again.
3. Spread this on a lined baking pan that fits your air fryer and press well.

4. Introduce in the fryer and cook at 300 °F, for 15 minutes. Leave mix to cool down, cut into medium bars and serve

Nutrition Facts: Calories: 121; Fat: 4g; Fiber: 7g; Carbs: 5g; Protein: 6g

Brown Butter Cookies Recipe

(**Prep + Cook Time:** 20 Minutes | **Servings:** 6)

Ingredients:
- 1 ½ cups butter
- 2 cups brown sugar
- 2 tsp. vanilla extract
- 1 tsp. baking soda
- 2 eggs; whisked
- 3 cups flour
- ⅔ cup pecans; chopped
- 1/2 tsp. baking powder

Instructions:
1. Heat up a pan with the butter over medium heat; stir until it melts, add brown sugar and stir until this dissolves
2. In a bowl; mix flour with pecans, vanilla extract, baking soda, baking powder and eggs and stir well.
3. Add brown butter; stir well and arrange spoonfuls of this mix on a lined baking pan that fits your air fryer.
4. Introduce in the fryer and cook at 340 °F, for 10 minutes. Leave cookies to cool down and serve.

Nutrition Facts: Calories: 144; Fat: 5g; Fiber: 6g; Carbs: 19g; Protein: 2g

Blueberry Pudding Recipe

(**Prep + Cook Time:** 35 Minutes | **Servings:** 6)

Ingredients:
- 2 cups flour
- 1 stick butter; melted
- 1 cup walnuts; chopped
- 3 tbsp. maple syrup
- 2 cups rolled oats
- 8 cups blueberries
- 2 tbsp. rosemary; chopped

Instructions:
1. Spread blueberries in a greased baking pan and leave aside
2. In your food processor, mix rolled oats with flour, walnuts, butter, maple syrup and rosemary, blend well, layer this over blueberries, Place the baking pan in your air fryer and cook at 350 degrees for 25 minutes. Leave dessert to cool down, cut and serve

Nutrition Facts: Calories: 150; Fat: 3g; Fiber: 2g; Carbs: 7g; Protein: 4g

Sponge Cake Recipe

(**Prep + Cook Time:** 30 Minutes | **Servings:** 12)

Ingredients:
- 3 cups flour
- 3 tsp. baking powder
- 1 ½ cup milk
- 1 ⅔ cup sugar
- 2 cups water
- 1/2 cup cornstarch
- 1 tsp. baking soda
- 1 cup olive oil
- 1/4 cup lemon juice
- 2 tsp. vanilla extract

Instructions:
1. In a bowl; mix flour with cornstarch, baking powder, baking soda and sugar and whisk well.
2. In another bowl, mix oil with milk, water, vanilla and lemon juice and whisk
3. Combine the two mixtures; stir, pour in a greased baking pan that fits your air fryer.
4. Now place the baking pan in the fryer and cook at 350 °F, for 20 minutes. Leave cake to cool down, cut and serve.

Nutrition Facts: Calories: 246; Fat: 3g; Fiber: 1g; Carbs: 6g; Protein: 2g

Ricotta and Lemon Cake Recipe
(Prep + Cook Time: 1 hour and 10 Minutes | **Servings:** 4)

Ingredients:
- 8 eggs; whisked
- 3 lbs. ricotta cheese
- Zest from 1 lemon; grated
- Zest from 1 orange; grated
- 1/2 lb. sugar
- Butter for the pan

Instructions:
1. In a bowl; mix eggs with sugar, cheese, lemon and orange zest and stir very well
2. In your air fryer baking pan grease some batter and spread ricotta mixture.
3. Now place the baking pan in the air fryer and bake at 390 °F for 30 minutes
4. Reduce heat at 380 °F and bake for 40 more minutes. Take out of the oven, leave cake to cool down and serve!

Nutrition Facts: Calories: 110; Fat: 3g; Fiber: 2g; Carbs: 3g; Protein: 4g

Orange Cookies Recipe
(Prep + Cook Time: 22 Minutes | **Servings:** 8)

Ingredients:
- 1/2 cup butter; soft
- 1 egg; whisked
- 1 tsp. vanilla extract
- 3/4 cup sugar
- 2 cups flour
- 1 tsp. baking powder
- 1 tbsp. orange zest; grated

For the filling:
- 1/2 cup butter
- 4 oz. cream cheese; soft
- 2 cups powdered sugar

Instructions:
1. In a bowl; mix cream cheese with 1/2 cup butter and 2 cups powdered sugar; stir well using your mixer and leave aside for now
2. In another bowl, mix flour with baking powder.
3. In a third bowl, mix 1/2 cup butter with 3/4 cup sugar, egg, vanilla extract and orange zest and whisk well.
4. Combine flour with orange mix; stir well and scoop 1 tbsp. of the mix on a lined baking pan that fits your air fryer
5. Repeat with the rest of the orange batter, introduce in the fryer and cook at 340 °F, for 12 minutes. Leave cookies to cool down, spread cream filling on half of them top with the other cookies and serve.

Nutrition Facts: Calories: 124; Fat: 5g; Fiber: 6g; Carbs: 8g; Protein: 4g

Poppyseed Cake Recipe
(Prep + Cook Time: 40 Minutes | **Servings:** 6)

Ingredients:
- 1 ¼ cups flour
- 1 tsp. baking powder
- 1/2 cup butter; soft
- 2 eggs; whisked
- 1/2 tsp. vanilla extract
- 3/4 cup sugar
- 1 tbsp. orange zest; grated
- 2 tsp. lime zest; grated
- 2 tbsp. poppy seeds
- 1 cup milk

For the cream:
- 1 cup sugar
- 4 egg yolks
- 1/2 cup passion fruit puree
- 3 tbsp. butter, melted

Instructions:
1. In a bowl; mix flour with baking powder, 3/4 cup sugar, orange zest and lime zest and stir.
2. Add 1/2 cup butter, eggs, poppy seeds, vanilla and milk; stir using your mixer, pour into a cake pan that fits your air fryer and cook at 350 °F, for about 30 minutes

3. Meanwhile; heat up a pan with 3 tbsp. butter over medium heat, add sugar and stir until it dissolves.
4. Take off heat, add passion fruit puree and egg yolks gradually and whisk really well.
5. Take cake out of the fryer, cool it down a bit and cut into halves horizontally.
6. Spread 1/4 of passion fruit cream over one half, top with the other cake half and spread 1/4 of the cream on top. Serve cold

Nutrition Facts: Calories: 211; Fat: 6g; Fiber: 7g; Carbs: 12g; Protein: 6g

Passion Fruit Pudding Recipe
(Prep + Cook Time: 50 Minutes | Servings: 6)

Ingredients:
- 1 cup Paleo passion fruit curd
- 3 ½ oz. almond milk
- 1/2 cup almond flour
- 4 passion fruits; pulp and seeds
- 3 ½ oz. maple syrup
- 3 eggs
- 2 oz. ghee; melted
- 1/2 tsp. baking powder

Instructions:
1. In a bowl; mix the half of the fruit curd with passion fruit seeds and pulp; stir and divide into 6 heat proof ramekins.
2. In a bowl; whisked eggs with maple syrup, ghee, the rest of the curd, baking powder, milk and flour and stir well.
3. Divide this into the ramekins as well, place them in the fryer and cook at 200 °F, for 40 minutes. Leave puddings to cool down and serve!

Nutrition Facts: Calories: 430; Fat: 22g; Fiber: 3g; Carbs: 7g; Protein: 8g

Maple Cupcakes Recipe
(Prep + Cook Time: 30 Minutes | Servings: 4)

Ingredients:
- 1/2 cup pure applesauce
- 2 tsp. cinnamon powder
- 1 tsp. vanilla extract
- 4 tbsp. butter
- 4 eggs
- 4 tsp. maple syrup
- 3/4 cup white flour
- 1/2 apple; cored and chopped.
- 1/2 tsp. baking powder

Instructions:
1. Heat up a pan with the butter over medium heat, add applesauce, vanilla, eggs and maple syrup; stir, take off heat and leave aside to cool down
2. Add flour, cinnamon, baking powder and apples, whisk, pour in a cupcake pan.
3. Place the pan in your air fryer at 350 °F and bake for 20 minutes
4. Leave cupcakes them to cool down, transfer to a platter and serve them.

Nutrition Facts: Calories: 150; Fat: 3g; Fiber: 1g; Carbs: 5g; Protein: 4g

Made in the USA
Middletown, DE
02 December 2019